The Butcher of Casper

Published by:
Powder River Publishing LLC
1014 Black Mountain Road
Thermopolis, Wyoming 82443

Copyright © 2022
ISBN: 978-1-956881-14-1
Printed in the United States of America

Powder River Publishing

www.powderriverpublishing.com

Dedication

To my friends, co-workers, and most importantly, Haley, who never stopped believing in me.

Contents

Dead End

I hate the day and the day hates me.

That is the thought that Clyde Holding had as he walked towards Martin's, one of the largest retail chains in the country. The one where he worked was in the city of Casper, located in Central Massachusetts. Clyde stood on the barely lit sidewalk as he waited for a couple of cars to make their way down Main Street. Martin's was about the half the size of a smaller Walmart, however, Clyde did not care. He already got paid and spent half of his check on rent and the other half went into the bank.

Of course.

Clyde walked across the street when it was clear. The city at this hour was not busy, however, people lingered about in the streets, walking, and sitting on benches. A few groups were scattered here and there, smoking, drinking, and creating small bonfires in large trashcans. The air was a little cool out and Clyde was happy with what he wore, which was his usual set of black sweat pants and solid back shirt. His long blonde hair was pulled back into a small ponytail that flapped when he walked. Clyde's blue eyes shifted in the dark, scanning the surroundings. Martin's was in Downtown Casper, and right across the street, was where Clyde lived. His best friend, rather only friend, Jeremy, owned the Brightcourt Place Apartment complex. Clyde lived in his own apartment rent free, however, he did help Jeremy with the maintenance of the place when his other worker Timothy couldn't make it. Jeremy would give him a few hundred dollars for the work. It was always under the table and Clyde would use the money for what he wanted. Clyde was twenty-six years old and had been on his own since he was sixteen. When Jeremy took over the complex from his uncle, he immediately gave Clyde an apartment to live in. Clyde was thankful and even though he didn't finish high school, he applied to Martins right away and worked there ever since.

Ten years. I can't believe it, Clyde thought.

He reached the other side of the street and walked towards

the back of the parking lot. The employees who drove cars had a separate parking lot to park. Only a few lights were on, and it was a miracle that Clyde was able to find his way in the darkness. The outside light to the door was on and Clyde rang the bell. The door opened and a man let Clyde inside.

"Evening Clyde."

Clyde didn't say anything. Jerry was a bigger fellow in his middle-ages. He had retired early from another job, however, he worked at Martins to get him outside of the house. Jerry only rolled his eyes as Clyde walked by. That kid says nothing, Jerry thought. Clyde walked through the backroom. Pallets were stacked high of boxes. Racks were full of product, ready to be put out.

Just another night.

Clyde made it into the employee breakroom, where the other overnighters were. Some of them had been here for years, decades even.

Others were just like Clyde.

Only here to make a few bucks, then leave.

Clyde went off to the left and found the employee lockers, then found his own. He always kept a steady supply of water bottles and snacks. Working overnight was boring. Not many of the workers talked to Clyde, even though he had been working overnight for eight years. Not many were pleased with his work. Clyde often chose to work alone in one section all night, however, it was good work and Clyde was proud of it, as he wasn't proud of a lot of other things. Clyde got his work done and went home in the early hours of the morning. His shift started at 10pm and he wouldn't leave until 5am. When Clyde punched in, he immediately went to see Brandon Young, the overnight supervisor. Brandon was on the sales-floor most of the time, however, these days he was hanging in the office with the other managers, which hadn't gone over well with a lot of the employees. This time Brandon was at the front of the store, where the customer service desk was. Clyde found a spot and stood by a line of carriages. A worker in the morning usually takes care of those. Brandon looked over at Clyde, sighed, then looked away. Brandon was a bit taller than Clyde, around

5'8, with brown hair, brown eyes, and fair skin. He wore a set of jeans and a solid-colored shirt, with a crooked nametag on his shirt.

"Can I have all third shift to the front please." Brandon echoed.

Clyde watched as the other third shift workers appeared, and they formed some sort of circle around the service desk. When everyone was here, Brandon hopped on the counter of the service desk and looked around at all the overnight workers. Clyde refused to learn the names of many of his co-workers, as he refused to work with any of them.

"Alright everyone, we have a lot of work to do tonight. Charlie informed me before he left, that the entire Seasonal section is to be ripped out and moved towards the back corner of the store...."

"What is going in that space?"

"The entire section!"

"And we have to do it in one night?"

Figures, Clyde thought, shaking his head. Brandon looked frustrated and waited for everyone to calm down. Brandon threw up his hands.

"Look, like many of you guys, I don't make the rules, I just follow them. I guess the entire Seasonal Section is going to be along the Back Wall of the store. The other sections that are there, must get moved tonight or have most of the sections empty. Charlie is coming in halfway through the night to oversee the progress, so I want no funny business. Agreed?"

Everyone nodded. Brandon continued.

"Now, everyone get your packets, look at the moves placed out, and get to it. I want a steady pace going by the time Charlie comes. Ok get going." Brandon said.

The overnight crew consisted of about fifteen employees and was one of the largest ones in the company, besides the flagship store. Clyde got his packet and went to leave when Brandon stopped him.

"Not you, Clyde. I got an assignment for you." Brandon said.

"What is it?" Clyde asked, softly.

Then a young girl appeared. She was skinny like Clyde, with black hair and brown eyes. She wore a solid-colored shirt, with a pair of jeans and wore sneakers. Her hair was pulled back into a single ponytail that stretched down her back a ways. The brown eyes looked up and down Clyde and he just looked at Brandon.

"Clyde, this is Jemma Sterling. She is new and you are going to be training her. It is her first night on overnight." Brandon said.

Clyde looked at Jemma. She's gorgeous, Clyde thought. Out of my league if I ever had one.

"Brandon. A word please." Clyde said, struggling to get the syllables out.

"Of course." Brandon said.

Clyde motioned Brandon off to the other side of the customer service desk. He watched as the other members of the crew went about their packets. The sounds of hammers and noises echoed in the store.

"What is it Clyde?" Brandon asked.

"You want me to train her? Why! Make Michelle do it or something. Make a women do it for Chrissake....."

Brandon put his hands up.

"Wait a minute Clyde. Hold up. I give you the opportunity to train someone and you turn it down." Brandon said, raising his voice.

Clyde angrily sighed.

"Look. If it was a guy, fine, but a girl? Everyone is going to be asking questions and I don't need to explain which ones." Clyde said.

"I know, let people think what they want."

"Brandon, that is not the fucking point..."

"Is everything ok here? I want to get to work sometime today."

Brandon bit on his lip and Clyde looked at Jemma. He furrowed his brow.

"Come on, follow me." Clyde said.

"Are you training me?" Jemma asked.

Clyde nodded.

"Yup and everyone doesn't like it, then they can do it and they can fuck themselves." Clyde said angrily.

Jemma followed Clyde and Brandon let out an angry sigh, then went to do his work. Jemma caught up with Clyde.

"So, have you worked retail before?" Clyde asked.

They were down in the Houseware section. The first part of the packet was to take all the tablecloths out and dump them in a large cage. The cage would then be moved in the front of the store. Brandon already did this. Clyde watched as the supervisor moved like lightning, going from one section of the store to the other. I wish I could have that energy, Clyde thought. He and Jemma got a few carriages and were taking the tablecloths out.

"I did years ago." Jemma said.

"Where?"

"Walmart. I was 18 and stayed for a couple years as a cashier, then left."

"Why did you leave?" Clyde asked.

"To much drama."

"You are gonna find that everywhere." Clyde said.

"It doesn't seem as bad here." Jemma said.

He watched as Jemma took her hands and pulled a huge section of tablecloths out. Clyde looked at the four carriages that were already full.

"Come on, let's get to that cage up front." Clyde said.

Taking one carriage in one hand, then grabbing the other one with his other hand, Clyde went to the front. Jemma grabbed the other two carriages and followed Clyde. When the two reached the front, Clyde spotted Michelle. She was one of the oldest members on the overnight team, having worked retail since she was sixteen. She had gone fulltime after working a few years and even though Brandon was in a supervisor position, he respected her like many others. Michelle was a shorter woman, with straight white hair that went down her back. She wore some work pants, with a gray shirt. Her brown eyes looked around and locked onto Clyde and Jemma. Michelle looked over as Clyde and Jemma dumped the tablecloths into the cage. She got off her ladder.

"I see you got paired with Clyde. I'm Michelle, nice to meet you."

"My name is Jemma, this is my first night. Nice to meet you too."

Michelle smiled, then looked at Clyde.

"I can see that you are training her well." Michelle said.

"She's good. She's going to need more instruction and in time, she will be good. I'm not worried at all." Clyde said.

"That is a reassuring thing to say." Jemma said.

Clyde looked at her.

"If you were doing anything wrong, I would have told you already." Clyde said.

Jemma took some of the tablecloths and dumped them into the cage. Clyde nodded.

"Impressive."

He took some from is carriage and chucked them into the cage.

"I'll leave you two be. I have to reset this whole wall and place everything summer in one section." Michelle said.

Clyde and Jemma continued to fill the cage with tablecloths. Michelle would look over occasionally, but other than that, the older worker kept to herself. Clyde and Jemma worked in silence and when the carriages were empty, they went to the next task of the packet. It was more of the same. Pots and pans had to be moved to the front wall where Michelle was working on. Everything kitchen had to either be placed in various cages or put into walls. The only one of the overnight workers that was a stickler about this type of stuff was Sarah. Like Michelle, Sarah had been working retail her whole life and refused to tolerate anything from anyone. Michelle was the only one that could reason with her. Clyde straight up hated her with a passion and one of the sections that she was working on, a wall full of garden tools, had to be replaced with the kitchen stuff. God knows why, Clyde thought. He and Jemma took down the pots and pans and pulled them to where Sarah was working. She was younger than Michelle, however, not by much, maybe a couple of years. Her hair was grayish silver that was short. Her attire was the same as Michelle, solid color shirt, with work pants, sneakers, and a nametag. Her blue eyes looked at Clyde and Jemma.

"We have to place the pots and pans where those garden tools are." Clyde said.

"I can see that." Sarah said.

"Want us to leave the carriages here?" Clyde asked.

"Why? So I can do your job?" Sarah snapped.

Clyde suppressed a comment. He then took the carriage of pots and pans and moved it to the side.

"You going to leave those there?" Sarah asked.

Clyde walked away. Jemma did the same and left the carriages.

"Hey! I'm talking to you! I expect an answer from you youngsters!"

Sarah's shouts were toned out by both Clyde and Jemma as they did the next tasks of the packet. The night seemed to be flowing nicely and soon, Clyde and Jemma took their lunch break. The two went to the back table and Clyde sat down in one of the chairs.

"I like to face the front. I hate having my back turned." Clyde said, sitting down.

Jemma sat on the chair that was on the end of the table. Clyde thought that Jemma was going to move the chair on the same side that he was on, however, this did not happen. Worth a shot, Clyde thought. He got up, went to his locker, and sat back down. He had a couple of water bottles with him and noticed that Jemma didn't have anything. He slid a bottle over to her. It was almost the beginning of summer, so it was not that hot yet. It will be soon. Jemma took the bottle.

"Thanks." Jemma said.

"Anytime." Clyde said.

The two of them sat in the breakroom. Jemma took out her phone and began to scroll through it.

"Nothing good." Jemma said, sighing and putting her phone down.

"Sorry to hear that." Clyde said.

Jemma looked at him.

"How long have you been working here?" Jemma asked.

"Ten years. The first two I worked as a closing cashier and then I moved to overnight and stayed on it for the last eight years. It will be my eleventh soon." Clyde said.

"Wow, ten years."

"Since I was sixteen. I have been on my own since...."

"Since what?" Jemma asked.

Clyde shook his head.

"Never mind. I said too much." Clyde said.

"Since what, I want to know." Jemma said.

"Not like you would care. You just met me for Chrissake." Clyde said, looking at Jemma.

Unbeknownst to Clyde, Jemma did want to know. Clyde got up.

"Lunch is over. Come on." Clyde said.

Jemma watched as he left the break room and she followed closely behind him. There is no way that I can tell her about my parents, Clyde thought. The girl just met me and there I was, about to tell her my life story. Do I need help? Am I really that lonely? These thoughts circled Clyde's brain. He hated when he overthought things. Clyde and Jemma punched back in and went out onto the sales-floor. The overnight workers seemed to let up a bit.

Charlie was here.

Clyde knew that Charlie was the store manager and he cared for his workers. The many other managers that were here before him, not so much. Many of them Clyde did not like to mention or even talk about. There had been numerous times that Clyde wanted to walk out because of some past managers and other workers. You can't like everyone Clyde, he thought. Charlie looked over at Clyde and motioned him over to him and Brandon. Jemma followed. Charlie was a bit older than Brandon, in his mid-forties. He wore a collared shirt, with dress pants and shoes. His collared shirt was short sleeve, and it was tucked in, where a blet lashed across his pants. A nametag was on the right side of the shirt, while a pen stood out in his right breast pocket. Charlie's hair was originally a brown, however, patches of grey scattered across his scalp. Green eyes looked at Clyde and Jemma as the two stopped. Brandon suppressed a retort.

"I can see we have our new worker tonight. How is your first night?" Charlie asked.

"It's going well." Jemma said.

"Jemma is a good worker. There isn't much more that she can learn from me." Clyde said.

"That's good to hear Clyde. I'm glad that things are going well with you and Jemma. I'll make sure that the both of you are on the same nights to get this work done. Brandon, help me move the all the Cleaning supplies. All of it has to go in the last section where Housewares ends."

"Certainly." Brandon said.

Clyde and Jemma watched as Charlie and Brandon went their own way. Clyde looked at Jemma.

"Come on, we have a few more things to do." Clyde said.

Jemma followed him as Clyde went over towards the middle of the store. According to the packet, the two had done all the moves from the Housewares Section. Now it was onto the Candle Section. One entire wall had to be moved to the other side, where all the frames were. The frames had to get moved to another wall that was already cleared by Michelle earlier in the night. Clyde and Jemma both looked at the wall. It was entirely full and the two got to work. This might be the only other move we could do tonight, Clyde thought. Even if he and Jemma could not finish it, then the early morning stockers would finish the job. Jemma grabbed some carriages without Clyde telling her too and the two got to work. Clyde watched as Charlie left the building. Brandon looked at the two of them, then went off in Charlies direction. Kiss ass, Clyde thought. He didn't like Brandon, however, to Clyde, Brandon was one of the other managers that he could tolerate. The others, not so much, Clyde thought. He just remembered all the other times that he wanted to quit in the worst way, but kept on because he needed the money for rent. Not like there is much rent to pay these days. Jeremy takes care of that department. Clyde and Jemma worked silently. Eventually, the entire wall of candles was empty and on the other side, the rest of the frames were taken and placed in that other empty wall. The two took another break, then when they were done, placed all the candles into the wall where the frames used to be. Clyde looked at the work that they had done. The entire wall was empty for the early morning stockers to fill up with product. Thank God it's almost over, Clyde thought. He knew that he was getting paid tomorrow, so tonight was just adding to the paycheck. He would probably get his usual amount, however, Clyde didn't seem to care. I get paid what I get paid and that is it, Clyde thought. Towards the end of the overnight, most of the other workers had already gone home for the night, their tasks done. We won't be able to get the rest of the packet done. It will have to be for the next night, Clyde thought. He looked at Jemma.

"It's best we go home. There isn't much we can do now." Clyde said.

Jemma nodded.

"Ok. I'll follow you."

Clyde went to the break room, with Jemma close behind. Clyde went into Brandon's office and dropped off the packet. By now Brandon was gone and the early morning manager, Sasha Landon was in. She was always nice to Clyde, however, since when the two never saw each other much, Clyde just did a wave and left it at that. Sasha looked up from her phone, smiled, waved, and the went back looking at her phone. Must be important, Clyde thought. Clyde turned around and left the office, almost colliding with Jemma. Awkwardly, Jemma shoved Clyde to the wall and Clyde shook his head.

"Jesus, you scared me." Clyde said.

"Sorry." Jemma said.

Clyde looked at her. Jemma looked embarrassed, as her face turned a bit red. Clyde ignored it and huffed.

"Come on. Get your stuff so we can go." Clyde said.

"No need to be like that." Jemma said.

Jemma disappeared into the break room. Clyde sighed. What the hell is your problem man? Why are you head over heels for this girl. You just met her and have no idea about her. Get your shit together.

Clyde couldn't.

He was really in love with Jemma in a way. Not like a complete crush. Maybe it could develop into something more? Clyde thought. Clyde walked over to the timeclock, punched in his numbers, and punched out for the night. Jemma appeared behind him, and Clyde's skeleton almost jumped out of him. She loves scaring me, Clyde thought. Jemma went over and punched out. It took her awhile for her to remember her numbers and put them into the computer. When she was done, she looked at Clyde.

"You ready?" Jemma asked.

Clyde was not paying attention, then snapped back to the present.

"Oh…….yeah.. let's go." Clyde said.

He let Jemma go in front of him and Clyde followed. The door opened and the early morning stockers were arriving. Clyde did not recognize them, however, he did say 'Hi' to some of them, in which the reply was a snort. Clyde shook it off and continued after Jemma. She already had her things in her hand. Clyde went into the breakroom, grabbed his bag, and then met Jemma at the doorway of the breakroom. She let Clyde pass him and he did. Jemma followed Clyde out through the back to the employee entrance. The last of the overnight crew had already left for the night and now the morning backroom people were coming in. Again, Clyde did not know many of them. After almost a decade and I don't know any of these fuckers, Clyde thought. He knew that he was not the most outgoing of people and he should have showed some initiative in saying hello. No, let them do that. Clyde thought. Too many thoughts were going through his head every time when he left. Did I do good enough? Did Brandon like it? Does Jemma like me or no? Do I like her? Too many Clyde thought. The backdoor was opened for both Clyde and Jemma as the two stepped out into the morning light. The sun was slowly rising, and the first rays of sun hit Clyde. He shielded his eyes and walked so he was out of the sun. Jemma looked at him.

"You don't like the sun?" Jemma asked.

"The sun doesn't like me." Clyde said.

Jemma nodded.

"So. I'll see you another time." Jemma said.

"Yeah, I'll be in the next time you come in. You technically must train with me for two shifts, but you don't need much training from me. There isn't much more to learn. It's now just practice." Clyde said.

"Understood. Have a good day."

Jemma fumbled with the keys to her car, which Clyde noticed a blue Honda Civic. At least she has a car, Clyde thought. Jemma walked halfway to her car, then turned around to see Clyde still standing there. She walked back to Clyde, who was scrolling through his phone. Nothing good on social media I guess.

"Do you need a ride?" Jemma asked.

Clyde jumped and almost dropped his phone.

"Jesus, you have to stop scaring me! No, I'm fine. I live across the street and walk to work." Clyde said.

Jemma was taken aback by Clyde's quick anger. He's strange, Jemma thought. Jemma sighed.

"Ok. I'll see you later." Jemma said.

"See you." Clyde said.

Jemma walked away. This might be your chance now, Clyde thought.

"Jemma!" Clyde shouted.

Jemma turned around.

"What?"

Clyde began to seize up. His throat was immediately dry, and he felt sweaty.

"What is it Clyde? I don't have all day." Jemma said, irritated.

Clyde sighed.

"Would you want to go out with me one day when we aren't working?" Clyde asked.

The look that Clyde got was priceless. Jemma looked at him, hands crossed underneath her breasts.

"I'll pay and I have a car, so I can drive too....." Clyde said.

Jemma rolled her eyes and sighed.

"No."

Clyde was shocked. She said no, Clyde thought.

"I'm sorry man. I don't know you and you don't know me. Besides, I just got off a relationship and I don't want to start anything new right now." Jemma said.

Clyde fumbled through his pocket. For the first time in a while, he lit up a cigarette, lit it, and blew the smoke out.

"Ok. Understandable." Clyde said.

"That's all you're going to say!" Jemma said, raising her voice.

Clyde sucked on that cigarette like it was the only thing left. He let the cigarette shut him up. Jemma let out an angry sigh.

"You guys are all the same! See you later Clyde." Jemma said.

Clyde blew out the smoke as Jemma left. She said no. Clyde put the cigarette out, then kicked a trash barrel. What the fuck! Clyde thought. He was lonely and now the emotions began to well up inside him. He went towards a small retaining wall and slumped down it, hands in his eyes. He hit himself in the forehead. Fucking stupid! Why can't you just leave stuff alone Clyde! Clyde thought. He looked over as Jemma drove away from him, shaking her head in disgust. Jemma hates me now. Clyde thought. Clyde got himself up and began the walk back to the apartment complex. The city of Casper was beginning to awaken, with the sounds of cars hitting the pavement and the footsteps of people crossing the sidewalk. Clyde wanted to light up another cigarette so bad, but he came close to a group of people and put the thought aside. Thankfully, the apartments were across the street and when the group crossed to the other side of Main Street, Clyde went with them, hoping that Jemma didn't see him walking. The last thing I need is her involved. I don't want to be with her anymore. Fucking girls. You always get into trouble with them, Clyde thought. He approached the apartment complex and went to the bottom floor. The door to it was open and Clyde furrowed his brow. No one should be in here, Clyde thought. He approached the door slowly and found out that the room was full of his stuff, just as he left it. Clyde then took his work stuff, threw it on the bed, and crashed right on the floor. He placed his hands to his face and felt tears coming down. Heart break was one hell of a pill to swal-

Full Day

"Are you ok?"

Clyde looked up to see Jeremy peering into the room. Clyde sighed. Shit, he saw me cry, Clyde thought.

"Clyde? Pal? You alright?" Jeremy asked.

Clyde sighed and got up from the floor.

"Yeah, I'm ok. Just tired."

"Then take a rest, pal. You need it. If you feel up to it, come by my room later and we can go around fixing some of the rooms that need it. I also need help with sorting the paperwork and permit crap." Jeremy said.

"Let me nap first, then I'll help." Clyde said.

Jeremy smiled.

"Thanks man."

Clyde watched as Jeremy walked out of the room and closed the door. Clyde then sat down on his bed.

"Fuck me." Clyde said.

He sighed angrily and went backwards on the bed. He placed his hands on his face and brought them down his face, bringing his cheeks down with him. I hate this, Clyde thought. The image of Jemma flashed in his mind. How could I be so stupid. I mean, I asked her out on the first night that I saw her and now it's all ruined. I need some sleep. Clyde reached down into his pocket and pulled out his iPhone. The time read 6:30am. Jemma is probably home and asleep right now, Clyde thought. He opened his phone and scrolled through his text messages.

There weren't many.

Figures, Clyde thought.

His friends were off doing other things and couldn't be bothered into texting or calling him. I sometimes wonder why I even have a phone, Clyde thought. His parents never kept in touch and that annoyed Clyde to no end. They abandoned me and I did the same to them. I don't care, Clyde thought. He forced himself to sit up in his bed. The sunlight began to go through the single window that Clyde had. Being on the bottom floor of the apartment complex meant that he only had one window. Doesn't matter to me anyways, Clyde thought. Sighing, he rubbed his hands in his face again, then went to get ready for a quick nap. Clyde walked to his closet, pulled out a set of pajamas and made sure that his apartment door was locked. When the door was closed, Clyde collapsed on his bed and closed his eyes.

A scream echoed in Clyde's ears. He shot straight out of bed, sweat all over his body. Jeremy was standing over him, eyes wide.

"Are you ok Clyde?" Jeremy asked.

Clyde looked up at him. He was breathing heavy, and he sighed.

"Yeah, I'm fine." Clyde said.

"You sure? You don't look fine." Jeremy said.

Clyde swung his legs over and rubbed his face.

"What time is it?'

"Noon."

Clyde looked at Jeremy.

"I only slept for five-ish hours?"

Jeremy nodded.

"Yup."

"Son of a bitch."

Clyde got up and stretched, letting out a yawn. Jeremy looked at him.

"So whenever you are ready, I need some help around here. I just collected most of the rent, so I can give you some after the other bills are paid." Jeremy said.

Clyde nodded.

"Sure, thanks."

Jeremy looked at him.

"You seem a bit down? Are you ok?"

"Not really." Clyde said.

"Why? Anything you want to share with me?" Jeremy asked.

At this point, Clyde hesitated. Clyde never told Jeremy much went on at Martins at night. Too much drama and little interest. It is best to keep it safe, Clyde thought. He looked at Jeremy.

"I am just having an issue with this girl at work." Clyde said.

Jeremy was shocked. I shouldn't have said that Clyde thought. Jeremy continued.

"A girl problem? Is it good or bad?" Jeremy asked, surprised.

"I would say it's bad."

"Why?"

"The girl is new and many at work are asking questions." Clyde said.

"Not the good kind of questions. The bad ones right?" Jeremy asked.

Clyde nodded.

"You bet. Not good."

Jeremy nodded.

"I see. So what are you going to do about this 'girl problem' of yours?" Jeremy asked.

Clyde shrugged.

"Nothing."

"Nothing!" Jeremy shouted.

Clyde nodded.

"Yup, nothing. There isn't much that I can do anyways." Clyde said.

"A shame."

"It doesn't matter to me Jeremy. The girl is younger and not my type, so I'm not interested in anyone now."

"For the moment. That doesn't mean that you won't be interested in her now."

"Shut up." Clyde said, raising his voice.

"I'm just kidding Clyde. I know that you don't want a girl. Just try to play it cool." Jeremy said.

Clyde sighed.

"I wish that she wasn't there. If she wasn't, then she would be doing the company a favor."

"Well, obviously they need her so there isn't much you can

do about it."

Jeremy went over and turned on the TV. The local news channel was on. Jeremy sat down on the couch and Clyde sat next to him.

"In a surprising shock last night, Police Sheriff Benton For-long has stepped down due to massive controversy over contracts with the police department. His second in command, Police Chief Mark Durn, is set to run in the Casper General Election….."

Jeremy shook his head.

"Unbelievable."

The TV showed both Benton and Mark shaking hands and other pictures as the newscaster went on. Clyde looked at Jeremy.

"I wonder if he will be able to fix this city. Lots of richer people moving out, low income coming in. The whole worlds going to shit." Clyde said.

"You are just saying that because of the problems with that girl. You need to get over it, Clyde. What I would do is go out and take a walk or something." Jeremy said.

Clyde nodded.

"I will. Do we have any beer left?" Clyde asked.

"Your Budweiser? I don't think so."

Clyde stood up and put his shoes on.

"Then, I'm gonna get some. I also need another pack of cig-arettes. Do you want anything?"

Jeremy shook his head.

"No and Clyde, smoking is a bad habit."

Clyde walked to the door and stood in the doorway.

"I'm always drawn to bad habits." Clyde said.

Clyde walked away as Jeremy loudly sighed and continued to watch the TV. Clyde didn't even bother to close his apartment door. Jeremy had the keys to every single room, so it didn't matter if Clyde locked it or not. He walked up the stairs and out into the main parking lot. Clyde had a car, a 2001 Subaru Outback. The car was a green color at one time, but with age, the paint had begun to chip off, revealing a silver color underneath. Clyde just saved up to get a whole new engine into the car, which cost him almost his entire bank account. Jeremy offered to help him out with the payment, but Clyde refused. Jeremy already has a lot to pay for, Clyde thought. The last thing Clyde wanted was for Jeremy to take on his financial responsibilities. Clyde fumbled for the keys of his car and unlocked it. He sat himself down and started his car. Clyde threw the vehicle in reverse and drove out of the apartment complex. He went down the driveway and took a left onto Main Street. Martins was on his right as rows of people went through the front door. Always making something, Clyde thought. Main Street was not developed as the rest of Casper. The only large building was Martin's, however, on Clyde's left were lots of small mom and pop places, which were mostly convenience stores. The one that Clyde liked going to be a place called Harry's, which was located on the better side of Casper. Clyde flew up Main Street. At this hour, not many people were out and about yet, which was a good thing because Clyde could not stand traffic.

He absolutely despised it.

Clyde hated living in Casper. The city was on the decline. As Clyde mentioned earlier, the city was losing people and the standard of living was terrible. The only two big employers were Martins and the nearby Market Basket, also on the other side of the city. The better half of the city, Clyde thought. The area that he lived in was dominated by apartments and run-down mill buildings. I have never seen the city go down this low before, Clyde thought.

As he drove, he looked on both sides of the street. People walked up and down the large sidewalks, sat on benches and walked dogs. As Clyde drove up Main Street, the landscape changed. Colonial and ranch style homes lined the streets. Nice lawns and picket fences appeared out of nowhere. A divide, Clyde thought. Clyde knew that no one could ever deny the fact that there was a divide between the people who lived in Casper. There were those, just like Clyde, who were barely making it, and others, well Clyde knew just by looking at their homes. They must have worked hard for them, Clyde thought. He knew that everyone worked hard just like him, just in other ways. Clyde noticed that there were other cars on Main Street now and he moved off to the right lane, letting others pass him if they wished. Main Street opened to two lanes that went eventually went down to one lane the further up you went. Clyde used to work there during the day when he was doing tiny overnight shifts. Then once when Clyde was working longer overnights, he couldn't work the two jobs. I wish I worked here instead, Clyde thought. He was a few years too late, and Martins still worked out for him to work. The Market Basket was packed as always, with the parking lot almost being half the size of a football field. Clyde remembered when the city put up a fight to try to not get the business here, but the mayor wanted the jobs and the cash flow. Now it was too late to change anything. Clyde took a right onto Mansion Drive and drove up the road, heading towards Harry's.

Harry's was one of the worst places to have a convenience store, however, the original owner, Harry Larson, believed that it was a good location. This was long before the Market Basket was there, and Casper was just a town then. It was one of the only solid brick buildings, with an architecture that screamed its era. Clyde had guessed numerous times that Harry's was built in the 50s or 60s and over the years, the building and the owners dumped money into improving the building substantially. Harry's was situated out of the way, with a few nice houses scattered about. The parking lot was just big enough to have thirty cars parked without any issues. There was always enough space to get in and out. When Clyde pulled in, he found the place busy, with almost every spot full except for a couple towards the end. Clyde waited for a few cars to pass him, then pulled into the establishment.

The parking spot that Clyde chose was a single spot and when he pulled into it, his car faced Mansion Drive. Clyde sat down in the car for a few seconds, then got out and headed inside of the store. Harry's was big for a convenience store, with about five or six registers. It sold a whole slew of products, which were also carried by nearby Market Basket, however, people shopped here all the time. It never ends, Clyde thought. He opened the door and let a family of three walk out, then went inside. The air inside of the store hit him like a truck. The cool air from the AC was on and it felt good for Clyde. I like it when it's cold for a bit,

Clyde thought. The good thing about Harry's was that nothing was moved around. This way, everything was in one place, and everyone knew where it was. While other stores moved stuff around, Harry's left it where it was. If people knew where the product was, then they will buy it, Clyde thought. Inside, the shelves were lined up with large numbers numbering from 1-10. The six registers were in the front of the store. The place had one exit and entrance for crowd control purposes. The owners wanted the customers to come in and out in an orderly fashion, whereas other stores did not have this luxury. Clyde went to the third aisle in the store, where the cigarettes were. He grabbed a couple of packets and even a new lighter that was blue. Fancy, Clyde thought. Clyde didn't even bother to grab a basket, as he only needed a couple of things. The cases of Budweiser were in the back, where all the cold stuff was. Refrigerators lined the back, with one section for beer, another for milk, ice cream, etc. Clyde reached in to grab a case and almost tripped inside in the process. He regained himself and pulled the case out with one hand. Struggling, Clyde went up to the register line. The line itself moved fast, with all six registers open. Harry's never had the workers stock the shelves. A separate crew did that.

  I could have worked here too, Clyde thought. He had thought about it many times, however, Clyde shopped here so much that he felt that it wouldn't have been a good job anyways. The only positions that were open were for the registers and Clyde didn't want to do that at all. Towards the front where the registers were, was a customer service desk and a TV that played the local news. Clyde was next in line, so he went to register four, where a teenage girl cashed him out. The girl looked Clyde up and down, however, Clyde didn't pay much attention. If I kissed her, then I would be in jail so fast, Clyde thought. Best not to get involved, I already have enough problems with Jemma at work. Then it hit him. The thought of going back to work. He didn't want to go in if Jemma was there. This is going to be so awkward, Clyde thought. The girl looked at him.

  "Your total is $30.45"

  Clyde nodded, got out his credit card, put it in, and paid the amount. The girl gave Clyde his receipt and smiled.

"Have a good day."

"Same to you." Clyde said in a raspy voice.

Clyde grabbed his things and proceeded to walk out when the TV caught his eye. It was that Mark Durn guy again. The headlines under it read: LIVE CAMPAIGN SPEECH FROM MARK DURN. So the guy is really taking this seriously, Clyde thought. He strained his ears to listen more.

"The city of Casper needs come control. Crime is not a problem, but fighting it has become a burden on our taxpayers. We need to reform the system, so it works for us, for the people. Vote for me and I swear, everything will get better..."

Clyde couldn't stand to listen anymore, so he left Harry's. He didn't want to linger there longer than he needed to be. He got halfway across the parking lot when he noticed someone.

It was Mark Durn.

The one that was just on the TV. He was giving the speech on a lawn across the street. How odd, Clyde thought. One of two things was wrong. Either the live coverage was wrong, or Mark Durn could teleport to different places. Either way, Clyde was rushing to his car now. He kept his vehicle unlocked and stuck the beer in the back seat, while the cigarettes and lighter were placed in the passenger seat. Clyde watched as Mark walked towards Harry's, with a group of people and news reporters following him. Mark was middle aged, Clyde guessed in his forties. Mark's eyes were the same color of blue as Clyde's, however, Mark had black hair and olive like skin. He wore a suit, tie, and dress shoes, as if he was going to some sort of press conference. Mark stopped at the door and so did the group. Clyde was already in his car, and he proceeded to drive out of the lot. He got halfway through the lot when Mark stopped in front of his car. What the hell, Clyde thought. Clyde slammed on the break and the car came to a screeching halt. Mark knocked on the window and smiled. Clyde had no clue how to react, so he rolled down the window.

"Can I help you? I'm trying to get home." Clyde said, a bit irritated.

"I'm just wondering if you would want to ask me some

questions. You seem to be a good fella." Mark said.

He held out his hand.

"Mark Durn, running for Sheriff of Casper." Mark said.

Clyde grabbed his hand and shook it.

"Clyde Holding. Nice to meet you." Clyde said, easing up.

Mark pulled his hand away.

"Nice handshake, Clyde. You seem to do well for yourself. What do you do?"

Clyde was not sure if he should open to this guy. He seems nice, Clyde thought. What the hell, you only live once.

"I work overnight at Martins." Clyde said.

"Is that all you do?" Mark asked.

"It's all I've been doing for the last decade."

"A decade? You are so young."

"I've been on my own for a while now. I only take care of myself." Clyde said.

Before Mark could ask another question, Clyde switched the car in park.

"So what do you think of the state of our city?" Mark asked.

Clyde shrugged.

"It is what it is. There isn't much I can do about it."

"That, Clyde, is where you are wrong. We can all change the course of history if we work together, right folks."

Clyde realized that the entire group was near him now. A news reporter and camera person were near him now. Clyde could feel the camera zooming in on him. I hate this, Clyde thought. He looked at Mark.

"Well, it was nice chatting with you, but I really have to go." Clyde said.

"What are you going to be doing?"

"That doesn't seem to be any of your business."

"Well, it is my business."

Clyde slowly got out of the car. Mark was shocked and so was Clyde. He went from being friendly to angry. Clyde got really close to Mark.

"I don't care if your Sheriff of Casper, but as of now, you aren't. You asked me some questions and I answered as best as I could. What I do is my business and if I were you, I would watch the way you talk to people."

Mark tried not to screw up his face in anger. The camera was still on the two of them and Clyde went back into his car and put it into drive.

"I'll see you later, Mark." Clyde said.

Mark didn't say anything and watched as Clyde left the parking lot. The crowd moved and let Clyde out and soon, he was back on Main Street in no time. Clyde could hear the beer bottles clanking in the back as he drove. He wanted to get back to the apartment complex soon. I have no idea about that Mark guy, but I think was onto me for some reason, Clyde thought. Why would he just stop and talk to a random guy in a parking lot. Was he looking for a running mate or some sort of campaign manager or something. Clyde shook his head. He ever tried to get involved with politics. Messy shit, Clyde thought. The last thing he needed was another mess. I already fucked up with work and now I have a feeling that this isn't going to be good either. Clyde pulled into the apartment complex parking lot, parked his car, and went back into his apartment. He took a couple of trips, first taking in the beer, then going back to get the cigarettes and the lighter. When he arrived at the apartment after the second trip, he found a note on the door in Jeremy's handwriting. Clyde took it and read it. The premise of the message was that Jeremy left to deal with the issue on another property.

Another property.

Clyde was not aware that Jeremy owned another apartment complex. The name of the town was unknown to Clyde, but that didn't matter. Jeremy said that he would be back in a couple of days, which didn't matter to Clyde. I'll just wait for him to come back, Clyde thought. He knew that when Jeremy was gone, that meant that Clyde oversaw the complex. Not a terrible gig to be honest. Clyde sighed and sat down on the couch. The TV was still on, and the news was still on. Clyde was not paying much attention to what the newscaster was saying. Clyde then got up, found one of his packs of cigarettes, and lit one up. It had been a while since he last smoked one. Clyde has been trying to quit for a long time, as he got hooked on cigarettes since he was nineteen. Many packs of cigarettes. Clyde's voice was raspy, however, it had smoothed out over the years because of his efforts to quit. He never smelled like smoke or at least Clyde thought that he didn't. Clyde tried to reduce his smoking habit with chewing on unpleasant snacks. Clyde would often buy cat food and eat it by the pound when he was craving a cigarette. The taste of the cat food would make Clyde throw up and he wouldn't dare grab a cigarette again. Now here he was, smoking in his apartment while the TV was going in the background. Clyde took a deep drag on his cigarette and slowly let the smoke out of his mouth and nostrils. He felt more relaxed than ever. At least I don't have to go into work until much later, Clyde thought. Another sigh followed another drag from the cigarette. Clyde kept the cigarette in his mouth as he found an ashtray and dumped the ashes into it. The cigarette was going down fast, as Clyde liked to use it all up quickly. When he finished, he put it out and found a can of cat food. Taking the can, he opened it, scooped out some, and ate it. The food didn't even reach Clyde's mouth as he hurled into the sink, arching his back, and heaving hard. Clyde took the can of cat food and dumped it down the sink. The strong smell was already enough to knock some sense into Clyde. I'll never learn I guess, Clyde thought. When he was done, Clyde reached into the fridge, pulled out a can of Budweiser, opened it, and downed it. The beer slid down his throat very easily and Clyde seemed to be ok. The last gulp of the beer he swished around in his mouth and spat into the sink, cleaning out his mouth. Clyde felt a little woozy, however, he was able to hold his liquor well to a degree and downed three more beers in a quick succession. There were only fifteen cans in a case and Clyde himself had already five of them-by-them time he began to struggle standing up. The TV was still on, and Clyde was lying flat on his stomach, one hand over the arm of the couch, while the other held onto his seventh beer. Clyde looked around and everything around him was blurry. His eyes were heavy, and Clyde felt like he was going to lose the feeling in his arms.

The feeling in Clyde's right arm was slowly going away and he dropped the beer can on the floor. The liquid spilled and Clyde just laughed and laughed. He had never laughed this hard about something so stupid.

"Hey Jeremy! I think the floor is a bit wet!" Clyde shouted, laughing even harder.

Clyde knew that he lost it. His laughter soon turned quickly to sadness and tears came down his eyes. He was drunk out of his mind, and he fought to get back up for his eighth or ninth beer. Clyde lost track of how many he had, and he rolled off the couch. Clyde then got up, his shirt and pants all wet. He didn't realize that he rolled right into the beer that ran all over in front of the couch.

"I'm wet!" Clyde shouted.

Clyde got up, soaking wet with stains from the beer. No matter, I'll get another one, Clyde thought. He went to the fridge and pulled the door open. Clyde grabbed another beer and downed it, followed by another and another. As Clyde tipped his head back to down his next beer, he fell backwards and slammed on the floor. His back felt cool, as his shirt was soaked in a mix of sweat and beer. Clyde dropped the can and the beer spilled all over his face. Clyde still held the can and chucked it at the ceiling. He moved out of the way as the can came back down and slammed on the ground. Clyde let out an angry sigh and began to cry again. He rubbed his hands to his face and cried and cried. Clyde never cried, but his drunkenness really took a toll on him. Clyde was on the ground, soaked in sweat, tears, and beer.

Clyde was also alone.

Clyde was thinking of Jemma.

And that was what was making him sad. Jemma Sterling. She's one hell of a girl that I'll never get to have at all, Clyde thought. I ruined it for us. I wish I just kept my fucking mouth shut. How in the world could he have kept his mouth shut. It wasn't Clyde's fault that he had to train a beautiful girl. It wasn't Clyde's fault that everyone at Martins was always gossiping and going through drama shit. That was his work in a nutshell. There was always problems with co-workers, but that was everywhere. Clyde sighed.

"Why can't I just die already! How many more beers does it

take to kill my liver!" Clyde shouted.

He rolled on the ground, so that the front of his shirt was soaked in the beer. He forced himself up and pulled the rest of the case of beer out. Clyde then finished the case of Budweiser. He was surprised that he was able to finish it, but Clyde did. He was now out of his mind, shouting things that didn't make sense. Clyde had locked himself in the apartment, hoping that no one would be able to get in. I don't want any of them around, Clyde thought. He looked at the time and couldn't read it because it was blurry. There is no way that it is 9:00pm already. No way that he would have to be for work. Clyde then took a step forward, then he felt himself falling. Clyde slammed his head on the side of the couch and then was nothing to the world.

Clyde woke up with a screaming headache. His shirt was still stained, and he took a whiff of himself. The strong smell of beer emitted from him and he almost gagged. Clyde got up and noticed that his phone was on the table and picked it up. Clyde scrolled through the messages.

Then it hit him.

"Shit! I missed work!" Clyde shouted.

He noticed that there were three missed calls and three voicemails. He played all three voicemails, and it was Brandon, wondering where he was and that he didn't show for his 10-6 shift and Jemma had to do all his work. Clyde got himself up and called the store number. By now it was 6:30am. Sasha picked up the phone.

"Clyde? Are you ok? Brandon told me that you weren't in."

"I know, I know. I overslept. Can I talk to Brandon?" Clyde asked.

"Yeah, hold on and I'll put you through."

Clyde waited for a few minutes, then Brandon picked up.

"You were late."

"I know. I overslept."

"I can guarantee some hours. Come by when you are ok."

"That's it? No yelling?"

"Not yet. Just get over here when you can."

Brandon then hung up the phone. Clyde let out a sigh. Fucking asshole. Clyde got up, went to his closet, and pulled out a solid shirt and jeans. Thankfully, the shower was in the same room, so Clyde went into the shower and hopped in. The hot water woke him up, however, he was still struggling from the headache and the hangover. Clyde didn't take long in the shower and when he was done, grabbed some waters and some food for a lunch, then left the apartment. The air outside was cool, however, since when it was the beginning of summer, it would get hot later. It was cold the previous weekend, however, the heat was coming, and it was on the rise soon. Clyde wasted no time in crossing Main Street to the back of Martins. When Clyde reached the back door, it was opened by Brandon. Clyde was in shock and almost ran into Jemma, who was leaving for the night. She didn't even look at Clyde. How rude, Clyde thought.

"Goodnight Brandon." Jemma said.

Brandon didn't say anything and let Clyde inside. The backroom was completely empty. Brandon only looked at Clyde, then locked the door.

"I can't believe you overslept." Brandon said.

Clyde shrugged, then touched his forehead.

"Sorry. I got a wicked headache and went to lay down for a few hours to try to get rid of it... ."

Brandon stopped in front of Clyde and sniffed.

"You've been drinking again." Brandon said.

"I haven't."

"Yes you have."

"Haven't and mind your business."

"I'll report you to Charlie."

"Go ahead. Then I quit." Clyde said, raising his voice.

Brandon was taken aback and sighed.

"Follow me." Brandon said.

Clyde followed Brandon from the backroom into the office. Sasha was nowhere to be found, so Clyde figured that she was out on the sales floor. Brandon sat down in his chair, while Clyde stood in the doorway.

"I have a project for you that will take you all morning. I

can only have you until 10, as customers will come in and mess up everything." Brandon said.

"Ok, what will I be doing?" Clyde asked.

"Jemma filled a lot overnight, however, she didn't get to do a section that I wanted done. Corporate is putting in a new Arts and Crafts section in every store and it must get done by tomorrow. The space is already cleaned out for you, and everything is good to go. The only thing that has to get done is for you to set it and then leave." Brandon said.

"I'm doing this by myself!" Clyde said, raising his voice.

Brandon nodded.

"Yup. I should have been gone an hour ago. Good luck. If you need Sasha, then call her and not me. Also next time when you want to drink, do it when you are off." Brandon said.

Arts and Crafts

Clyde watched as Brandon left the office. That asshole, Clyde thought. He now had to do an entire section by himself and only had until 10am to do it. Three hours isn't enough time for just one person. I need help.

There was no help coming.

Clyde was the only one from the overnight crew that was here. Most of the early morning stockers took Thursday's off, so Clyde was stuck in a hard place. Sighing, Clyde got himself together, put his stuff away, then went right to work. The racks of the arts and crafts stuff were out in the backroom, lined up in a way that would allow for anyone to take them out in an orderly fashion. Clyde grabbed the first rack and pulled it out onto the salesfloor. It was 7:00am and the customers would not be in the store for another hour. Martins always opened at 8am and usually closed around 7, although the employees wouldn't go home util around 9 or 10 to clean up the store. The shoppers were usually messy all the time and Upper Management wanted the stores to close early so the salesfloor could be cleaned more. They wanted a clean store rather a messy one. When Clyde stepped out onto the salesfloor, he saw the lines of carriages of the returns that had to get put away. Thankfully I don't have to do that, Clyde thought. It was almost as he was psychic, as the morning stockers grabbed the carriages and began to put the stuff away. Good do something for once. Clyde dragged the first rack to where the Arts and Crafts room was going to be. An entire section was cleaned out towards the back middle of the store. Martins had a large middle section where lots of the smaller sections where, however, the Arts and Crafts area was going to be in a section where all the candles used to be. Clyde had no idea where they decided to put them, but he was not focused on that. Not my problem, Clyde thought. He only had three hours to put all the stuff out, so he started with the rack that he had and placed it in the middle of the section. This entire rack was all boxes of art stuff. Sketch books, coloring supplies, crafting kits, and more stuff that Clyde did not recognize. Must all be new, Clyde thought. He placed the boxed stuff on the shelves, while underneath, he filled bins and smaller sections with the sketch books and other small things. When Clyde was done with the first rack, he returned it and got the next two racks. These racks contained coloring supplies from colored pencils to markers to crayons and weird gel things. Clyde put them out in a good fashion, hanging most of the stuff up on a wall behind him. He moved a lot of the boxed stuff into one whole wall and the remainder that didn't fit, he placed somewhere else. The second rack that he tackled, was a rack of yarn, crochet hooks, and crafting books. Weird, Clyde thought. He didn't hate stuff like this, however, he just found it strange that Martins was now getting this stuff. As if they don't have enough shit to sell, Clyde thought. The yarn and other stuff fit on the second wall where Clyde was working. Clyde then noticed the first few customers, the early morning shoppers. They have nothing else better to do, Clyde thought. He really hated people sometimes, however, he couldn't say much about it. They give me my job. Clyde finished the other two racks and returned them to the backroom. By now, it had taken Clyde about three hours to get the stuff out and he was shocked.

Most of the stuff was already out now. Clyde only had one more wall to fill, then tiny bins and other spaces to place random stuff. Then I can go home hopefully, Clyde thought. There were a couple more racks left, so Clyde grabbed the next one and brought it out to the salesfloor. This time it took a while to get to the section because a wave of customers moved down near him. Some of the customers grabbed at the stuff that he just put out and Clyde had to suppress a lot of comments, so much that he felt his tongue bleeding. Clyde then wheeled the rack into the section, near the last empty wall. This was a mix of craft and art supplies, more focused on painting equipment, clay modeling, and more art stuff for kids. In no time the wall was full. Clyde was proud of himself. When he set his mind to his work, then he got it done. There was something inside Clyde that wanted to work, like he was missing something.

Or someone.

The image of Jemma popped in his mind, and he really

wanted her to work with him. Why are you thinking in that way? Clyde thought. She has brought you nothing but trouble, so why would you want more trouble? Clyde shook his head. He had no idea why he was so fixated on this girl, when he ruined it for him and for her. Now the co-worker relationship is not going to be good at all. It is ruined, Clyde thought. When he returned to the back room, he couldn't find any more racks of the arts and crafts stuff. I put everything out. I can't believe it, Clyde thought. He had placed the empty racks back the way that they originally were and was happy to leave them there. Whoever is back here can fill them up again, Clyde thought. He let out a sigh of relief and pulled out his phone. It was nearing 10am and Clyde couldn't find anything else to put in that section. Clyde stood out on the salesfloor, leaning up against a column. Already customers were buying the stuff that he put out. Figures, Clyde thought. At least he knew that he was making some sort of sales. That was a good thing and Clyde smiled. Clyde then went through the backroom and into the office. Brandon, Sasha, and Charlie were all talking amongst themselves when Clyde came into the office. Brandon just gave Clyde a terrible look and Clyde only acknowledged Charlie and Sasha in the room.

"The Arts and Crafts section is done." Clyde said.

Charlie nodded.

"Good. I want to go see it. Come with me." Charlie said.

Sasha and Brandon remained seated as Charlie got up and led Clyde out to the salesfloor. The two walked in silence, until they reached the Arts and Crafts section. Charlie looked at the full walls and the product. Clyde was always skeptical of Charlie and how he operated the store, however, since when the company liked him, Upper Management never bothered them too much. Charlie then looked at Clyde.

"You did a great job, Clyde." Charlie said.

Clyde was bit shocked.

"That's it. A good job?" Clyde asked.

"Did you want something else?" Charlie asked back.

"I would like to go home."

"Then you may go..."

"Clyde!"

Charlie and Clyde looked like Brandon came over pulling a rack. It was full of arts and crafts stuff.

"What is the meaning of this?" Brandon asked, raising his voice.

"Now, now. Let's not get upset. Clyde, do you know about this?" Charlie asked.

Clyde furrowed his brow and screwed up his face. Brandon started to smile. He hid it on purpose, Clyde thought. In a freak movement, Clyde rushed for Brandon and shoved him against the rack. Brandon was about to fight back, but Charlie stood between them.

"Relax!" Charlie shouted.

Clyde and Brandon were both taken back. Charlie had never gotten upset before and it was a bit scary. Brandon stood up and brushed himself off. Clyde kept his fists clenched, as if he was about to knock someone out.

"Now, does anyone know where this rack came from?" Charlie asked.

"I only have five racks. If I had known there was another, I wouldn't have come back and said that my work was done." Clyde said.

"Clyde is just making excuses. He just wants to go home..."

"Wouldn't you also want to go home." Clyde said, raising his voice.

"Enough!"

Brandon and Clyde waited for Charlie to speak again.

"What we have here is a problem. The section is full, so we can't put out the rack until the section is sold down. Brandon, I would have you fill it as the section sells down, however, since when there is no overtime, I have to send you home...."

"What!" Clyde shouted.

Charlie looked at Clyde.

"Let me finish." Charlie hissed.

Clyde sighed. Brandon smirked. Charlie continued.

"Clyde, I'm going to have you fill the section as it sells down. There is also other things from Kitchen to Furniture that have to go out, so I would like you to stay and complete some of that for another four hours, then you can go home, and since when you are staying here during the day, you will have the overnight shift off."

A night off!

"What! Charlie you can't be serious!" Brandon shouted.

"Did I stutter Brandon? Let me remind you that it was you who found the rack, so I am beginning to get suspicious that you set up poor Clyde here. Did you? It would be a shame if Al found out...."

Clyde watched as Brandon's eyes went wide.

"Please, don't tell Al..." Brandon begged.

"I'm getting closer to it. Now, the both of you scram and get your work done. I have to be on a conference call in the next hour, so don't bother me." Charlie said.

Clyde had never seen Brandon run off the salesfloor. Charlie waited a couple of minutes, then left as well, leaving Clyde behind. Clyde was not angry anymore. Extra money for me I guess, Clyde thought. He sighed and looked at the rack of Arts and Crafts stuff. Brandon hid it from me, but why? Clyde thought. Brandon had given Clyde problems in the past, but nothing to the extent of framing him for not doing his work. Is he jealous of me? Does he want Jemma in the same way as I do? Clyde shook his head. I'll never know. He noticed that a couple of the sections that he just put out were low, so he filled them with some of the stuff from the rack, then proceeded to the backroom. As Clyde approached the doors to enter the back, he stopped. Brandon ran through the backroom, not even paying attention to anything around him. Charlie was not too far behind and watched as Brandon left. Clyde watched as Charlie stopped, then turned back around to head towards the office. Ok, coast is clear, Clyde thought. He entered the backroom and grabbed a rack full of rugs. Heavy stuff takes a long time to fill.

Clyde was right.

The rugs were not in their own room, rather, they were standing up in cages. The rugs were varying lengths, which made it a pain in Clyde's ass to put them out, however, Clyde was killing time. I have already done my work, Clyde thought. He was just waiting for Arts and Crafts to be sold down so that he could put more out. That was the only thing that he cared about. Other than that, nothing else matters, Clyde thought. The rugs took Clyde longer than he expected and he filled one of the cages, then went to the back to bring out a cage to the floor, and filled that cage. And that was all from rack of rugs. Most of them were indoor/outdoor ones, however, there were other ones that were just strictly indoor ones. Some were big and others were small, however, Clyde filled the cage in a way that the bigger rugs were towards the back, while the smaller ones were towards the front. Thankfully the cage was up against one of the back walls of the store, so the larger rugs could lean on the wall. Charlie didn't seem to care if it was this way, as the other cages of rugs were like this. Across from where Clyde was standing, was a section were some of the rugs could be displayed out flat. People went through this section like no other, as Clyde witnessed customers throw the rugs on the ground. Pathetic, Clyde thought. He even watched as some people stepped on the rugs and wiped their shoes on them, as to test them out before buying them. Ever heard of a return? Clyde thought. He wanted to say it so bad to some of these people, however, he bit his tongue, so blood flowed in his mouth again. Clyde went over to the rack and brought it towards the back room. It took his longer to get to the back, as more people were in the store now. Usually Martins was busy in the afternoon and Clyde was happy that he was leaving. After dropping off the rack, Clyde went over to the Arts and Crafts section. The entire first and second walls were almost half empty. God Damn, Clyde thought. Thankfully the other rack was still here, and he proceeded to fill up the section. Clyde them turned around as Charlie appeared.

"It's time for you to leave. I can see that you are pretty much done." Charlie said.

Clyde nodded.

"Yeah, I just have those crochet hooks left to put out." Clyde said.

Charlie nodded.

"Interesting. Ok, do that, then punch out and Clyde, please

enjoy your night off. You deserve it." Charlie said.

Clyde was about to respond when Charlie disappeared. Clyde got up off his knees and went over to the rack. Clyde then was shocked. I thought I had more crochet hooks. In the last basket on the rack, there was only one pair of the hooks. Clyde pulled out the basket to get a better look of the hooks. They were a large size and were jet black. Clyde grabbed one of the hooks and realized that it was wood. It felt heavy in his hand and Clyde almost fell. Strange, Clyde thought. He picked up the second one and it seemed to even out. The hooks were about the size his arm, which was strange because they looked a lot smaller in the basket.

"These are weird." Clyde said.

As he held the hooks, an older lady came around the corner.

"Do you have any more of those?"

Clyde looked at her.

"The crochet hooks. No, this is my only pair."

The old lady let out a laugh.

"What's so funny?" Clyde asked.

"You must be blind there sonny, because I found them."

The old lady pointed to a section on the second wall right across from Clyde. An entire slew of crochet hooks were hanging from the pegs. Odd, Clyde thought.

"I guess I do have more. Take whatever ones you want." Clyde said.

"Thanks sonny."

Clyde watched as the old lady grabbed some yarn and a pair of crochet hooks. This is getting strange, Clyde thought. He looked at the hooks and then looked back at the wall. There is no way that those could have just appeared. No fucking way, Clyde thought. He never believed in God or magic or anything, so this was freaking him out. Clyde put the hooks down and went over to the wall of crochet hooks. He grabbed a medium sized pair that were made from wood. Clyde held the package in his hands for a second and he pulled back. The hooks fell to the ground and shattered into tiny beads that rolled across the floor. What the fuck! Clyde thought. He backed away from the crochet hooks and slipped on a couple of beads that were under his shoes. Clyde grabbed the end of the rack and held onto it, hauling himself to his feet. Clyde scanned the area for customers and let out a sigh of relief. No one is around. Clyde then looked at the ground and noticed that the beads were all gone. What is going on here! Clyde thought. He rubbed his hands on his pants, then went over to the crochet hooks. I'm going to buy them, Clyde thought. Clyde went over to the hooks and moved the rack into the backroom. There was just enough space for the rack to go and when he placed it in the backroom, Clyde almost had a heart attack. He held the hooks and then the rack disappeared right in front of his eyes. Clyde's eyes went wide.

"What the fuck!"

"Clyde are you ok?"

Clyde turned around to see Charlie standing there, arms crossed over his chest. Clyde did a double-take, and then looked at where the rack was.

"I had a rack and now it's gone." Clyde said.

"Are you sure?"

Clyde nodded.

"Charlie, would I lie to you? I brought in the last rack and had it here. The crochet hooks are all out."

"Did someone lose a rack?"

Clyde and Charlie watched as one of the early morning stockers brought in a rack. It wasn't just a rack, it was the rack. The basket that had the crochet hooks were on the rack, empty.

"This is strange." Clyde said.

"What do you mean?" Charlie asked.

Clyde shook his head.

"Never mind. I'm just tired. I'm going to punch out and buy some things before I go." Clyde said.

Charlie nodded.

"Whatever floats your boat." Charlie said, walking away.

The early morning stocker also left the backroom, leaving Clyde standing by himself. In his right hand, he gripped the hooks and let out a sigh of relief. Clyde then went to the timeclock and punched out. Immediately he went to the registers. He looked for a price tag, but there was nothing on the hooks at all. Strange all the other ones did. Clyde hustled to the Arts and Crafts section and found a set of crochet hooks that were of similar size. Clyde then hopped into the line. There were at least five registers open and Clyde never recognized the cashiers during the day. None of them were young, as most of them were retired and just working at Martins to get out of the house. Good for them, Clyde thought. He was called to Register 8 and went over to the cashier.

"I want these ones here, but it had no price, so scan the other set please."

"Do you work here?" The cashier asked.

"I do."

"Numbers."

Clyde told the cashier his numbers. The cashier grabbed both sets of crochet hooks and fumbled with them in her hands. Clyde was beginning to get impatient, but the cashier had a confused look on her face. After five minutes of silence, Clyde spoke.

"Anything wrong?" Clyde asked.

"Well, the one you want me to scan has nothing on it." The cashier said.

"What. Gimme that." Clyde said.

He grabbed both sets of the crochet hooks out of the cashiers hands. Some people waiting in the line looked over, but didn't say anything. Clyde searched up and down the crochet hooks, looking for the packaging and the price. What the fuck! Clyde thought. He let out an angry sigh and shook his head.

"This can't be happening. I thought there was a price on it. Just make up one, I only want the black wooden ones." Clyde said.

"How about $7.99?"

"Works for me."

The cashier punched in the numbers and Clyde only ended up paying $5 or something because of his discount. The cashier put the crochet hooks in a bag and the other ones were placed in a basket underneath. Clyde took the receipt and told the cashier to have a great day, in which she mumbled something under her breath. Clyde went to the breakroom and got his things, then went out through the backroom. By now, the backroom was full of employees that he did not recognize, however, he was not going to start getting to know them now. A guy opened the door and Clyde left. When Clyde was away from the backdoor, he fumbled for a cigarette and cursed. I left the blasted things at home, Clyde thought. He walked back to the apartment complex so fast that Clyde was in his apartment before he knew it. The sun was at its highest point and the city of Casper was fully awake. Cars and trucks drove up and down the busy Main Street, while people walked about on both sides of the sidewalk. Clyde went into his apartment and closed the door. He flicked on the lights and opened the single window. Clyde then found his cigarettes, lit one up, and grabbed the crochet hooks. He sat down on the couch and took the hooks out of the bag. Strange things they are, Clyde thought. He felt a gust of wind brush past his neck and turned around. There was nothing. No wind came from the only open window.

Strange. Clyde held the hooks in his hand. It was a strange feeling that he had. He felt somewhat weaker for some reason. He tested this by placing the hooks on the table in front of the couch and laid back. When Clyde was not touching the hooks, he felt dizzy and empty, that something inside him was not complete. Clyde then leaned forward and grabbed the hooks. It was almost as a lightning strike went through him. He had energy to move, to get up and do whatever he wanted. Clyde hopped to his feet and grabbed a beer from the fridge. Except he didn't. The beer came to him. Clyde ducked as the beer can almost hit him. In a quick movement, Clyde caught the beer can. It was a Budweiser can.

"I thought I finished the case last night." Clyde said.

He looked in shock. In front of the fridge, were at last ten cases of Budweiser. What in the hell?! Clyde thought. Swallowing, Clyde walked over to the fridge and opened it. All the food and the snacks were still in the fridge, except for the beer that just appeared out of nowhere. I wish I had a bigger fridge, Clyde thought. He jumped as the fridge door closed rapidly. The fridge expanded. The metal stretched itself out, making strange noises and sounds that echoed in Clyde's ears. Clyde backed away and put his hands to his ears, trying to block the noise, but the noises still seeped in. Clyde then let out a scream and then was silence. He looked up to see that the fridge had expanded from floor to ceiling. The cases of beer were gone, but when Clyde opened the fridge, then entire fridge was lined with beer. Every shelf of it. Clyde looked at crochet hooks that were still on the table.

"What did I buy?" Clyde asked.

He went over to the hooks and touched them again. The energy ran through him like lightning. Motivation seemed to emit from him, and he held the hooks in his hand. This is so strange, Clyde thought. He turned around, held his arm out, and opened his palm. The fridge door opened wide. Clyde smiled and closed his palm. The fridge door closed. He tried this multiple times, with each time getting better and better. Clyde they sat on the couch and tried this. The fridge door opened, and he extended his reach more to get a can from the fridge. The can flew in the air and after many tries, Clyde got it down to where he could move the can in the air and catch it as it came towards him. This is cool, but very strange. Clyde thought. Clyde still didn't know what to think of this, but there was one thing that he knew.

He needed the hooks near him for anything.

The energy that allowed him to do these things, required the hooks for some strange reason. Clyde tested this multiple times, as he tried to open the fridge and levitate cans without the hooks nearby and nothing happened. Clyde also began to feel sleepy, like he hadn't slept in over a hundred years. His eyes were heavy, and his movements were sluggish, however, when he picked up those hooks, all those effects were gone, and he felt like he was the same. Clyde then wanted some rope so he could tie the hooks together. He made a motion with his hands and out of his fingertips, came a rope that coiled at his feet. The rope coiled until he stopped moving his hands and picked up the rope. It was solid. Clyde bent down and took the rope. He coiled some of it at the middle of the hooks, then cut the rope in pieces to tie the top and bottoms together. Now it looked like that Clyde had a scroll in his hand. Great, Clyde thought. Clyde then took the remaining rope and wrapped it around the middle rope, so that the hooks had a bit of a string attached to them. Clyde then sat down on the couch with the hooks next to him. When they were on the couch near him, Clyde felt fine. Then Clyde thought of something else.

He had his night off, which was a good thing, however.

The next night, he would need to have the hooks with him.

"Great." Clyde thought.

Clyde was no stranger to having nights off and when he did, all he would do was either drink or watch TV. The TV was going, however, Clyde was not in the mood to really watch anything. Also Jeremy was still out fixing that issue, so Clyde was really stuck. He drank a few more cans of beer and even made the trash-can expand to contain all the cans. Clyde also moved the trashcan closer to the end of the couch, so that he wouldn't have to get up all the time. Clyde finished some more beers, then decided to order some food from Door Dash, in which a pizza showed up at his door. There was a knock at his door and Clyde got up. Then everything hit at once. Clyde fell to the floor and slammed face first on the floor. Struggling, Clyde turned around and crawled towards the couch. As he got closer, he felt the energy coming back into him.

"Hello! Anyone there!"

It was the pizza guy, but Clyde didn't care. He reached for the hooks, and he finally got up and brushed himself off. Clyde went to the door and opened it. Clyde held out one hand with the money, while the hooks were in the other. The pizza guy looked at him.

"You ok man? This is one large tip for a single pizza."

Clyde looked at the money in his hand and noticed that there were 3 twenty-dollar bills in his hand. Clyde nodded.

"Take it and keep the change." Clyde said.

The pizza guy didn't object, took the money, and ran away. Clyde struggled to hold the pizza with one had at first, however, he put it down on the table and sighed. The hooks were still firmly grasped in his right hand and Clyde shook his head. What is going on with me! I need to find out about this, Clyde thought. He looped the rope with the hooks to one of his jean loops and surprisingly, he felt the same. The energy pounded in him, like something had opened. Clyde felt better than he did. He felt younger, more vibrant than usual. It's all because of the hooks. This can't be right, Clyde thought. The thought of him having more energy was a concept that Clyde was not used to. Clyde then got a paper plate and ate some slices of the pizza. He flipped to his Netflix account and put on one of the movies that was in a the top 10 spots. He didn't really care for the movie, however, he just wanted background noise. Clyde had to admit, that eating with crochet hooks next to you was one of the most interesting experiences ever. For one, he couldn't take off his jeans because he was eating. Clyde looped the rope tied to his jean loop and put the hooks next to him. Clyde felt the energy pulsing through him and as he ate his pizza, he felt the same. Even though these hooks had attached to him, Clyde still felt the same. He knew that the hooks didn't have to be right next to him, however, they had to be within arm's reach. Clyde tested this and sure enough, even if the hooks were an arm's reach from him, Clyde felt the same. Now I don't need to have them near me all the time. Good, Clyde thought. It took Clyde a few hours to eat all the pizza and flip through the Netflix Movies. By the time he was done, he was wiped. Clyde was not energy tired.

He had plenty of energy.

Clyde was bored tired.

The type of tired that hits you like a truck. The type of tired that makes you want to go to bed when you really don't want to. Clyde moved from the couch, but the first thig he did was grasp those hooks. Clyde still felt the energy in him and when he stood up, felt like he could take on the world. I'm not in the mood mentally, Clyde thought. He didn't want to do anything, so he went to his bed, put on his pajamas, and crashed on the bed. The last thing he did before closing his eyes, was place the hooks within arm's reach. He still felt the energy pulsating from the hooks, and it was enough for Clyde to crack a smile. Clyde closed his eyes and took in a deep breath, then let it out and sleep overcame him.

"Clyde! Clyde! Get up man!"

The rapping at the door jolted Clyde awake. The next thing Clyde did was look at his phone. It was 10:00am and the rapping at the door continued. Suppressing a groan, Clyde let out a sigh and got off his bed. Clyde gripped the crochet hooks as he walked towards the door. He was still tired from getting up, however, the energy had begun to emit from the hooks and transferred itself into Clyde's body from his fingertips. So the energy starts when I am awake. Interesting, Clyde thought. He stopped at the door and opened it. Jeremy stood at the front of the door.

"You look terrible, Clyde. What the hell happened to you?" Jeremy asked.

Clyde did not know how he looked, but Jeremy noticed that there was something off about Clyde. He had some circles forming under his eyes. His body seemed a bit smaller, and it showed in his pajamas. Was he dieting, Jeremy thought.

"I feel fine." Clyde said, straightening out in the door way. Jeremy nodded.

"Sure you do. Let's go for breakfast. I'll drive." Jeremy said.

"Where are we going?" Clyde asked.

"Valerie's in North Casper." Jeremy said.

"Let me get dressed and I'll be right out." Clyde said.

Clyde closed the door and went to get dressed. Thank God he hasn't noticed the hooks yet. Now Clyde was in trouble. How was he going to explain to Jeremy about the hooks? It makes me look suspicious when I carry them around, Clyde thought. I need to find a way to bring them without him thinking about it. Clyde returned to the door dressed in his jeans and a solid color shirt.

Jeremy smiled and the two left.

"I'll drive." Jeremy said.

Clyde followed him to his car, which was an older model of the Corolla. The two friends got in and drove out of the apartment complex. North Casper. Clyde felt a shiver go down his spine. It was not the best of places. Clyde didn't think that it was even part of the city. It was a whole separate town all together, with its own local government and everything. It all had to deal with the history of Massachusetts. Some towns and cities were so big, that they wanted to be separated from the main town or city and become their own. North Casper was one of these places and Clyde sat in silence as Jeremy drove. He was not much of a talker in the morning, but he would open after he got his breakfast. Like me,

Clyde thought. The entire drive he gripped the hooks in his right hand. I'm not sure if Jeremy even knows that I still have them. The energy pounded through his body, as if it was trying to get him to do something.

Create something.

The voice pounded in his head. This was the first time that he heard this voice. Clyde could not tell if it was a female or a male voice, but he knew that it was a voice. It was also very loud and when Clyde heard it again, he pressed his hands to his ears. Jeremy looked over at Clyde, puzzled.

"Are you ok Clyde?" Jeremy asked.

Clyde nodded.

"Yeah, just a bit of a headache that is all."

"Want me to turn around? We can go someplace else?" Jeremy asked.

"No, we are already halfway there. Might as well continue." Clyde said.

Jeremy nodded and continued driving. Clyde waited for a few moments, then took his hands from his ears. The voice was not there. Where are you, Clyde thought.

In your head.

The voice startled Clyde again, however, he just looked right at the dashboard, not moving, or saying anything. The last thing he wanted was to tell Jeremy about the voice. The itch was there, bugging him like nothing that Clyde had experienced before. He then felt it. An itch on his ankle and Clyde reached down to itch it. He kept itching and itching. Jeremy looked over at Clyde.

"Leg itchy?"

"Yes, very." Clyde said in a hurry.

Jeremy continued driving. Clyde continued itching. His fingers began to hurt, and his arm was getting sore. Why won't it stop, Clyde thought. Then it stopped and Clyde let out a sigh of relief and sat back up in his seat. Thank God, Clyde thought. Valerie's was a medium sized breakfast place, located off Main Street in Downtown North Casper. The parking lot was decent enough to have at least forty cars in the lot at one time. The early morning hours were always packed and by the time Jeremy pulled in his car, half the lot was full. Jeremy found a spot to park in and the two stepped out of the car. Clyde gripped the hooks with his hands, hoping that Jeremy would still not notice. He hasn't noticed this whole time, so why would he now? Clyde thought. If anything, Clyde was going to place the hooks next to him. The energy pounded through him like an endless cycle of drums. Every heartbeat was like the footstep of an elephant, pounding through him. Blood rushed in his body and Clyde felt more awake. Jeremy noticed this as the two walked to the front door.

"You seem more awake now." Jeremy said.

Clyde nodded.

"Yeah, a lot better now that we are out of the car. I don't use the car because I'm always car sick at times." Clyde said.

"I know. I hope that you can overcome that someday."

"Why?"

"I wanted to go on a road trip with you. You know, as friends."

Clyde almost burst out laughing and he snorted when he held it in.

"What's so funny? I can't take my best friend places." Jeremy said, irritated.

Clyde shook his head.

"No, it's not that, it's just, where would we go?" Clyde asked.

"I don't know Disney Land. Universal?"

Those places sounded better than Casper, Massachusetts. Jeremy opened the door and the two friends stepped inside. The building itself was a mix of vibrant colors. It had that 1950s era look, with the tables, floors, and wallpaper to match the era. The waitress's wore whatever clothes they wanted and wore name tags on their shirts. Clyde's eyes shifted to a few of them that were pretty....

Get your head out the gutter, Clyde thought.

You want them don't you?

It was that voice again. The mix of male and female voices coming together to form one sound that irritated the fuck out of

Clyde. A hostess came over.

"Two?" She asked.

"Yes please." Jeremy responded.

"Follow me."

You want her don't you Clyde. Tied down and naked.

No! Go away! Clyde thought.

"Clyde let's go!" Jeremy said.

Clyde snapped into the present and followed Jeremy. The hostess looked annoyed as she led the two down a main walkway and off to the right, where a booth was. The booth looked out to the parking lot, where the windows let in a lot of light. Clyde was not paying attention and hit his body on the side of the table. Jeremy rushed to help Clyde sit down.

"I'm sorry, he isn't really awake this morning." Jeremy said, apologizing to the hostess.

The hostess just placed the menus down and told them to enjoy their breakfast. Jeremy handed one to Clyde and Clyde watched as the hostess went to the front to sit more guests.

You want her more than your food. Who's a hungry boy?

Fuck off.

The voice went away for the second time. Clyde had only been to Valerie's a few times. I can't remember the last time I was here, Clyde thought. It didn't matter. Clyde was starving and when the waitress came over, the two friends ordered right away. Both got the same thing, which was a combo breakfast order with pancakes, scrambled eggs, bacon, ham, toast, and a plate of home fries to share. Other patrons came into the establishment and by the looks that the two were getting, it seemed to everyone else that Clyde and Jeremy were some gay couple having breakfast. Let them stare, Clyde thought. He looked at Jeremy.

"So, what was the emergency that you had to take care of?" Clyde asked.

The waitress brought over some water. The two friends did a toast and the glass clinked louder than they expected. A few heads turned, then went back to their morning conversations.

Jeremy sipped his water, then spoke.

"The other complex had a break in. A bad on if I might add.

One of the tenants is now out of over ten-thousand dollars' worth of stuff and she is so pissed."

Ten-thousand dollars, Clyde thought. What the hell is someone doing to make that kind of money. And why live in an apartment?

"Did they ever catch who did it?" Clyde asked.

Jeremy shook his head.

"No, a few leads at first, but now the case is cold for some strange reason."

"What was that person doing, if you don't mind me asking?"

"She was some sort of artist Youtuber. Originally from New York City. She moved out to MA because it was cheaper. She had another studio apartment next to her that she used as an art studio. Think of that Clyde. The girl lived by herself and had enough money to afford two studio apartments. That is a lot of money."

"So she lost artwork?" Clyde asked.

The food came and was placed in front of them. Saying their thanks, the two friends dived into the food.

"She had a collection that was getting ready to be shown at that Casper Art House tomorrow. I don't know how much of a following she has out here, but by the looks of the art ticket sales and stuff, she lost a lot." Jeremy said between mouthfuls of food.

"So what happens now?"

"Well, she basically has to clean up her apartments and that is why I took so long. She introduced herself as Alexandria and the two of us got along very well..."

"Don't tell me you hooked up with this artist girl?" Clyde asked, smiling.

Jeremy smiled. Clyde pointed his finger.

"I knew it. You went to bed with her, didn't you." Clyde said, raising his voice.

"Shhh! Not so loud. Yes we did, but there also is something else...."

Clyde raised an eyebrow. Something else.

"We want to get married, Clyde." Jeremy said.

Clyde couldn't believe it. Jeremy's getting married. Jeremy

had his fair share of girls in the past. Clyde could only remember one or two and Jeremy always made sure that if he was in with a girl, then there was protection involved. Kids are not Jeremy's thing, but if he is with this Alexandria girl, then maybe it would be a possibility? Clyde thought. He couldn't see Jeremy being a father, but then again, Clyde thought that anyone with kids could never be a father.

"Well, I'm happy for you man." Clyde said.

"Just think man, the three of us living in same apartment complex. I would just have to work on the maintenance, and you could still help with the books. We got it made. Alexandria and I can get our own room and you can have the whole apartment to yourself. It's a win-win situation." Jeremy said.

Clyde only smiled and ate his food.

"I'm still so happy for you man. That's great. Now, it's my turn." Clyde said.

That hostess wants you so bad Clyde. You can feel it from here.

It was the voice again, whispering in his ear.   I'm trying to eat, go away.

You can't resist her. You want her.

Leave me alone!

If you have the hooks, you are mine!

I will never be anyone's.

We will see about that.

"Clyde, are you ok?" Jeremy asked.

Clyde snapped back to the present.

"Yeah, I'm fine." Clyde said.

Jeremy gave him a confused look.

"Are you sure you are fine because you have a vein sticking out of your forehead. Are you stressed out about something?" Jeremy asked.

Clyde looked at him, then touched his forehead. He could feel the bumpy vein beneath his fingers. Stressed is more like an understatement, Clyde thought. He was stressed out, but couldn't tell Jeremy what the issue was. Clyde sighed.

"I guess the food is good and fills me up, but I am stressed out."

"Why?" Jeremy asked.

The perfect time to lie, Clyde thought.

Lie to protect your friend. That is interesting. I'm all ears.

Clyde sighed.

"Jeremy, I'm just stressed at work." Clyde said.

Clyde waited for the voice to come into his head, but it was not there. For once, silence reigned supreme in his head. Jeremy looked at Clyde and nodded.

"Yeah, I can tell that you have been stressed at work. Is it because of the new girl?" Jeremy asked.

The waitress came by with the check and left it. Jeremy fumbled through his wallet for cash to pay.

"I think it might be more than that." Clyde said.

"I think you have said this before." Jeremy said.

Clyde put his hands in his face.

"I can't like this girl, Jeremy. I mean, I saw her for one fucking night and now I'm girl crazy. It doesn't make any sense to me!" Clyde said, raising his voice.

Heads turned.

"Clyde, shut up!" Jeremy said, raising his voice too.

Clyde realized the heads looking at him and Jeremy. Clyde nodded.

"Fine, but you get what I mean? There is no way that I could love this girl. She is different than me. She works hard and isn't a bum, whereas I... ."

"You think that you are bum?" Jeremy asked.

The waitress came to take the check and smiled.

"Yes, I'm a bum, Jeremy. I mean look at me. I live in your place, your life, and everything in between and you don't have to include me, but you do... ."

Jeremy leaned back.

"You are jealous of me and Alex?"

"I'm not jealous of anyone." Clyde said.

Jeremy leaned forward.

"Now Clyde, pal, tell me the truth." Jeremy said.

Clyde could not avoid his stare. The Jeremy Stare is what

he called it over the years. When Jeremy looks at you like that, he wants an answer, Clyde thought.

"Ok. I am a bit jealous, but it's going to make me want to work hard so I can find someone for me." Clyde said.

"I'll hold you to that, Holding. Let's get out of here."

The two got up from the table and left Valerie's. As the two left, streams of people were coming in and the hostess seemed a bit ticked off that it was busy. Tough, Clyde thought. He gripped the hooks so hard, that at first he thought he left them in the restaurant, however, when he got to Jeremy's car, he placed them at his feet. The energy bounded through him still and he was not going to let them out of his sight. Jeremy pulled his car out of the parking lot and began the drive back to Casper and Brightcourt.

"Clyde? I never knew that you had those with you until now."

At first, Clyde was not sure of what Jeremy was talking about, until he looked down. Across his lap, where the crochet hooks. Fuck, Clyde thought. Clyde smiled sheepishly.

"Yeah. I bought them at the store, and I like carrying them around." Clyde said.

Jeremy let out a laugh.

"What? Is it a good luck charm?" Jeremy asked.

He is a fool? Doesn't he know about the power of the hooks!

He doesn't need to know.

He should know. Or you can show him.

No then it would end badly for the both of us.

"What do you mean?" Jeremy asked.

Clyde didn't realize that he was talking out loud. The voice seemed to go away from his head. Fuck you, Clyde thought.

"These hooks. Well…"

How could he explain it to Jeremy? Oh yeah, they are magic! That would be the stupidest thing that Clyde could say. It sounded stupid in his head and probably even more stupid out loud.

"Clyde, I get it man. It's ok." Jeremy said.

Clyde was confused and he furrowed his brow.

"You do? You understand?" Clyde asked.

Jeremy nodded.

"Yeah man, I totally get it. It's 2021 and you don't want anyone to know that you are crocheting stuff on the side. I get it. It must be a new hobby. I totally support you man." Jeremy said.

Clyde's mouth almost dropped. If he could have laughed he would, but Clyde held it in so much that he began to choke on his own spit and cough. Then he laughed. Jeremy laughed nervously in the driver seat as Clyde laughed, his face becoming red and tears coming down his eyes. This is most ridiculous thing that I have ever done, Clyde thought. When he was done laughing, he sighed, and spoke.

"Yes, man. I can't keep the secret anymore. I have been crocheting on the side and I would like to make you something, but I'm not very good at it yet, so I don't know how it is going to come out." Clyde said.

Jeremy smiled.

"I would like something from you Clyde. A blanket. You know, one of those big ones for two."

Clyde gulped. How was he going to do that, when he didn't know shit about crocheting and yarn and measurements and stuff. God Damn it all, Clyde thought. He could only smile.

"Say no more, I will try to my best and make a blanket for two. It might take a while though. I don't think I'm very fast at it yet." Clyde said.

"That is fine man. Take your time. I would rather you do that so you can focus on your craft."

Craft. That is what Jeremy called it. A fucking Craft. Clyde knew that these hooks were much more than a craft. Clyde looked down at the hooks. They stared back up at him, seemingly lifeless in his lap to Jeremy. To Clyde, the hooks presented something that Clyde was waiting for. A life where he could escape from what he was doing. A jump into his own mind was a good thing occasionally. The drive was in silence for the last few minutes as Jeremy pulled into Brightcourt's parking lot. He put the Corolla in park, then pulled out his phone.

"Alexandria texted me. She's asked me to appear in a video, so I'm going to help her out. Want to come?" Jeremy asked.

Clyde shook his head.

"No. I'm feeling a bit tired this morning so I might hang out here. I want to figure out how to do that blanket, then I have work tonight from 9pm-6am." Clyde said.

Jeremy nodded.

"I understand. Well, I'll let you off here and make that blanket." Jeremy said.

Clyde stepped out of the car and fumbled for the keys. The first things in his hands were the hooks. He could not forget the hooks. That would be the last thing that I would do, Clyde thought. Jeremy pulled the car out and rolled down his window.

"Clyde I'll text you with updates and if I don't see you tonight, then I will tomorrow morning." Jeremy said.

"Sounds good man. See you later."

Clyde had never seen Jeremy speed out of the parking lot before and you could have sworn that in another life, Jeremy was a NASCAR Racer. Clyde watched as Jeremy's car disappeared and was lost in a mess of cars that were on Main Street. Clyde used the key to get into his apartment and the first thing that he did was lie down on the couch. He placed the hooks on the table in front of the couch within arms-reach. He sighed, rubbing his hands across his face. How am I going to make this blanket, Clyde thought. He knew that he couldn't just make the whole thing, as Jeremy would find that suspicious. How to do it? Clyde then sat up on the couch and grabbed the hooks in his hands. He unwrapped them, holding one hook in each hand. Clyde took the hooks and started to rub the fronts of the hooks together in a motion. Without even realizing what he was doing, yarn sprung from the space and began to form itself into a series of rows. Clyde was shocked but he couldn't stop his hands from moving. He tried to move his body, but it was stuck. There was no feeling in his legs. He could feel himself breathing, but when he tried to move anything else, he was struck. Clyde moved his head around, looking about the room. He was the only one that was here that was awake. As far as I know, Clyde thought. He could feel his hands and arms moving in a motion, the hooks rubbing back and forth. The yarn grasping and moving together, forming patterns and shapes. When Clyde looked down, he had an entire stripe of a blanket. The colors were blue, grey, white, and green. Each section was a square and each square had the mixture of colors involved. There were no squares that were only one color. Why can't I move, Clyde thought. He then tried to get up again and he used so much force, that he launched himself forward and over the table in front of him. Clyde landed hard on the floor and in a panic, let go of the hooks. The hooks rolled across the room, well out of arm's reach of him. Suddenly Clyde felt cold. A draft swept through the room, but he knew that no windows were open. He reached out his arms slowly in front of him, trying to reach the hooks. The hooks stopped rolling and were at the front of the door.

Now you want me Clyde.

Clyde's mouth was dry, as if he was in a desert. The temperature of the room continued to change from extreme cold to hot in a matter of seconds. Shaking his head, he tried to crawl towards the hooks. His legs dragged right behind him, as if something came with a sledgehammer and broke them while he was on the ground. Clyde coughed and sputtered, sending out phlegm that built up inside of his system. The coughing fits continued as Clyde crawled forward, sending his body into convulsions. He reached out for the hooks, his eyes building, his tongue out of his mouth, gasping for water, air, and life itself.

I think you can go a bit further.

There was that voice again. It bothered Clyde. He hated these hooks, but hated how dependent he had become on them in the span of almost a couple of days. Clyde rolled onto his back, coughing madly. The phlegm sprung from his mouth and when it launched into the air, it fell back on his face like rain drops.

"PLEASE!!!!" Clyde rasped.

His voice shook the room and Clyde knew that it was no use. Letting out a scream, he rolled over on his stomach and crawled towards the door. Tears streamed down his face. His entire face was red with sweat and exhaustion. I hate this, Clyde thought. The hooks were in reach now and when he grabbed one, the other one seemingly fell into his other hand. Then everything was back to normal in a snap. The temperature was normal. Clyde didn't feel sick at all. The energy that pounded through him was so hard that it launched him to his feet and Clyde sailed in the air, crashing into the couch. The force was so great, that Clyde caused the couch to flip over and slam into the back wall of the apartment. Thankfully Clyde was face down on the floor when the piece of furniture sailed in the air. Clyde put his hands to his chest, as if he was trying to calm his heart that beat repeatedly in his chest. Clyde got up and let out a huge sigh, then stretched out his right hand, opening his palm. The couch floated from the back wall and Clyde guided it to where it was before. When he placed the couch down, Clyde looked at the wall. There was dent in it and again, Clyde just had to look at it and hold out his hand. The ground shook for a little bit, but after a few minutes, the wall fixed itself. Clyde could see the inside of wall working and coming back together. Wood, wiring, insulation. All the components of a wall, Clyde felt them and saw them fix itself. My God, Clyde thought. When the wall was done fixing itself, Clyde felt like something was drained from him. He was tired. I've never experienced this before.

You Created something.

Again it was the voice. Clyde would have turned it off, but this time he was eager to listen.

What do you mean Created?

You used your Energy to Create something. Everything you make, it takes your Energy.

Why?

It's always been like this. It will always be like this, Clyde.

Can I get the Energy back?

You tell us. How do you feel?

Not good.

You can't lie to us Clyde. We know that you aren't feeling well.

This was true, Clyde thought. I can't lie to this voice or these voices in my head. They know my every move before it's even out.

We know that you want something. Something that your friend has.

I don't know what you are talking about.

The voice let out a laugh. It was so loud that it startled Clyde and he fell to the floor, placing his hands over his ears.

That's funny Clyde. We know what you want. We know what you seek. Why don't you see for yourself. Look in the sink.

Clyde looked over to see the sink full with water to the point that it was overflowing. Jeremy is going to kill me, Clyde thought.

He will never know.

That was the voice speaking to him again. Clyde got a hold of himself and went over to the sink. The water was almost to the top of the sink, just so that a little bit of water would flow out ever so slightly. Clyde looked in the water. Surprisingly it was clear, and ripples appeared. Clyde at first struggled to see what was in the ripples, but the ripples stopped, and they formed a figure.

That figure was Jemma.

Clyde pulled away in shock.

"I don't want this!" Clyde shouted.

The voice laughed inside of Clyde's head.

Look.

Clyde tried to pull away from the sink, but a force held him still. His palms were spread out, forced on the counter. His head was only looking at the figure of Jemma. At first, she was completely clothed, then the next moment, she only had underwear on.

Then she was naked, and she smiled at him.

Clyde threw up inside his mouth and struggled to spit out, so he moved his head to the side and let it out in a pile on the floor. The voice laughed in his head.

You see. We know what you want, what you desire. We can help you achieve want you want, but only if you learn to control the power of Creation and harness your Energy. We believe in you Clyde and with our help, we can get you this Jemma of yours.

Clyde struggled to speak for a second, as he choked on his own spit.

I don't believe this.

Search yourself. You know that you desire her. You knew it on the first day that you met her.

This is true.

You can't hide the truth from us Clyde. We know it be true.

I want her in the worst way.

The water rippled and soon, Jemma was completely clothed. She smiled and waved at him, then she disappeared.

There is much to learn Clyde. Much to learn.

How do I learn?

Practice.

Practice.

There is no manual for Creation. The thoughts that go in your head fuel this and the Energy that flows through you. Only practice will help you gain your powers and use them for whatever you want.

Whatever I want?

Whatever you want.

Even torture? Even sex?

Yes.

It was one of the worst 'yes's' that Clyde had ever heard. It was sinister. It was full of evil, like something out a legend. Clyde gulped, then sighed. To have the power to bend a girl to my will. What the hell? Clyde thought.

You are nervous.

I've never done anything like that before. I don't think I would be good at it.

There is always opportunities to learn. You don't have to be good at being bad to do bad if that makes sense.

Clyde just nodded.

I find this strange that I'm talking to a voice.

Would you rather talk to a person.

Clyde couldn't answer back as he was in shock that a girl appeared in front of him. He was now able to move his head and hands. He turned around to face the girl. Her skin was white, with flashing yellow eyes. Her brown hair was halfway down her back. She was also not wearing any clothes. Her arms were crossed over her chest, and she levelled a look at Clyde. This girl was skinny, but not too skinny to the point of seeing her bones.

I'm right here, you know.

I'm sorry.

Yes, let me get something to wear so you aren't distracted.

This wasn't how Clyde pictured this girl. Clyde watched as the girl put on a set of fall clothing, with jeans, Ugg Boots, a shirt, and a sweater. I'm expecting some fall flavor coffee.

Very funny, Clyde.

What is your name?

Serena.

That's a new name.

What were you expecting Jane or Jill or Mary or Barbara? Come on now.

Sorry.

Don't be sorry.

So will Jeremy be able to see you or just me? Clyde asked.

Serena shook her head.

Only you can see me. Even if Jeremy would want to see me, he can't.

Why?

The Hooks only have one master and that is you Clyde. There is one rule that is very important. You cannot let anyone touch The Hooks. Only you can touch them.

What happens if someone else touches them?

Serena sighed.

If someone else touches The Hooks, then you will be back to normal and all the power that you have will be transferred to that new person. The downside is that everything that you Created will be undone.

That doesn't sound too bad.

It is bad! Imagine if you used The Hooks for years, then lose it and someone else has them? We witnessed something like the end of the world one time when a guy lost The Hooks. Our last Master sold The Hooks when he.....

Go on.

Serena didn't want to look at Clyde.

Tell me, Serena.

Serena let out a huff.

The last Master that we had is here in Casper now. I believe you know the man. You had run in with him at the convenience store.

This can't be true.

Serena nodded.

Search yourself Clyde. You know it is true.

Clyde then remembered. Mark Durn.

That is why he wanted to talk to me. That's why he was following me.

"Clyde I'm home!"

Jeremy's back!

Clyde watched as Serena faded away and Clyde turned around. Jeremy walked into the apartment.

"Clyde. Did you have the sink on?" Jeremy asked.

Clyde looked to see that all the water was gone.

"Yeah, I ran the dishes while you were gone." Clyde said.

Jeremy nodded.

"Good."

"I thought you were going to be gone for a while. What happened?" Clyde asked.

Jeremy took some steps forward.

"Well, Alexandria needed some stuff for her new video, then I got a call while I was at Tanner's Arts and Crafts, and came back here. Turns out the entire incident was only a false alarm and I figured I would check in on you while I was gone." Jeremy said.

"When will you be back?"

"Why so many questions?" Jeremy asked.

Clyde could sense the irritation in his voice, and he shrugged.

"I don't know. I just wanted to know so I can plan my sleep schedule. I'm working from 9 to 6 tonight." Clyde said.

Jeremy nodded.

"I should be back in a couple of days. Alexandria is a beautiful handful. While I'm gone, if you aren't doing anything, could you watch the desk for me. You know, take the calls and stuff?" Jeremy asked.

Say no.

It was Serena's voice. Clyde as sure of this. The voice had a lingering whisper to it that snaked through his ears and stayed in his brain. I really should say no. Say NO. This time the voice was louder.

"Clyde?!" Jeremy asked.

Clyde snapped into the present and blurted out the first words that came to mind.

"Yes. Yes. I'll do it."

Fool. Jeremy smiled.

"I'm delighted. Thanks Clyde. I'll pay you for your trouble, this time legit and not under the table so it's all legal. Thanks pal. I'm off." Jeremy said.

Clyde had never seen Jeremy run out of the apartment door so fast and he let out a sigh of relief. Thank God.

Finally.

Clyde turned around to see Serena manifesting in front of him, arms crossed over her chest.

What was that about?

He's my friend. Clyde said, letting out a nervous laugh.

Serena only stared harder at Clyde. Clyde knew that he couldn't win with that stare, so he rolled his eyes.

He own's the complex.

Oh does he. What else does he own?

None of your business.

If we are going to be 'together' then it is my business Clyde.

I can't control him coming and going. He is an adult, and he can do what he wants. And what about this 'together' thing. Does that make me your master orrr...

Serena let out a laugh. Her mouth and whole body was moving, but the voice itself bounced in Clyde's head.

Master? Jeez, I would never think of you as my master sort of speak. No Clyde, we are partners. I help you use your Energy to Create what you want and in turn, you prevent anyone from taking The Hooks. Deal?

That's the deal. Nothing else.

Serena shook her head.

Nothing else.

I want to make something.

What do you have in mind?

Clyde didn't have the foggiest idea, however, there was something itching at him, something that really bugged him to bring to life. Serena looked at him, puzzled at the whole thing, then smiled. Clyde looked at her.

I think I know what you want.

How can you tell?

I can read your mind Clyde. Once bound to The Hooks, you can't hide anything from me. I'm your partner. Do you remember that or are you not that bright?

I know that you are my partner, but I don't know how to ask of this.

Ask away Clyde. The worst I can do is say no.

I want walls inside the apartment, like around my bed so I can have my own room. I'm sick of just having one whole room.

Ok, use your Energy.

How?

Serena rolled her eyes.

Think of the walls and how you want to form them, then place your right hand out and move it in the motion you want. I promise that the walls will form.

Clyde hesitated. How do I know that this is the truth?

Just do it, Clyde! Stop thinking about it.

Clyde sighed and stretched out his right hand, spreading his palm and fingers out wide. Serena smiled as the floor moved. The ground shook and Clyde stepped back as materials burst from the ground, forming a wall. At first, Clyde was in shock, but as he moved his hand around his bed, the materials formed a wall, a solid wall of wood, then sheetrock, then painted the same color of grey. Soon Clyde's bed was surrounded by a thick wall and before Clyde sealed it off, he thought of a good place for the door and so it appeared. Clyde then stopped and closed his hand. The ground didn't shake anymore. He looked around to see if anyone was going to barge in the door and see what he made. Nothing. Clyde looked at Serena.

I did it.
Serena clapped.
Congrats. How do you feel?
Better. Like I could do this all day.
Serena shook her head.
Don't get used to it. Energy doesn't replenish all that fast.
I hope that you aren't right.
Serena gave him that stare.
I'm always right.

Clyde looked at his phone. It was only 3pm. He didn't feel hungry and noticed the throw up that he left behind on the floor. With a wave of his hand, it vanished into dust. Clyde looked at Serena.

Can you eat or drink anything.
Can I do that! Of course I can.
Want something.
Sure.

Clyde went over to the large fridge and a pulled out two cans of Budweiser. He tossed one to Serena and watched her as she downed the whole can. Clyde liked to take his beer slow and when he was only halfway done, Serena waited on the couch and flicked on the TV. Clyde had no idea what to make of her. She's a ghost, yet she's watching TV and the volume is on, making it seem like I'm watching it when I'm not. Strange. Serena turned around.

You done thinking about me?

Clyde almost shit himself when she spoke and choked on a sip of his beer. Serena just watched as Clyde fumbled for breath and spat out his beer, coughing and wheezing. Serena only smiled. Clyde looked at her.

That wasn't funny you know.
Serena had turned completely around now.
How do you know it was me?
I know it was you. Who else would use power like that?
I don't think it's wise to accuse me Clyde Holding.

Clyde finished his beer, then walked right over to Serena. Serena did the same thing, so the two were standing in front of each other. Serena smiled.

I think I know what you want, but I don't know if you can even say it to me.

Clyde watched as Serena put her hand near the button of his jeans. Clyde felt himself grow. Serena undid the button and slipped in her hand slowly, touching his underwear. Clyde smiled. So did Serena.

"I think we should take this to the bedroom." Clyde said.

"I agree." Serena said.

It was the first time that Serena spoke. Her voice was lovely. Serena took her hand out of Clyde's pants and went towards the newly made bedroom. She smiled as Clyde followed her. The door was open, then Clyde closed it and locked it shut. Serena was stretched out on the bed, waiting for Clyde. Clyde slowly went onto his bed and soon, he was on top of Serena. They locked lips, kissing passionately. Clyde found his hands under her shirt, grabbing her tits and squeezing them. Serena wrapped her hands around Clyde and soon his shirt was off. They locked tongues and violently took their clothes off, huffing, puffing, and moaning. Soon Clyde put the sheets over the two of them and proceeded to get inside of Serena. She was extremely wet and moaned every time Clyde went in and out repeatedly. As Clyde continued, Serena wrapped her legs around Clyde, forcing him to stay in. Clyde continued, focusing his energy into coming inside her and after what seemed like an eternity, Clyde finished, and Serena moaned as loud as she could. Clyde found his hands holding her down on the bed as she flailed, the orgasm forcing her to struggle against Clyde.

"That a girl. That's a good girl Serena." Clyde said, holding her down as he finished.

Serena didn't say anything and continued to flail around. She kicked her legs in the air to get Clyde off her, but Clyde's weight was too much, and she was forced down. Clyde got a good look at her. Serena was beautiful and even more so when her arms were forced over her head. Her chest rose and down slowly and Clyde wanted to squeeze her tits, but didn't want to let her up. Clyde then kissed Serena, forcing her mouth open and shoving his tongue as far as it would go. Serena gagged a bit, but didn't fight

Clyde. He then pulled away.

"Are you done with me?" Serena asked.

It was a serious question. Clyde had no idea and he smiled.

"Just a bit longer, my dear." Clyde said.

Serena nodded.

"Ok."

The words sounded so innocent. Clyde then noticed that her wrists were tied in a crisscross and forced over her head. Clyde didn't have to hold her down. He then noticed that she was tied down. Her ankles were tied and forced her legs wide open.

"Does this make it easier for you?" Serena asked.

"Of course." Clyde said.

Clyde then touched Serena's chest and he was hard again. He felt in between her legs to find that she was still wet. Clyde then began the process again, with the intent of coming inside of her. Serena thrashed in the bed, moaning, and struggling. Clyde kissed her passionately as he continued his job. Serena moaned and kissed back, trying to match Clyde's strength, but it wasn't enough and soon, Clyde was dominant again. Before Clyde was about to finish, Serena thrashed with all her might and moaned. This was Clyde's que to hurry up and when he did, he squeezed Serena's chest so hard that she screamed. Clyde forced his mouth on her to muffle the scream and that helped as he stayed inside her. Clyde and Serena continued to kiss, passionately at first, then began to slow down bit by bit. Before Clyde knew it, he and Serena were wrapped together in the sheet. No more ropes and Serena didn't try to get away this time.

"Is this what love is like?" Clyde asked.

Serena brushed his hair out of his face.

"Yes. Pure love doesn't need force."

Clyde smiled and kissed her.

"I could stay here forever."

"Me too."

Clyde then took the sheet and wrapped it over the two of them as they enjoyed their time together.

As 8pm rolled around, Clyde and Serena were still in the

room, completely naked. The two went at it again for another hour and this time it felt more natural. Clyde could tell that he was slowing down and when the two orgasmed they knew that they were done for the night. Well for now that is, Clyde thought.

Think again man. I love you, but I need some rest.

Sometime before, Serena entered back in his head.

You must learn that I am a figment of your imagination. I'm only real to you, no one else.

This was a hard pill for Clyde to swallow. For the first time in years, he thought he finally found a girl that was for him. A girl that understood him. He leaned up on the pillow and looked at Serena. She was so beautiful, and Clyde couldn't get enough of her.

Serena could I make you real?

That all depends. Why?

I'm in love with you, that's why.

Serena blushed.

Clyde that's so sweet but...

What?

Clyde. You must remember I'm just a manifestation of The Hooks. I'm The Hooks remember.

That was right. Serena was not a real person. The Hooks were real.

If there was a way that I could be Real, you know that I would but....

For now you are just my imagination.

Serena nodded.

I'm afraid so Clyde.

Clyde sighed. He wasn't sure if he was to be angry or sad. Serena drew him close to her and held him tight.

Even if I'm not real, we can act like this for as long as you want. If you love me back, I'll love you and we can do this. It can be our little secret. No one must know.

Clyde pulled back enough so that he could kiss her. The two kissed for a long time and Clyde ran his hand down Serena's chest.

I like keeping secrets.

I do too.

For as long as I want.

Serena nodded.

For as long as you want. I'll always be with you Clyde.

The two kissed and touched each other more, until Clyde got up.

It's time for work.

Serena smiled.

Ok. I'm coming with you.

Clyde watched as Serena disappeared. He could see her impressions on the bed, where she lay and where she was a second ago. Then the impressions disappeared.

I'm back in your head. Don't forget The Hooks.

How could I forget?

You don't want to forget. That would be terrible.

Clyde went through the door and out into the apartment. He was still shocked that he Created another room for him and Serena to be in. Clyde found The Hooks, which were on the table in front of the TV. He grabbed them and looped them to his jeans. Clyde rummaged through the fridge, finding only beer and a few snacks. Clyde only had a few minutes to get out of the apartment, so he cut up some chicken, vegetables, and fruit. He then mixed it all together and grabbed some waters. This should be enough.

Yum.

He could hear Serena's voice echoing in his ears.

This is for me you know.

I know, but you can share. Remember, I'm a part of you, partner.

I know you are.

Then let's get going. You don't want to be late for work.

Clyde gathered the rest of his things and stepped outside of the apartment complex. The air was cool as it hit Clyde and wrapped around him. The Hooks slammed against his legs with every step and Clyde was tempted to take them off and hold them. Keep them there, Serena said, and Clyde obeyed like a dog. He kept on walking through Brightcourt and made it to the sidewalk. Main Street was up ahead and since when it was late, not many people were out driving. This was a good thing, as Clyde could easily cross the road and head towards the back where the employee entrance was, and he did this with ease. The Hooks slammed against his legs as he walked and in his left hand, he held his bag with his lunch and waters. Working overnight was such a strange experience. The sleep cycle was really messed up and Clyde knew that he would never get a 'normal' cycle ever again. I could work days, but then I would lose the differential.

That is why Clyde stayed on the overnight crew. It was only for the money.

The other crap Clyde could care less about. The profit of the store, the emails, the ads, the sales, etc. Everything like that was not in Clyde's department, so there was no reason to care. I didn't get anything out of getting people to receive coupons and ads. I still got the same wage like everyone else during the night crew and it was only when I moved to overnight, that I saw a difference in pay and in attitude for myself. Clyde didn't particularly like working on the second shift. That crew was a different one altogether, a tighter knit crew that Clyde was not too fond of. They disliked new people and only kept to themselves, gossiping about others that were not there to defend themselves at all. This bothered Clyde, but there was nothing that he could do about it. Above all, I hate gossip.

I agree.

Clyde had forgotten for a moment that Serena was still in his head, her voice echoing on the walls of his brain.

I can hear your thoughts.

Well, now you know that I hate gossip.

Good to know. Let's hope that it doesn't start tonight.

Clyde made it to the employee entrance and rang the doorbell. Jerry poked his head out and let Clyde in. Clyde just rushed past Jerry without saying a word and Jerry closed the door in disgust.

I guess you hate that guy.

Jerry is not a nice person anyways.

Clyde could hear Serena laugh in his head as he made his way to the breakroom. By now, the second shift was getting close to leaving, as it was almost 9. Martins had strange hours for a re-

tail store. Most stores were open until 9pm, but not Martins. 7-8
Sunday-Saturday were the standard hours of operation and during
the holidays, it would be 6am-9pm every day. Clyde did not miss
those holiday nights when working second shift. The store was
always hot at night and with large crowds, it did not help. Clyde
would be fishing out summer clothing when 2-3 feet of snow was
outside on the ground. Clyde made his way to his locker. He didn't
recognize the second shift people and when they waved, he waved
back and gave no response. They don't need to say anything to
me.

Do you not like them?

They aren't friendly. Let's just leave it at that.

Ahh, I see said the blind man.

Clyde smiled as he went to his locker and put his things
away, then gathered what he needed for the night. He put on his
nametag, then brought out his gloves, knife, and water bottle.
Clyde then went into the breakroom and almost had a heart at-
tack. Jemma was at the back table in the breakroom, her body
completely facing forwards. Jemma slitted her eyes and furrowed
her brow.

"Nice to see you here, Clyde." Jemma said, steely.

This is Jemma.

Yes.

Clyde gulped, then spoke, his voice cracking a bit.

"I didn't expect to see…you here Jemma. I thought….you
had the night off?" Clyde asked.

Jemma nodded.

"I did, but Brandon called me and asked me to come in to-
night. Said that there was a big project for me to do."

"Did he say anything about me?" Clyde asked, sitting down.

Jemma shook her head.

"You can ask him."

Clyde turned his chair around, so he was sitting sideways.

I hate my back turned.

Gotcha.

Jemma looked at Clyde, puzzled.

"You talking to someone else Clyde?" Jemma asked.

Clyde let out a laugh.

"Me! Talking to someone else? You must be joking." Clyde said, astounded.

"Well, it just looks like from here that you are in a conversation."

I am.

In your head.

Clyde shook his head.

"I have no idea what you are talking about. Must be seeing things, Jemma. I hope that you are ok."

"I hope for your sake that you don't tempt me, Clyde Holding."

Clyde turned and faced her completely.

"And what are you going to do to me, Jemma Sterling?" Clyde asked, raising his voice.

Jemma was shocked at the tone of his voice. I caught her off guard, Clyde thought. He furrowed his brow and pointed a finger at her.

"Don't you ever threaten me again." Clyde said.

Jemma sighed and looked down. Clyde still pointed his finger at her and slowly leaned back in his seat.

Keep your cool. You shouldn't use your powers around people.

Thanks for the warning.

Jemma looked at her iPhone, then got up.

"Time to punch in and actually do some work." Jemma said.

Clyde screwed up his face in frustration and watched her leave the breakroom. The other overnighters were not here, which was puzzling to Clyde. After waiting a few minutes or so, Clyde got up and punched in for the night. The air on the salesfloor was cool for once, as the A/C was going. Even in the fall, it always seemed that the A/C was working the best. It was during the summer that it would not work and was always broken.

Stupid company.

They would rather profit over comfort.

Most companies in America were like this. Clyde walked out towards the customer service desk, where Brandon was. He was talking with Jemma in detail and the two seemed to be in deep conversation. Just as Clyde got close enough to hear what they were saying, Jemma walked away towards her assignment. Brandon grabbed the lineup sheet, marked that Clyde was here, then looked at him.

"Clyde. I have a lot for you. I hope that you don't screw up this time." Brandon said.

"That rack was not my fault, Brandon.." Clyde started.

"Let's not get into it Clyde. For the love of God, just drop it. I need two sections moved tonight, The Beach stuff must go up here because it's all 75% off starting tomorrow. Charlie wants that done more than anything. The second thing is all that Arts and Crafts stuff must get refilled. I guess a lot of the other local craft stores in Casper closed, so that means their customers are coming here for that stuff. There are 10 racks of Arts and Crafts that have to get put into that section..."

Ten Racks! That'll take weeks to put out!

"Brandon, you can't be serious. Ten Racks! That'll take weeks to put out, even a month. And besides, you know that all of it will never fit in that small section. I'm going to need tools and movers to move the walls out, maybe even put a whole new wall down the middle to get it all out..." Clyde said, raising his voice.

Brandon held up a hand.

"I don't want to hear complaints. This all came from Charlie, and he found out from the Upper Management, so he wants it done tonight."

Clyde sighed, looked around, then back at Brandon.

"Where is everyone else? If we are going to have a big move, wouldn't H.R have scheduled more people?" Clyde asked.

"Most of the overnight had to take today off for paid vacation time that they had to use up or else it would be gone. It was a blessing that Jemma came in and Charlie won't be in until 4am to help. I guess Upper Management wants him in earlier to help with more projects that they are sending down from Corporate. You know how it goes, Clyde. We both do. We've been playing the game long enough to know the rules." Brandon said, sighing.

For once, Clyde agreed with Brandon. As much as he hated

the son of a bitch, Brandon was a good worker and Clyde knew it too. Brandon knew that he was good and what made him so good was that he jumped at every chance to be a kiss ass when Corporate people came in to look at his work. Charlie groomed him that way, which is why Brandon could get away with what he did. Clyde nodded.

"Sometimes, I think I've been playing it too long."

"You and me both. I'm going to see if I can make some more phone calls for others to come in. I would focus on the Beach Stuff, then Arts and Crafts. Maybe I can convince Jemma.."

"Don't!" Clyde shouted.

Brandon was taken aback, and he almost fell off the desk. Clyde inhaled, then exhaled deeply.

"Sorry.. just let me do my work alone this time, Brandon." Clyde said.

Brandon nodded.

"If that is how you feel, then be my guest."

Clyde watched as he hopped off the service desk and proceeded to go into the office to make some phone calls. Clyde sighed and went over to the front of the store. Most of the Beach stuff had been in the Seasonal section, however, when Clyde looked over, he noticed that it was out already in cages and the entire Seasonal Section was full of Fall Décor and other Fall things. Martins was always behind in some of the seasons, but it was not a store issue. It was a Corporate issue, as they controlled what went into the stores, the quantity, what could be ordered, and what stores got the stock. It was a strange system, but Clyde never questioned it. I don't get paid enough to ask those questions. The first thing that Clyde did was assess the situation in the front. He had a bunch of cages of fall décor that he could move where the Beach cages where and that is where he started. He moved all the Beach Cages off to the side, effectively making a wall. Clyde looked up to see Jemma trying to get past his blockade of cages. He heard her snort.

"You going to move these or what?" Jemma asked.

Clyde looked up at her and wiped his forehead.

"You know, it is hard work moving cages by myself. I would

ask you for help, but I think that you would punch me out. I will move when I'm ready." Clyde said, crossing his arms over his chest.

"Fine! I'll go around the other way." Jemma said, scoffing.

Clyde stuck out his tongue as she turned away.

This was the one you loved. Serena asked.

Used to love.

Not anymore.

Clyde shook his head.

Not anymore.

More time with me.

Yes, more time with you.

Clyde moved the rest of the cages to the front of the store. As he gripped them with his hands, he felt a renewed strength in his body, something that he had not felt in a long time. To test his theory, he pulled one of the cages out with his might and pushed it hard. The cage rolled across the floor and Clyde was certain that it was going to crash into the wall. In a moment, Clyde's hand was stretched out. The cage stopped immediately in its tracks, the wheels underneath screeching to a halt. Clyde stood there, stunned in amazement.

You forget that you have me with you, Clyde.

I'll never forget.

You seemed to just a minute ago.

Clyde then realized one thing. For the first time in his life, he couldn't think to himself anymore. Serena, The Hooks, they have taken over him completely. Everything that he was doing now, was not of his own doing.

I'm not me anymore.

The cage was still there, and Clyde moved his arm back towards him. The cage rolled forwards and when Clyde stretched his palm out, as if he was telling someone to stop, the cage stopped in its tracks.

You are part of us now, Clyde.

Serena's voice echoed through his ears, bouncing off the walls of his brain. His body, his movements, were not his own. Clyde looked up to see Jemma staring at him and Clyde put his arm down. Scoffing, Jemma walked away.

I hope she didn't see that.

I wouldn't worry about it Clyde. What is the saying from the Catholic Church? 'Blessed are those who have not seen, but have believed'?

Yeah, something like that. I wasn't much of a Church Person.

I can tell. Come on, we have more work to do.

Clyde walked over to straighten the cage to where he wanted it, then went over and placed the second cage next to that one. Soon, he had about seven to eight cages of Beach Stuff lined up in the middle of the Front Section, which was the area where the customers walked in. The customer service desk was off to the left of the entrance doors and then the Front Section was in front of that. All along the front wall was fall décor stuff, which didn't make any sense to Clyde, as the other fall stuff was in the Seasonal Section. Clyde shook his head and continued with his work, working faster than he wanted to. In the span of three hours, he finished the first task that Brandon gave to him. He felt the energy pumping through him. With every step he took, Clyde felt like he could have done this forever, as if there was an untapped part of him that was just beginning to rise from hibernation. Clyde looked around at his work. He was surprised that he was able to get all of that done and decided to look and admire what he had done. Jemma came up with a couple of carriages and took out the fall décor from the front wall.

"Where are you going with those?" Clyde asked.

At first, Jemma ignored him, as if he was not that. Clyde cleared his throat and Jemma turned around.

"Oh? You are talking to me?" Jemma said, sarcastically.

"Yes I am talking to you. Where is all that going? What is going to be on the front wall?" Clyde asked, irritated.

"None of your business. Go talk to Brandon." Jemma said.

"Whatever." Clyde said.

He watched as Jemma continued to knock stuff off the pegs and shelves, filling up the carriages like it was nothing. Jemma took the carriages and placed them in the Seasonal Section, lined up in the middle of the area, near some cages. Clyde sighed. Time for the Arts and Crafts section.

That shouldn't be too bad to do.

Easy for you to say. You aren't the one doing the work.

Think again, Clyde. I'm the one helping you do the work, so therefore, I am working.

Just not getting paid for it.

Exactly.

Clyde stood there for a few seconds, then walked towards the backroom. He knew that Jemma was watching him walk away, but he didn't care. Let her stare. She can go to hell.

Strong words for someone that you used to love.

I don't want anything to do with her anymore.

Whatever you say.

Besides, I've grown to love you Serena.

That's comforting to say, Clyde.

Clyde opened the doors to the backroom. As Brandon mentioned, ten whole racks of Arts and Crafts stuff were already processed, ready to be put out onto the salesfloor.

There is no way I can do this in one night.

There is always a way.

Easy for you to say.

Just trust me. We can Create space.

Then I would be the only one who will see it, right?

Wrong.

Wrong? I thought you told me that I was the only one who could see what I Create? Is that not true?

Well, I told you a lie. I partially told you the truth. There is a difference between the truth and the partial truth if that makes sense.

Nothing is clicking. You are going to have to explain, Serena.

There was a sigh that echoed through his brain and Clyde put his hands to head, trying to block out the noise.

Yes, what you Create, only you can see, however, since when you have me then there is no reason to hide this. The Hooks are on your person, right? Therefore whatever we Create Together, everyone can see it.

So you are suggesting that me, we, Create space for every-
one to see?

How are you going to get all this stuff out? That section is
too small. Only a couple of walls and a middle section of cages.
It's not an ideal space. I mean, come on Clyde. I've never worked
in retail, but I can tell you right now that putting this out in that
space will not work at all.

Makes sense.

Makes sense my ass. You are just agreeing with me because
I am right.

Maybe that is true.

Maybe?

I haven't told you the whole truth.

Ughh, just stop and let's get to work. You aren't hungry
yet? I'm starving.

Clyde was not hungry, however, after Serena mentioned it,
he began to feel a strange way, like he was empty.

Let's get at least two racks out, then we can eat.

Good enough for me.

Clyde went to the first rack that he found, gripped it with
his hands, and pulled it out. The racks were stationed in a way
that would allow anyone to get them out without much trouble.
There were two rows of five racks each, which made it easy for
Clyde to count how many racks he had left. Good, Clyde thought.
He brought the first rack out to the Arts and Crafts Section. Down
where the cleaning stuff was, Clyde could see Jemma moving more
product somewhere else. Must be another job given to her by
Brandon. Clyde shook his head and parked the rack in the middle
of the section. Clyde stopped the rack and looked at the walls of
the section. When he first put the stuff out, it sold very well, how-
ever, this was not the case. Between the last time he was here and
now, some of it was not selling well. A few of the bins down below
the shelves were empty and Clyde could stick some yarn there, but
there was nothing else that he could put into the section. The art
supplies still occupied an entire wall, while the other wall was full
of crochet hooks, more yarn, crafting supplies, toy kits, and much

more. Clyde could not even recognize half of the shit that was in the section now.

"Must have been filled."

Clyde nodded to himself. Besides talking to Jemma, he was talking in his head to Serena and the words that rolled off his tongue were more of a croak. He found his water and downed the bottle, putting it on the top of the rack. That was good, Clyde thought.

How are we going to do this?

Clyde shrugged. I don't have the foggiest idea.

Well, we must figure out a way.

Clyde looked around.

The only other way that I could see this working, is if we Created another wall and put it where the cages are.

That could work.

It must work. There is no other way.

Whatever you say.

Clyde focused his attention on the cages. He stayed put as one by one, the cages rolled out of the way, out into the main runway that ran around the store. Clyde watched as the cages slammed into the other cages and a scream erupted. The scream interrupted Clyde's concentration and he realized that Jemma almost got squished between the cages he moved. Jemma folded her arms across her chest.

"What the hell!" Jemma said, raising her voice.

"Don't get in my way, Jemma!" Clyde shouted.

Jemma let out an angry moan and walked away.

"You are crazy, Clyde Holding! Completely bat-shit crazy!"

Clyde couldn't tell what else she said as Jemma walked away, her voice drowning out. Figures. Get the fuck out of here, Clyde thought.

Don't worry about her. We have a job to do.

Clyde nodded and looked towards the second wall. He stretched out his hand. The ground shook and Clyde almost lost his balance, but he regained himself and his focus. The second wall moved out of position and lifted in the air. Clyde couldn't believe that this was happening and laughed. He laughed so hard that his face was red, and tears came down his cheeks. It was a joyous laughter, that he was able to overcome something inside of him. Clyde almost lost his focus and pushed the wall back until there was space for a whole new wall. Clyde let the wall fall gently to the ground and then aimed his hands at the ground. Again, the floor shook and soon, a whole new wall fixture came out of the ground. Clyde imagined it in his head, with shelves, pegs, and bins on both sides, with two endcap sections on either side. It's beautiful, Clyde thought.

We Created this, Clyde. Remember that.

I'll remember.

The ground finally stopped shaking and Clyde stood in amazement. He was not laughing anymore, but the joyous feeling was still inside of him, the feeling of accomplishment that he hadn't felt since his days at school. Clyde sighed. What a relief. He turned to face the first rack and outstretched his hand, opening his palms. The arts and crafts stuff from the rack flew in the air, levitating towards the wall. All that Clyde had to do was keep his focus on the rack and point to the wall. In a matter of minutes, the first side and two endcap sections were full. Clyde wanted to bring out the other racks. The feeling of Energy rushed through his system. With every movement, it felt like Clyde always had this power. You are helping me do great things, Serena.

We are working together Clyde.

In an instant, Clyde heard the backdoors open and soon, the rest of the racks rolled out onto the salesfloor in single file. Clyde thought that he had to look with his eyes to accomplish this, but he only had to think about it. Just thinking about the Energy and the Power allows me to do what I want, Clyde thought.

Within Reason. You still need me.

Clyde nodded. I'll always need you.

That's very reassuring Clyde. Very reassuring.

The racks lined up in the main walkway, completely blocking anyone or anything from moving about. Clyde forced the cages that he moved into the middle section, then with his mind, morphed them into the spaces in the first wall. Sick, Clyde thought. He was enjoying the usage of the power, that he forgot to take his lunch.

Lunch time.

Ok.

Clyde went to the breakroom and had his lunch. He longed for Serena to manifest beside him and watch him eat, however, Serena told him that it would be too risky. Jemma was nowhere to be found, however, that didn't mean that she was not in the building.

Always hiding.

I know. It seems like that girl wants nothing to deal with you. What did you do to her?

I can't hide anything from you, can I?

Nothing. I'm a part of you now, partner.

I asked her out and she said no.

Serena laughed.

And that is why she hates you? Because you asked her out.

Clyde tried to answer, but Serena' laughter echoed in his brain, and he waited until she was done.

I'm sorry, continue.

Thank you. No I asked her out, she said no, and then it just became awkward from that moment on. I think she might have had problems with other guys, which is why she didn't want to be.....

"Clyde? Who are you talking to?"

Serena was gone from his thoughts. Jemma stood in the doorway of the breakroom and Clyde realized his mistake. I was talking out loud right? Yes you were. Fuck me. Later.

"Jemma…...I thought you were still on the floor…I'm not talking to anyone, just myself." Clyde said, nervously.

I can't hide this forever. Yes you can. I believe in you. Jemma came over to Clyde, pulled up a chair and sat across from him.

"Ok, let's cut the shit. I know that you are doing some strange stuff Clyde. I've noticed and so has Brandon. So, spill it." Jemma said.

I can't tell her. No!!! Don't give us away. Clyde gulped. He felt sweaty and when he tried to get out of his seat, it was as if he was stuck there, bound by the weight of Serena and The Hooks that were strapped to his belt.

"What is it Clyde? What is it with the moving wall and the cages. I know that you don't have that much strength in you."

Clyde didn't respond and drank more of his water. As he lifted the bottle, his hand shook and he spilled half of it on the table. Jemma jumped up and cursed.

"Jesus! Here, let me get you a napkin. Are you going to talk to me!?" Jemma asked, annoyed.

Clyde wanted to speak, but he moved his mouth, and nothing came out. His throat was dry, the saliva in his mouth was all gone. Jemma cleaned up the mess, took the bottle, and gave it to Clyde. Clyde reached out for the bottle and grasped it with his hands. Jemma came on the other side of Clyde, tilted his head back, and gave him the water slowly. Clyde took it slow at first, then grasped the bottle with both hands and drank it like he did with his beer, downing the liquid as fast as he could.

"Clyde! Clyde stop!" Jemma yelled.

Jemma tried to wretch the bottle from Clyde, but he was stuck in this state and Clyde fell to the ground, hitting his head on the floor. Whether it was something else or God, Jemma would never know, but Clyde gasped, choked, and muttered on the floor. Something had clicked in him, and he wriggled on the ground, covered in water. Jemma stepped away, hoping not to get wet. She then hauled Clyde to his feet.

"What the hell Clyde! Are you going to tell me what the fuck is going on or not!" Jemma screamed.

Clyde looked up at Jemma, then launched from his seat, grabbed her, and pushed her against the wall. Jemma's face was in shock and so was Clyde. This strength is not my own, Clyde thought. He looked at Jemma in the eyes.

"You don't know what this is, Jemma Sterling, you will never know, you hear me!" Clyde shouted.

Jemma tried to cower in the wall, but Clyde put his face close to hers, so that his breath echoed off her ears.

"It has me, Jemma. It has all of me, like a dangerous criminal. It has my family, my friends, my wellbeing. For the last day, it has me by my balls, pushing, prodding, attacking, willing. It has me! Me! Of all people, it has me! You will never understand, but do me a favor. Don't ask about it. Don't tell anyone about it. Just leave it alone and I'll leave you alone, how about that?! I'm sorry Jemma, but it has me."

Jemma had no idea what to say and Clyde pulled away from her, leaving her cowering up against the wall. Clyde looked to see Brandon standing in the door way.

"What has you Clyde?" Brandon asked.

Clyde only had to look at him once to tell that Brandon was scared. He noticed that Brandon's eyes were wide and there was a fear that Clyde sensed, a fear of the unknown.

"It has me Brandon. That's all I can say. It has me." Clyde said.

Brandon gulped and nodded.

"Then I'll leave you two be. Charlie should be here in an hour." Brandon said.

Before Clyde could respond, Brandon stepped out of the room, shocked at what he had seen. Jemma slowly moved along the wall, then stopped when Clyde looked at her.

"I won't tell Clyde. I swear....." Jemma started.

Clyde looked at her. He was still deeply in love with her, but something pulled him to think about Serena and the time he spent with her. Clyde shook his head and let out a sigh.

"It has me. It doesn't attach to anything else. One person at a time." Clyde said.

He turned around and stretched out his hand. The thought of a clean table and breakroom flashed in his mind and soon, his food and his mess were clean, wiped from view. Jemma still slid along the wall and stood right in front of the breakroom doors.

"I'll see you Clyde." Jemma said.

"I'll see you too." Clyde said.

Clyde watched as Jemma walked out of the room. When he was sure that he was by himself, Clyde went into the men's room and threw up in the only stall. He felt hands on his back, rubbing him as he heaved and retched into the toilet.

"It's going to be ok, Clyde."

Clyde turned to see Serena behind him. She was standing

naked, and Clyde suddenly felt his urge rise in him, but Serena looked at him.

"No more, big boy. We still have work to do. I'll reward you when we get home, how about that?" Serena asked.

Clyde was about to respond, when Serena flicked her fingers and Clyde heaved up more throw up into the toilet. Serena rubbed her hands on his back.

"That a boy. That's a good boy. Let it all out. Good."

She repeated these words, all the while teasing him by running her hands on his body.

"I don't like this. Why are you doing this?"

Another retch racked his body as Serena stood on the other side of him, watching him throw up. Clyde was all red now, sweat pouring down his face.

"I want you to be completely honest Clyde. Were you going to tell Jemma about us?"

"I would never."

Another retch, another heave and Clyde gasped for air. Serena grabbed him by the shoulders and turned him to face her.

"I want your unwavering loyalty Clyde. I don't like cheaters."

Clyde tried to get Serena's hands away from him, but her hands found his crotch and she squeezed. Clyde tried to yell, but Serena closed his mouth with a vicelike grip with her other hand. Serena moved her face to Clyde.

"I want your loyalty, Clyde. I want you and your loyalty. I love you, but as a mother loves her child, some things must be done to make sure that this loyalty stays. Can we agree?" Serena whispered.

Clyde nodded and writhed as Serena squeezed him again.

"Don't make me do this ever again Clyde. I would hate to have to hurt you. You have such a pretty face and body. It would be a real shame if it was ruined." Serena said.

"Clyde!! Clyde are you in there?"

The voice of Charlie echoed in the breakroom. Serena pulled away and planted a kiss on his cheek.

"I'll have you when we get home." Serena said.

Clyde could only stand in shock as Serena disappeared. Clyde sighed and got himself together and went out of the men's room. Charlie was standing in the breakroom.

"Clyde are you ok? You look like you saw a ghost?" Charlie asked.

Choose your words carefully.

Clyde nodded as if Serena were here, but it was only Charlie and him in the room.

"So you are saying that you are ok?" Charlie asked, confused.

"Charlie I'm fine. Just a bit under the weather, that is all." Clyde said.

Charlie nodded.

"Right." Charlie said, slowly.

The two stood in silence, until Charlie broke it again.

"The arts and crafts stuff has to get finished. I'll come over and help... ."

"No!" Clyde yelled.

Charlie was taken aback.

"No, I'll do it, Charlie. I mean, it's only fair. I started it so I should be able to finish it." Clyde said.

He suspects something. Don't be a fuck up Clyde.

Charlie just stood there and nodded.

"You are right. You finish it and I'll come over to check on your progress. I need to ask Brandon about a couple of things before he leaves for the night."

Clyde was about to say something else, but Serena stopped him but making him cough. Clyde coughed, then straightened as Charlie left.

Be a good boy and finish Clyde.

Fine, but you need to stop.

I'll do what I want. Remember, this is only because I love you Clyde.

Clyde suppressed a retort and went out to the salesfloor. The last few hours of Clyde's shift went by very fast. Clyde created two more walls and soon, all the racks of the arts and crafts stuff were out on the salesfloor. Clyde worked in silence, as if Serena stripped him of words and his vocabulary. One by one, the racks went into the backroom, empty as if nothing was put on them in the first place. The Arts and Crafts section had grew by two walls and a bunch of endcap sections. It seemed that the other sections around Clyde got smaller as he made the Arts and Crafts bigger. Of course, no one would notice, and Clyde was hoping that he would not get in trouble for doing what he did. Clyde looked around for Jemma and concluded that she went home for the night.

Stop thinking about her! Only me!

Every thought about Jemma was squashed by Serena, who had a hold on him like he never experienced before. As Clyde worked, The Hooks slammed against his thighs. Clyde couldn't think about getting them off his jeans, as Serena would pick up on this and do something terrible to him.

"Clyde?"

Clyde jumped as Charlie stood in the main walkway.

"Can you come with me please?" Charlie asked.

"Sure." Clyde said, weakly.

Charlie was shocked that Clyde even responded and the two men made their way to the office. Brandon was in the office as well, waiting impatiently.

"About time." Brandon scoffed.

"Drop it." Charlie said.

Brandon got up and closed the door behind him, leaving the three men in the same room. Charlie looked at Clyde.

"Clyde. Is there something that you aren't telling us?" Charlie asked.

I'll allow you to speak, but don't ruin it or I'll ruin you.

The thought ran through his brain like no other thought and Clyde gulped.

"What do you mean?" Clyde asked.

Charlie went over to the computer and pulled up the camera footage. Clyde almost shit himself, but he could feel Serena preventing from even doing that. The footage showed Clyde moving the cages, then the talk with Jemma. Then it cut to Clyde making the wall and putting out the arts and crafts stuff. Then more footage of the racks coming out of the backroom one by one, lined up in single file. Charlie looked back at Clyde.

"Do I need to show more?" Charlie asked.

The tone of his voice was almost as identical to Serena's voice when she was mad at him moments ago. Charlie leaned back in his seat

"I'm waiting, Clyde." Charlie said.

"Ok, I'll talk." Clyde said, choking on his words.

"Explain?"

"I'm not sure if any of you will believe me, but I got this cold and for some reason, I can move stuff and make stuff. I don't know what it is, so I went to the doctor, and he told me that I'm in some sort of trial for this cold. They are calling it The Clyde for now because there is no name for it...."

Charlie nodded understandably. Brandon, on the other hand, shifted in his chair.

"Go on." Charlie said.

"Well, there isn't much to say. I can just do this stuff now and I don't know what is happening to me."

Clyde wanted to mention everything, but her voice sounded in his brain.

Mention me and you die!

Clyde shook his head.

"You ok?" Charlie asked.

"Headache. That is a common side effect." Clyde said.

Charlie looked at Brandon.

"What do you think?" Charlie asked.

"I think it's a pile of horseshit." Brandon said.

"I don't think it is, but if it's a new sickness, then let's hope to God that it doesn't spread amongst the others." Charlie said.

"What am I to do?" Clyde asked.

"Well, we can either fire you or keep you. You aren't in trouble Clyde.."

Not in trouble! Clyde couldn't believe it! YESSS, Serena screamed.

"Not in trouble?" Clyde asked.

Charlie nodded.

"You put out more freight in one night than all the team

combined. Your new side effects could be of use to us. I think this is going to be a new normal for you Clyde." Charlie said.

Brandon got up.

"Charlie! You can't be fucking serious! Clyde is a freak now and now he endangers us all!"

"Sit down, Brandon! I'm the store manager and what I say goes! Clyde and his powers will stay. I'm going to put in a raise for him now. Clyde, take the next two days off and come back in early and we can figure this out together. There is going to be a bright new future for you." Charlie said.

Clyde couldn't believe the words coming out of Charlies mouth. Brandon stormed out of the room, fuming, and cursing like a sailor. Clyde sat in the chair, not knowing what to do next.

You and I are going to have a good day.

Clyde felt shivers go down his spine as the words echoed in his mind. Charlie turned around and sent an email, then turned to see Clyde.

"Clyde, go home. You look pale and you need some rest."

"Good night, Charlie. Thanks." Clyde said.

Clyde got up from the chair, went to the breakroom, grabbed his things, and went home. The morning person for the backroom was waiting for him and the door opened. Clyde turned around to see Brandon following him, still angry at what had happened in the office. Clyde watched as Charlie disappeared, probably going to the salesfloor. Clyde stepped aside as Brandon rushed by him, then stopped and looked at Clyde.

"This isn't over, freak." Brandon said.

"You can stop calling me that Brandon." Clyde said.

"You can fuck yourself, Clyde. I knew you were strange the first time you stepped in, but now it's all coming back to me. Enjoy your next two days off. I'll be here wasting my life away."

"Good, then maybe I won't have to deal with a piece of shit like you." Clyde said, raising his voice.

"You better watch your mouth." Brandon snapped.

Clyde got close to him and gave him a shove.

"Make me you son of a bitch!" Clyde shouted.

Brandon was about to retaliate, but walked away. Charlie

stood at the backdoor. Clyde turned around and saw him. Charlie shook his head and walked back inside. Jerry, the morning back-room guy, followed suit.

Can we finally go home?

It was Serena's voice again, echoing in his ears.

Might as well.

Don't give me that. You've missed me haven't you.

I'm not in the mood.

We'll see when we get back to your place if you are in a God damn mood or not.

I'm tired.

So am I. I did a lot of the lifting.

I got paid to do it, you didn't.

Then you owe me.

I don't owe you jack shit.

You better watch your words Clyde.

Closing Time

Clyde walked back through the parking lot and across Main Street. The sun slowly rose behind the clouds that drifted in. The air was cooler than usual, and Clyde knew that it would only be a matter of time before winter set in. Not looking forward to that. Serena or rather, Serena's voice, had been quiet on the lonely walk home. Clyde looked around for a trace of Jemma, but there was nothing around. Cars were in the employee lot, however, Clyde didn't recognize any of them. Must be for the day and after-noon crew. Clyde couldn't think of the last time that he ever drove to work because if he was aware, he always walked. Rain, sleet, shine, or snow, Clyde walked, and he would dress for the occasion too. Clyde was waiting for Serena to echo something in his ear, but she was silent. Clyde knew that the fight with her was not over, however, he was not going to think about it, as she will read his every thought. The Hooks slammed against his thighs as he moved across the street. He waited for a few cars to go down the road, then crossed into Brightcourt, then entered his own apart-ment. Clyde put down his bag by the sink, then untied The Hooks from his jean loop. As he did this, Serena manifested in front of him, wearing only a bra and panties.

"So?" Serena asked.

"So what? I'm tired." Clyde said.

Serena latched onto him, wrapped her arms around him in a hug. She began to kiss his chest.

"What's your issue?" Clyde said, irritated.

Serena looked at him with her flashing yellow eyes, then kissed his chest again.

"I just want to make sure that your needs are fulfilled." Serena said.

"My needs are fulfilled. I want to go to bed. I'm tired."

Serena continued to kiss him, reaching his neck, then his cheeks, then his lips. Clyde let Serena kiss him, but he didn't kiss back. Serena tried to slip in her tongue, but Clyde stood still.

"What you did embarrassed me at work!" Clyde shouted.

He grabbed her and threw her up against the bedroom wall. Serena was shocked, but also turned on at his strength.

"I'm sorry if I was a naughty girl. You gonna do naughty things to me to get your anger out?" Serena asked, smiling innocently.

It was that smile that irritated Clyde the most. This girl is wacked.

Wacked is right, but I'm your whack. You can do whatever you want with me, yet you say that you are tired.

"When have I ever heard or met a men who has had enough of sex, huh?" Serena asked.

Clyde still held onto Serena. He felt himself bulge in his pants. Serena smiled.

"You see Clyde. Your mind says no, but your body is telling me yes."

She slipped her hand in between his pants. Clyde almost had a stroke. Serena then kissed him, and he returned the favor. Soon the two of them were in the new created bedroom, under the sheets and having the time of their lives, and when it was over, Clyde let out a huge sigh of relief.

A few hours went by, and Clyde was sleeping on his side, naked in his bed. Next to him, also naked, was Serena. Clyde slowly got up and pulled her closer, his arm wrapping around her and his hand on her left tit, holding it in his hand. The two had fallen asleep for hours now, locked in a spooning position. This was the only opportunity that Clyde had to think. She's finally asleep, Clyde thought. The Hooks were in the apartment somewhere and Clyde was happy that he was able to function without them having to be near him. Thank God, Clyde thought again. Serena stirred, then went back to sleep. I hope she stays asleep. I rocked her good. Clyde only wanted to go around once this time and dragged it all out. It played out the same as before. Serena didn't have to tie herself down this time, but Clyde still felt forced into it. She's using the one thing that men like to get what she wants.

Control.

The idea of being controlled was something that Clyde

hadn't come to terms yet. It was one of the many reasons why Clyde couldn't have a girlfriend or get married. The idea of having a nagging wife always stuck with him and that was the last thing that he needed. I don't want that. Then what do I want? He remembered Serena asking him that, then forcing him to investigate the sink where he saw Jemma. Is Jemma what I really want? Clyde sighed. I'll never know. All I know is that I have sex with this girl whenever I want and in exchange, I can Create shit out of thin air. It's taking over me and I must find a way to get rid of this but....

There was a part of Clyde that stopped him in his tracks, the part of the Clyde that was on the darker side. The possessed side of Clyde Holding. He looked at Serena. She was so peaceful sleeping next to him, her chest rising and down with every breath. I can do what I want to this girl. Think of it Clyde. Your very own slave. Yes, a slave. To do your bidding. No! I'm in love with Serena.

Are you in love or is it a forced love?

Clyde had never thought of that.

Serena would force something like this on me.

She's going to force me to love her and in exchange, I can live.

Live.

Now that was a thought that never crossed Clyde's mind until now. Clyde could do what he wanted to Serena and in exchange, Serena would have some sort of control over Clyde. The usage of Energy and Creation, that was all Serena's doing. After all, Serena was not real. But she is! She's sleeping next to me naked for Chrissake and you are trying to tell me that she isn't real! Get the fuck out of here! The problem was that Clyde knew he was right.

Serena was not real.

Serena was all in his head and when she wanted to make a presence, here she was. Serena wasn't around physically when he wasn't working, but had been inside of his head the entire time that he worked. Serena shifted in the bed, rolling over to face him. Clyde took her close and ran his hand through her hair, then cupped one of her breasts in his hand. Serena smiled and looked up at him.

"I can see you want to go again?" Serena asked.

She was so beautiful, Clyde thought. He didn't want to go again, but his urge was too great and soon, he was on top of her and when he finished, he slumped back over. Serena smiled as she wrapped her hands around him. Clyde lay on top of her. Serena moved her hands on his back and touched his ass as she slid her hands down.

"Clyde? I've been thinking that this would be a lot harder to do." Serena said.

"What do you mean?" Clyde asked.

He was sweating now, the kind of sweat that happens when you get nervous. Serena continued to stroke his back with her hands, then wrapped her legs around his lower back, forcing him in a grip.

"We've already had sex two times in the span of a couple of hours and I've noticed that no matter how tired you are, you get right in and finish. Remarkable that when I want it, it happens right?" Serena asked.

Clyde pulled away, propping himself with his front arms. Serena smiled.

"You see Clyde. I always get what I want, and I want more from you. I'm going to tire you out until you can be a good boy. You gave away our secret and now you have to pay."

Clyde was not listening. He was angry, pissed off to the core. He tried to get out of the bed with Serena, but she had him in a grip.

"Come on, you really don't want to avoid me. I'm all for you Clyde. You see, I know that there is a part of you that loves women that are helpless. I'm helpless without you Clyde, so come on. Do me again."

As if on que, Clyde's arms stopped holding him up and instead, clasped onto Serena's shoulders. Clyde screamed as he tried to pull away, but he was rock hard and plunged himself into Serena again. Serena moaned, but it was an evil moan that echoed in Clyde's ears every time he went up and down and when it was done, he slumped over, gasping for air, and groaning in pain. Serena ran her hands through Clyde's hair, sending shivers down his spine.

"Are you going to be a good boy Clyde?" Serena asked.

Clyde struggled to answer. His throat was dry, and his body felt weak with fever. A headache rapped his brain. He tried to concentrate, but it was no use and he slumped on Serena's chest, his head rising and falling with her chest and her breathing.

"You see Clyde. You have no choice but to love me back. I control you and give you what you want. It's only fair that it be this way, but you must be a good boy and not an asshole, you understand. No one will ever know about us again, so in two days you must quit your job. I can't have anyone know about this. The Hooks are supposed to be mysterious, not seen at all. I think in time you will grow to love me, and I hope that this is the case soon. I love you very much Clyde. You are the more interesting of the owners that I have had in the past. Clyde? Clyde are you awake? I'm talking to you, ya know."

Clyde groaned. His body writhed as he struggled to get up and move. Serena smiled.

"I want you again right now. Come on, let's go."

Clyde then had sex with Serena on que. Serena knew that he couldn't be pushed anymore so when he was done, she turned him over and strapped him down to the bed.

Clyde woke up a couple hours later dressed in his pajamas. Serena was still naked, and she held a bowl of soup in her hand. Clyde tried to get up, but she sat down next to him and placed a hand in between his legs. Clyde writhed. Her hands were cold.

"I have some soup Clyde. Are you hungry?" Serena asked.

Clyde hated her voice now. It wasn't sweet or innocent or anything.

It was pure evil. Serena smiled.

"You hate my voice now."

She squeezed. Clyde tried to scream, but nothing came out of his voice. Serena stopped and propped his head up with her left hand. With her right, she fed him soup. Clyde took the sips at first, but then reached out for the bowl and yanked it out of Serena's hands. Serena watched as Clyde sucked down the soup, then threw the bowl at Serena. Serena thankfully ducked and the bowl turned into dust when Serena looked at it.

"What a rude Clyde." Serena said.

"Listen bitch! You can go to hell. We have a partnership, but don't blame me for something that was out of my control. How was I supposed to know that they would catch me doing stuff on camera!" Clyde screamed.

Serena was shocked. Clyde continued.

"I would never betray the secrets of The Hooks, so you can stop torturing me and calling me a good boy. I hate it and I don't like getting hurt for no reason."

Clyde propped himself up and sat up in the bed now. Serena shifted in her spot.

"Well, I wanted to make sure that you would never do such a thing. I hated seeing you hurt Clyde, but I did it out of love..."

"Love my ass. You loved every second of me getting hurt, you good for nothing...."

"Clyde? Clyde I'm home!"

Jeremy.

Serena disappeared. Fuck you, Clyde thought.

Another time perhaps.

Whatever.

Jeremy came into the apartment and Clyde was lucky to have his pajamas on and not be naked.

"Did I hear another voice in here Clyde?" Jeremy asked.

"No, it was my mom. She finally called me, and I told her to go fuck herself." Clyde said.

Jeremy watched as Clyde came out and stood in front of the coffee table in front of the TV.

"Ok, but Alexandria is moving in with me in my apartment. Maybe if you can get with this Jemma girl, then we can go on a double date?" Jeremy asked.

That won't work. Working on it, Serena.

"I don't think that is going to happen, Jeremy." Clyde said.

"Why not?"

"She doesn't like me back, so who would I go on a date

with?" Clyde asked.

"New co-worker?" Jeremy asked.

Clyde shook his head.

"No, I don't want anything to do with co-workers." Clyde said.

"Well, suit yourself. I think it might be time for you to get a girlfriend man. You've been alone for too long."

Is that what he thinks that I've been alone for too long.

You are lonely without me, huh, Clyde?

Stop it.

"Stop what?"

Jeremy looked at him, confused. Clyde shook his head.

"Sorry. I woke up with a headache and if I yell at myself, sometimes it goes away." Clyde said, nervously.

Jeremy furrowed his brow.

"You've never done anything like that. Clyde what's going on?" Jeremy asked.

Don't do it.

Serena's voice shattered his skull, echoing louder than before. Clyde was so tempted to tell Jeremy.

He's right there, right in front of you.

If you tell, then everything will be undone.

Clyde sighed.

"I've just been a bit down in the dumps lately. All I do is sleep and I don't do much other than work. I feel like I'm wasting away. I also got into a fight with Brandon at work, so that caused a war and a half. Charlie, my boss, wants me to work more because we don't have the people." Clyde said.

All lies, but some of it is partially true.

Even though Clyde was not happy with Serena, he had to admit that for once, both were on the same side, which was the side of trying to throw Jeremy off. Jeremy stood there for a bit, as if he had to process what Clyde had to say.

"Well, I can see that a lot is on your mind. Why don't you go outside and take a walk? The fresh air might be good for you and its always so dark in here." Jeremy said.

Clyde nodded.

"I'll go for a walk, but now I'm hungry."

"When do you go back to work?"

"Two nights from now. Charlie gave me the time off. I was supposed to work the next two nights and get my weekend off, but that doesn't seem like it is happening."

Jeremy nodded.

"I see."

Clyde then noticed that he wasn't looking at him, but he was looking at the pair of crochet hooks that were on the ground. Jeremy moved towards them and picked them up. Serena was not talking now. Where are you?! Nothing. Jeremy looked at Clyde.

"These are strange things. Have you made anything with them?" Jeremy asked.

As if on que, Clyde saw on his bed a blanket of yarn appear.

"Oh, you mean this." Clyde said.

He went over and showed Jeremy his blanket.

"Ahh yes. The dreaded blanket. Are you going to be doing more of that in the coming days now that you have them off?" Jeremy asked.

"That is a possibility, but I have no idea yet. I might want to go for that walk, then see if I can clean up anything around here. You know, make it presentable." Clyde said.

"Well, I wish you the best of luck with that."

Jeremy handed over the Hooks and Clyde felt a sigh of relief go through him. Jeremy then went to the door.

"I have to help Alex move in. She should be here in a couple of hours, so when she gets here, maybe you can help me bring in all her stuff and meet her. She's anxious to meet you."

"Meet me? Why me?" Clyde asked.

Jeremy didn't answer Clyde's questions, as he was out the door, leaving Clyde by himself. When Clyde was sure that Jeremy was gone, he closed the door and Serena manifested again, sitting up on his bed, completely naked.

"I hope that for your sake that you don't jump into bed with this Alexandria. She sounds like nothing but trouble." Serena said.

Clyde looked at her.

"Sounds like someone else that I know." Clyde said.

Serena let out a laugh.

"Come on, Clyde, baby, I'm not all that bad."

"Well, you are close to it."

Serena hopped off the bed and stood in front of Clyde, caressing his body with her hands. She then looked up at him and planted a kiss on his cheek.

"You and I are bound by the same fate, Clyde. The Fate of The Hooks. It's the one thing that I forgot to tell you about."

Clyde suddenly tensed up. This can't be good, Clyde thought. For once, Serena didn't read his thoughts and just hugged him, her arms wrapping him in her embrace.

"I know that you want to get away from me Clyde, but it is not that simple. The Fate of The Hooks is a terrible fate. We are bound together, from the first moment you touched those hooks, you have sealed your own Fate. If you try to leave me Clyde, you will die a terrible death. There is only one way to release yourself from this mess. It is to kill yourself. By doing this, only then you will be released from your Fate, but you don't want to do that, do you Clyde? You would miss me so much, I can already tell...."

Serena stopped and smiled. Clyde felt himself grow again. Not again. Serena touched him and Clyde almost had a stroke.

"You would miss me too much Clyde, which is why we are bound together, not only as partners, but as lovers. I think that you are beginning to get used to this, like a pet that is being trained." Serena said.

Oh please stop! No more! Clyde thought. Again, Serena didn't enter his thoughts and stood there. Serena stopped touching him and soon, had her fall clothes on. She looked beautiful either way and Serena smiled.

"You are so easy to manipulate Clyde. I bet you are thinking of me without any clothes on, even though I am clothed." Serena said.

Clyde nodded and struggled to get the words out. His throat was dry again.

"I'm getting some water." Clyde croaked.

Serena hopped on his bed and watched him fumble through

the fridge. Clyde pulled out a water bottle and downed it, crushing it in his hand, then throwing the plastic in a bin next to the trash. All the while, Serena just watched him, not moving at all. Clyde looked at the time. It was only 10am and Clyde felt like he was up for an eternity.

"Are you going to help Jeremy with Alexandria?" Serena asked.

Clyde looked at her.

"I guess so. Do you want any breakfast?" Clyde asked.

Serena nodded, a smile spread across her face. She jumped off Clyde's bed and ran to him.

"Can we make the food together this morning? How about omelets or something?"

Clyde had never seen Serena this excited, and she asked more questions that blended in with her other ones. To get her to stop, Clyde hugged her and planted a kiss on her head.

"Ok, ok, relax. We can make the food together." Clyde said.

It was like calming a kid and Clyde was surprised that Serena listened to him. She hugged him back, then the two pulled away from each other to make food. It didn't take long for them to make the omelets. Serena produced the ingredients from the air and soon, the two were sitting on the couch, watching TV, and eating their food. Serena eat surprisingly fast, as if she hadn't eaten at all. Clyde took it slow and ate his food. Serena flipped through the channels on the TV, but couldn't find anything good. She went onto Netflix, found a random Top Ten Movie, and put it on. Clyde the felt her on him, her head up against his shoulder. Clyde tried not to do anything but eat his food, but it was so hard.

Hard to resist me, huh, Clyde?

Her voice cut through him like a knife, sending a chill down his spine. She's crazy, Clyde thought.

I know I'm crazy. Crazy in love with you, Clyde.

Clyde didn't respond and continued eating his omelet and when he was done, put the plates away in the sink. Serena watched him move, her entire body shifting around to watch him work at the sink. Clyde decided to do the dishes. Less tempting when I'm over here.

"Clyde can I ask you something?" Serena asked.

Clyde shut the water off.

"Depends. Will you like my answer, or will you torture me for the right one?" Clyde asked.

This made Serena think and Clyde almost let out a laugh in triumph. Serena screwed up her face, thinking of the right words to say. Come on, answer me. Clyde thought.

"How come you never had a real girlfriend?" Serena asked.

Clyde couldn't hide his thoughts and sighed.

"I was a very shy kid growing up. My parents were no bargain either, so when it came to having a girlfriend, I never got the chance because at 16, I was living here..."

"You were here at 16?"

Clyde nodded.

"All by myself. Jeremy was and still is my only friend. He's let me live here for nothing and in return, I help him out with the complex. I then went to work for Martins and have been there for ten years, a long time to work in retail." Clyde said.

"I'm sorry that this happened to you Clyde. I didn't know..."

"You knew. You know my thoughts Serena..."

"No Clyde, I really didn't know."

Clyde looked at her. She was looking back at him now, eyes flashing and staring at him. Clyde tried to detect a lie, but there was nothing to indicate this.

"So you never knew." Clyde said.

Serena nodded.

"Yes. Just because I can read your thoughts and live in your head, doesn't mean that I know your secrets Clyde Holding." Serena said.

"I thought you could read my thoughts. Is this not true anymore?" Clyde asked.

He moved and stood behind the couch. Serena got on her knees and stretched as high as she could to face Clyde.

"It's partially true, Clyde." Serena said.

"Partially true...."

Serena nodded.

"Yes, partially true."

"I guess I underestimated what you can and can't do."

"Well, what I can do and can't do are two different things. I can love you or hurt you because I love you. Does that make sense?"

"It's like you said, Serena, we are bound by the same Fate."

Serena wrapped her arms around Clyde and pulled him forwards. Clyde collapsed and landed on top of Serena on the floor. Before he could do anything, Serena kissed him, and Clyde kissed back. Soon they were wrapped up in each other's arms, kissing each other passionately.

"I love you." Serena said, gasping for air, then taking another kiss.

"I love you too." Clyde said, in between breaths.

They stayed on the floor for some time, then both got up when a knock came at the door. It was Jeremy again and Clyde felt Serena disappear from underneath him. Clyde got up and dusted himself off.

"Clyde! Can you help me!"

"Yes, just let me get my clothes on." Clyde said.

Clyde thought he heard Jeremy say something, but it was muffled as Clyde rummaged through his clothes. He put on a pair of jeans and a solid blue shirt. Clyde then went to the door and saw Jeremy and Alexandria standing outside. Alex or Alexandria was of average height, with flashing brown eyes. She wore typical fall attire, which was a sweater, a shirt underneath it, a pair of Ugg Boots and a scarf. Typical for an artist, Clyde thought.

You can say that again.

Serena hopped inside of his head. Alexandria was not that skinny, as she had some weight to her. Despite this, she was still beautiful in Jeremy's eyes and Clyde was happy for both. Alex had to look away from Clyde when he opened the door.

"Alex this is Clyde. Clyde this is Alex." Jeremy said.

Clyde held out his hand.

"Clyde, nice to meet you. Jeremy has told me so much about you." Clyde said.

Alex took his hand and shook it.

"Nice to meet you too Clyde. Jeremy has told me a lot about you too Clyde." Alexandria said.

She's pretty.

He's mine. Back off sister!

Clyde tried not to laugh in both Jeremy and Alex's faces.

"We have everything for Alex outside. Care to help?" Jeremy asked.

"Sure, let's go."

Clyde got his shoes on and followed Jeremy and Alexandria to the parking lot. A single U-Haul was parked in Jeremy's spot. The back of the U-Haul was already open, full of boxes of art supplies and boxes of clothes. Jesus, she's packed her entire wardrobe. Clyde thought.

Yeah, no kidding.

Clyde shook his head and helped Jeremy and Alexandria. Jeremy's apartment was on the same floor as Clyde's which was on the first floor. The only thing was that Jeremy's room was on the other end of the first floor. In between that, were other rooms, a common room, and a community kitchen. Clyde never came out here because he liked to stay in his room. Also if I stay in, it gives me more time for Serena. More for me? Later. Yes, I like that. The sound of her voice echoed inside his brain as he lifted one box after the other, bringing one by one into Jeremy's apartment. It was the largest one on the first floor and being the owner of the complex, Clyde expected it to be big. The apartment had a couch and a TV off to the right, with a coffee table. Towards the back, was the sink and cabinets for the food. A single fridge was in the corner. Two windows were above the sink, letting light in. Off to the right was a large bed, with pillows, blankets, and all of it. The closet was off to the left, where Jeremy hung his clothes. Clyde could see that Alex had already brought in a lot of her own clothes a while ago, as some of her shirts, pants, and other articles were hanging about. Alexandria looked embarrassed when Clyde looked around as he dropped a box.

"I'm sorry that I didn't put anything away, Clyde." Alexandria said.

Clyde shrugged.

"It's fine, don't worry about it." Clyde said.

Alexandria was still embarrassed, and Clyde just left the room. It took about a couple of hours for Clyde to help Jeremy and Alexandria bring in all the boxes. I can't believe all the shit that she has. They are going to need a house. Yeah, no kidding. For once, it was nice to hear Serena's voice inside of his head. Clyde got one of the last boxes, when he noticed something.

The Hooks were not on his person.

And he felt fine.

Clyde almost leaped with joy, but Jeremy came into the U-Haul and took the last box. The two friends walked out of the U-Haul and into Jeremy's apartment. The last of the boxes were placed down and Jeremy let out a sigh.

"Thanks for all of your help Clyde. I really appreciate it." Jeremy said.

He then went over to Clyde and gave him $300. Clyde tried to send it back.

"Jeremy, man, it's fine. Keep the money." Clyde said.

"I insist. Take it." Jeremy said.

Clyde's hand was forced open, and Jeremy put the money in it. Alexandria stood off to the side, putting her stuff away. She looked at Clyde, then at Jeremy. Clyde guessed she had to be at least 23 or 24, so a couple years younger than Jeremy.

"Are you going to have lunch?" Jeremy asked.

Clyde nodded.

"I'll make something. I have the next two nights off for now. You never know about Martins."

Jeremy nodded.

"Well, we are gonna eat something quick, then we both have to get to work. Alexandria is going to do a video on her new setup."

"Alright. I'll leave you two be. Have a great guy."

"Goodbye Clyde, it was nice to meet you!" Alexandria said.

"See you later Clyde." Jeremy said.

Clyde walked out and Jeremy closed the door behind him. He then heard rustling and knew that the two were not going to work. Sex. What else did you think that they were going to do,

Clyde? They were waiting for you to leave. For once, he agreed with Serena and went back to his apartment. By now, it was lunch time and Clyde was hungry. He entered his apartment and Serena manifested herself again. Clyde noticed that the bedroom that he made a while ago was not there anymore.

"Puzzled?" Serena asked.

Clyde nodded.

"Yeah, on a couple of things. One, why is the bedroom gone and two, why was I able to function without The Hooks near me?" Clyde asked.

Serena smiled.

"Ahh, good questions and thankfully, I have the answers." Serena said.

Serena sat on the couch and put her feet on the coffee table.

"Well, explain please." Clyde said, almost raising his voice.

"Well, you and I have been bonded for some time so after a while, you don't need The Hooks on your person. The Power and Energy just becomes a part of you, like how I am a part of you now. Also, the stuff that you Create has a limit. After a while it will go away if it is not used all the time or properly..."

"What!!! So you mean that the walls at Martins will be gone!" Clyde shouted.

He was sweating now, a nervous sweat came over him and he sighed. He sat down on the couch, placing his head in his hands. Serena just laughed and rubbed his back with her hand.

"Why are you laughing!" Clyde said.

That made Serena laugh harder.

"Clyde, relax. Nothing at Martins is going to be destroyed. If people shop in the store, then those things won't fail. Trust me, I knew that this was going to happen, so when we Created those sections. I made sure that the Creation was permanent." Serena said.

Clyde looked at her.

"Serena! Don't you ever do that again! You got me all worked up for no reason!" Clyde said.

Serena kissed him on the lips. It felt good and Clyde sighed as he kissed her. Serena then pulled away.

"You don't have to be so loud all the time. Relax, Clyde. Everything is going to be fine." Serena said.

Clyde looked at his iPhone.

Martin's number lit up on the screen and Clyde sighed.

"Pick it up." Serena said.

Clyde sighed again, grabbed the phone, and answered the call.

"Clyde! Clyde, its Sasha!"

"Hi, Sasha, how are you?" Clyde asked.

Sasha sighed. Clyde noted that she had never called her before. Good to know. Serena's voice echoed.

"I need you to come in tonight, Clyde. Just for a few hours. From closing time until 1am. That should be enough hours right."

"That would be fine. What about the rest of the night?"

"Don't worry about that. I have Michelle and Jemma coming in when you leave, so don't worry about it. Just come in at 8 and find me. I am going to be there until we close tonight."

"Ok I'll see you then."

"Thanks Clyde."

The line went dead. Serena now was leaning up against the end of the couch, her legs spread out over Clyde's lap. Clyde looked at her and ran a hand up and down her legs.

"You have to go to work?" Serena asked.

Her voice was innocent again. The tone of 'Please don't leave me alone another night.' Clyde nodded.

"I have to go in for a few hours. Then I'll be home." Clyde said.

"Did you eat? You might want to, then go to sleep for a few hours before you go to work." Serena said.

Clyde nodded.

"Yeah. Want some grilled cheese and soup. I think that is all I have of actual food in the fridge." Clyde said.

Serena leaned close, just enough so Clyde would look down her shirt.

"That would be lovely." Serena said.

Clyde took a quick look, then got up and made the food.

Surprisingly, Serena did not cook with him this time and that was fine with Clyde. He took the bread, grilled it the way he wanted, then sliced the sandwich in two triangles. Clyde cooked the cheese to a point that it was hot enough to be melted, but not enough to spill out onto the stove. The soup, which was a can of Campbells Chicken Noodle Soup, was done before the sandwich's. Clyde motioned for Serena to come over and she grabbed two bowls from the top cabinet.

"You know, I think we need a table for this occasion." Clyde said.

Serena smiled and raised an eyebrow. Clyde felt a small rumbling and when he turned around, a solid wood table appeared, with two solid wood chairs.

"Man, I love you." Clyde said.

"I love you too, Clyde." Serena said.

When Clyde was done, he turned the stove off, got some small plates and gave one grilled cheese to Serena. He pulled out two glasses, filled them with ice and water. He gave one glass to Serena.

"Thanks." Serena said.

Clyde liked her a lot more when she was happy, not when she was upset. Clyde took a munch out of his sandwich, then looked at Serena.

"You know I wish that you were real." Clyde said.

Serena sipped some of her soup, then a bit out of her grilled cheese before responding.

"You want me to be real?" Serena asked.

Clyde nodded.

"Yes. I want nothing to do with Fate or The Hooks or anything. I want to find a way to make you real, so that I can feel complete. You complete me Serena and that is something not to take lightly. I mean, I've been alone for all these years, then you show up and I lost my virginity to a girl that only I can see. There has to be a way to make you real, to make this whole thing real." Clyde said.

Serena looked at him, her eyes full of sadness. She's thinking of the same thing, Clyde thought. For once, she was not in her thoughts and Serena sighed.

"I know Clyde. I want this to be just as real as you want it, but we are bound to The Hooks. I'm The Hooks in the flesh. There isn't a way to make me real if you wanted to." Serena said.

"There has to be way. Can I make someone dead come back to life?" Clyde asked.

It was a serious question and Serena seemed to struggle for the answer.

"Well, can I raise the dead or not?" Clyde asked.

"There is a way that you can do it, but Clyde, why would you want to?" Serena asked.

Clyde could tell that she was getting scared now. Clyde sighed and leaned back in the chair.

"There has to be a way to break the Fate." Clyde said.

"What do you mean?" Serena asked.

Clyde leaned forward.

"You know how most cursed things are cursed because of a reason. Well, there must be a reason behind why The Hooks are the way that they are. There has to be a way to break it, but I don't know what it would entail." Clyde said.

Serena nodded. The two of them were now done with eating their food.

"You are right. There has to be a way to make this real." Serena said.

"See what I'm saying. The hold of The Hooks can't be that strong. You said that there was another owner and whoever it was dropped it like a dime. I feel that The Hooks are weakening. You and I can both feel it." Clyde said.

"This is true, but there is still a power that is holding on, something that is giving The Hooks the motivation to live." Serena said.

"Is that motivation me?" Clyde asked.

Serena nodded.

"It is." Serena said.

"Then there is only one way to break it. It's to sacrifice myself for the sake of The Hooks."

"Clyde don't talk about this." Serena begged.

"If I die, then the hold will be gone. You will be real, a real fucking girl...

"A real girl without a real love! Can't you hear yourself and what you are saying!" Serena shouted.

Clyde was taken aback by her response.

"You're right. A real girl without a real love." Clyde said.

"How do you suppose we go about this?" Serena asked.

"So you are on my side then? You aren't going to try to back out or anything?" Clyde asked.

Serena shook her head.

"No. I want this Clyde and I know that you do too. I'll do my best to keep The Power at bay. There is only so much that I can do myself, but I feel its hold weakening. If I can control it completely, then the two of us will be able to take on anything that we want." Serena said.

Clyde nodded.

"Good."

"How do you want to go about it Clyde?" Serena asked.

That was a good question, Clyde thought. How to go about my own death, so that my ghost girlfriend can resurrect me and bring me back to life? Clyde shook his head.

"I have no idea."

"Then we are going to have to experiment first." Serena said.

Clyde saw that the smile on her face was wicked, not the innocent smile that she usually had on her face.

"Experiment? With a dead body. You can't be serious." Clyde said.

Serena nodded.

"Clyde, that is the only way that we can do this. It would be the only way that we would be able to test out our theory. If we can raise someone else who is dead, then there is the chance that we can do the same to you."

"Shit."

"What?"

"I don't feel too good about talking about death over lunch." Clyde said.

Serena got up and cleared the table. Clyde insisted, but it was her payment for having him cook the food. Serena sat back down at the table and looked at Clyde.

"You work at 8pm?" Serena asked.

Clyde nodded.

"Yes."

"Then we can spend some time together before then. Maybe go on that walk that Jeremy was talking about?" Serena asked.

"We can go to Freeman's Park. It's not a long walk from here." Clyde said.

"Then let's go." Serena said.

Clyde watched as Serena disappeared.

I'll be with you in your head, silly.

I know that you were going to do that.

Jeez. Are you guessing all my secrets and tricks now?

I have been getting very good at this type of stuff.

I bet you have.

Clyde got himself together, then exited his apartment and went outside. Freeman's Park was on the other side of Main Street, going in the opposite direction of Martins. Clyde walked on the sidewalk avoiding eye contact with the people that walked in the opposite direction. The sun was out, and it was hanging high in the sky. The sky was a bit cloudy, however, Clyde did not really pay any attention to it. A crowd of people walked on the sidewalk, heading his direction. Clyde stepped off the sidewalk and let them go by. They obviously were not paying attention to him, and he didn't give a fuck if one of them was the Pope. Freeman's Park was a place for little kids, however, adults seemed to be gravitated towards it. It was a large area with walking trails and nice mowed lawns. It was a pleasant place and Clyde could remember the many times that he would go here as a kid and play on the playground. He looked up as he entered the park and walked through the large parking lot. All the spots were full, and a line of cars were exiting, as if a kid had a party and then decided to leave. Clyde could remember all the times that he would come home with scraped knees. The good old days, Clyde thought.

I wish I experienced those things.

Serena's voice echoed in his head and the Clyde acknowledged that she was here by nodding. Clyde saw that the playgrounds were a lot bigger, some of them were even connected to each other. Good for the kids. It's always for the kids and not for me, Clyde thought. He passed a group of adults who were walking with their kids, and he avoided eye contact with them. The walking trails began on the right and made many twists and turns around the park. Clyde went off to the right and continued the trail. The sun hurt him, and it felt warm on his skin. The air that he breathed was different and it filled his lungs with every breath. Clyde looked around, the began to jog on the trail. He hadn't jogged in a long time, so he started slowing at first, then it was a full-on run. The trees closed in on him from both sides and Clyde was swallowed by the shade. Ahh, much better. Clyde thought. Serena was silent and Clyde expected her to say something at least. Nothing. The trail that Clyde was on twisted off to the right, up a hill that went straight down into another section of the park, where more playgrounds were. Clyde sprinted up the hill and then stopped when he got to the top. He was surprised that in a city like Casper, there could be so much green space for everyone. Casper was a large city, probably about 100,000 people all together and this was the greenest space around. To find more green space, the next place to go was to go to the other surrounding towns that were near the Quabbin Reservoir.

It's beautiful. The view.

I know. It's just as beautiful as you.

Don't flatter me Clyde. I know that I'm beautiful.

Ok, just checking.

Clyde continued his jog and finished the trail back where he started. He already killed at least a couple of hours by doing this and it was still the early afternoon. Clyde sighed and found a shady bench to sit in. He watched as the groups of adults and kids walked on the grass, the trails, and played in the playground area. Clyde knew that by all accounts, he shouldn't have been there. Some of the adults watched him with suspicion, but he paid no attention to them at all. Let them look all they want. I'm not going to do anything to them, Clyde thought. That's right, let them look. Thanks for the confidence Serena. You're welcome. Another group of adults walked by him. They looked at him, then left without saying a word. Rude, Clyde thought. He then got up and went on the same trail. When he got to the fork in the trails, he took the left, this time skirting to another edge of the park. When Clyde was a kid, he was only in the front section of Freeman's Park. He had never been to the other side where the other fields were. That place was off limits to kids at the time and only the older kids were allowed in there. Figures, Clyde thought. He continued his way, jogging on the trail. Some others were jogging as well, however, they were going back the opposite way. A horse and rider passed by Clyde and Clyde almost fell forwards in shock. He continued his way and the trail opened to a large baseball field. The trail continued the other side of the field and Clyde decided to turn around. A baseball game was happening, with kids that Clyde guessed where about 11-12 years old. Young kids, Clyde thought. He couldn't stand the loud screaming when they hit a ball or when they ran. Clyde could hear everything that was going on at the game. The crack of the bat hitting the ball echoed in his brain, the rumbling of feet on the ground, the sliding of body on dirt. Clyde could hear it all.

Suppose you want to know why you can hear it all?

Serena always came at the strangest of times.

Why?

The Power allows it, that is why you can hear more. Have you noticed that your senses are a bit stronger now?

I never really paid any attention to it.

Well now you know why.

Thanks Serena.

"Hey, buddy. You going to come watch the game?"

Clyde was jolted back to the present. An older man approached him, dressed in an umpires uniform.

"What was that? I'm sorry. I'm kind of daydreaming." Clyde said.

"Well, I'm sorry to hear that, but you either come watch the game or get away from the field. Some of the parents are getting a bit uppity. They think you are some pervert or something. I think you are harmless, but if you are going to come over, I have a spot next to the batter's box for you."

"Oh, no thank you. I'll just be going. Sorry to bother you. I used to come here a lot as kid, but I never was allowed down here so after a while I decided to come back here and see what is up." Clyde said.

The man nodded.

"Well, whenever you are in the area, come and stop by. Other than that, get off my field so the teams can play."

During this conversation, Clyde looked off to the right and noticed that both teams stopped, and all the players were looking in his direction, wondering what was going on between their Umpire and this strange guy.

"Well, have a great day." Clyde said.

The man was taken aback as Clyde left.

"Yeah. You...you too man." The man said, shaking his head.

Clyde went back on the trail and jogged back to the main section of the park. He felt the eyes of the man on him the entire time and didn't stop until he know for certain that he was not being watched anymore.

That was strange.

I know. No kidding. That guy thought that I was going to hurt his kids and told me to either watch the game or get the fuck out of here.

He should have sworn at you. You seem to answer those very well.

Whatever Serena. I'm just glad that it's over.

Me too. I hate confrontations with strangers.

Clyde went to the front section of Freeman's Park. By now, most of the day and afternoon people were going home and the night people were coming in. Just like work, Clyde thought. He left his iPhone back in his apartment, so he decided to head back. When he got there, he had spent over four hours at the park, killing time and dreading going into work. When he entered his apartment, Serena appeared again. The first thing that the two did was hug and kiss.

"I missed you." Clyde said.

"I was with you the whole time." Serena said.

"I know, but you weren't with me, holding my hand."

"I know, Clyde, but I was still with you. I still love you and always will love you, you know."

They hugged for a few more minutes, before Clyde pulled away. It was only 6pm. Serena watched as Clyde gathered his things for work. He changed out of his clothes in front of her and he could only watch her smile from the corner of his eye. When Clyde was done, he turned to Serena.

"We have an hour or so to kill." Clyde said.

"Just an hour?" Serena asked.

Clyde nodded and Serena came towards him. She sat herself up on the wood table near the sink and stretched out her arms.

"Want to take me to bed for a bit?" Serena asked.

Clyde came over to her, picked her up, and placed her on his bed. Serena put her hands over her head as Clyde slowly undressed her. She let out a little moan as Clyde put his hand in between her legs, the slipped off her jeans, then her underwear. Clyde then reached under her shirt and soon, Serena lay naked on his bed, waiting for him. She smiled and Clyde came on top of her, then pulled the sheet over the two of them.

"I love you, Serena."

"I love you too Clyde."

Serena's back arched and she and Clyde moaned.

The hour passed quickly, and Clyde got out and was ready. Serena was awake, lying on her back, naked. The sheet stretched across her body, while her arms were still over her head. Clyde had put them there so that he could grab her chest easily and she just left them there, as if she was tied to the bed itself. Clyde could remember the first time that he came inside of her. The ropes, the moaning, the grunting, the struggling. It was as if Serena wanted to get away from him, but she couldn't.

She was tied down.

Now both Clyde and Serena were bound together. Tied by the Power that reigned supreme because of The Hooks. Clyde dressed himself and looked back at her. This is not real. None of it is. It feels real, but it's not real.

"What's the matter, Clyde?" Serena asked.

Her voice was still so sweet, so innocent. Clyde sighed.

"Are you ready to go to work?" Clyde asked.

Serena groaned and rolled over on her stomach, her head looking back at Clyde.

"I guess so."

A smile spread across her face. Clyde came over and cupped his hands around her back and touched both of her breasts, squeezing them in his hands.

"I know, but you have to help me. The faster I work, the faster we can get back. I also get paid tomorrow morning, which is a plus for me." Clyde said.

Serena rolled around and wrapped her arms around his neck, pulling Clyde to her.

"You mean I help you work, and you are the only one that gets paid. That doesn't seem fair, now does it." Serena said.

Clyde kissed her.

"Well, if we figured out how to make you real, then you can work and get paid, how about that?" Clyde asked.

"I don't like it one bit, but I want to be real with you, so I guess that I have no choice." Serena said.

The two kissed and Clyde helped Serena up. It was only 7pm, so Clyde had plenty of time to get ready. He stood Serena up and as he touched her with his hands, he slowly dressed her, as if she was going to work for the first time. First the underwear, then the bra, then the jeans, and finally the shirt. All the pieces fit together. Clyde ran his hands through her hair and tied it back into a long ponytail. Serena smiled and turned around.

"You definitely know how to dress up a girl." Serena said.

"I haven't had a lot of practice, but I guess that is where you come in right." Clyde said.

"Let's go." Serena said.

Clyde got the rest of his things and when he was ready, he opened the door. He looked back at Serena, but he was already gone.

You can give me a kiss when we get home, how about that?

Maybe more than a kiss.

Fine, two kisses. That is the limit.

No sex?

No sex. I think it's break time. I don't want to ruin you.

Fine.

Clyde walked out into the summer night. The air was hot this time, different from the cool spell that gripped Casper for a week. Clyde knew that Serena was inside his head this time. The Hooks were not with him, and it seemed like it was a blessing.

Well, a blessing and a curse.

Serena was the only thing that was representative of the Power and of The Hooks. He felt the energy coursing through him and there was an urge to Create something from thin air, but Serena interjected.

Think about going home, not making stuff. Too many witnesses.

Clyde looked around and Serena was right. Groups of people were going out, shopping, and enjoying the nice weather. Why would people be out on a Thursday? It doesn't make any sense to me, Clyde thought.

Nothing makes sense, Clyde.

You got that right.

Clyde made it to the crosswalk and waiting for a random stranger to hit the cross button. When the button came on and stopped the cars, Clyde walked with the group, staying towards the back of them. He didn't want to give them the wrong impression that he was with any of them. Most of the group went off to the left, heading towards Freeman's Park and the other local shops that were down that way. Clyde headed down the sidewalk and went around the back of Martins. Clyde did this on purpose, as to kill more time. There was no need for him to go in early when it was not worth it at all. I hate this place, Clyde thought.

Keep your cool.

I'll try.

That was a lie and Clyde was surprised that Serena didn't catch onto it sooner. When Clyde reached the back, he had about fifteen minutes left until he could punch in.

I'm killing for a cigarette right now.

You don't need those Clyde.

You don't know how long it's been since I had one.

You don't need it.

Just one.

One turns into one hundred. The answer is no.

Fine.

Clyde waited a few more minutes, then went to the door. If I go in now, then I have five minutes to put my stuff away, then punch. Plenty of time. The door was opened by someone that he didn't recognize.

"Hi there."

"Hi. Where is Jerry?" Clyde asked.

"Jerry? Oh he quit. Moved up someplace in Maine. Small town that has nothing left in it for retirement."

"I see. I'm Clyde and your name is.."

"Jared."

"Well, it's glad to meet you Jared. I hope that you stick around, and I'll see you soon."

"See ya."

Clyde rushed to the backroom. It was not that he wanted to work, but he wanted it to be over so that he could go home.

So we can go home, you mean.

Yes, so we can go home.

Who's a good boy?

I wish you wouldn't say that.

What? It's ok for you to call me a good girl, but not ok for me to call you a good boy. Why?

It's just weird that's why.

Whatever. We are both weird together, Clyde Holding.

Clyde put his things in his locker, then punched in. When he went into the office to see if Sasha was there, he only found Brandon. He looked up at Clyde, upset and pissed off.

"Sasha was moved to another store." Brandon said.

"What?" Clyde asked, raising his voice.

"She was moved to another MA location, some place called Shrewsbury. Have you heard of it?" Brandon asked.

Clyde shrugged his shoulders.

"No clue."

"It's in the eastern direction. Not as far west as we are. Anyways, I'm the overnight manager permanently and Charlie will be on all day from now on, until we can get some more managers in the store."

"Great." Clyde said, rolling his eyes.

"Don't do that to me, Clyde. It's not my call and not my fault. Upper Management came down on all the stores, moving the managers like chess pieces like they always do." Brandon said.

"Then what are we doing tonight?" Clyde asked.

Brandon handed him a list.

"This is all the stuff that has to get moved in the next week. Take a crack at it for the next few nights. I don't care how much of it gets done, just do what you can and leave." Brandon said.

"Who else is coming in?" Clyde asked.

"Jemma and Michelle, right when you leave." Brandon said.

Clyde nodded.

"Ok, I'm going to get some of this done before I leave." Clyde said.

"Fine with me. I going to have a cigarette, then I'll be back." Brandon said.

Clyde let him out of the office first, then Clyde punched in, got his water, the packet, and went out to the salesfloor. He had never been here at 8pm before, so it was a shock to see some of the second shift workers still here. They had to stay an hour after the store closed to get everything together before they could leave. I always thought that staying after the store was closed was stupid.

Was that why you moved to overnights?

It was one of the reasons.

I see.

Clyde looked at the first thing that was on the packet that Brandon gave to him:

Move the remaining Beach/Summer Stuff out front

Fill empty Beach/Summer cages with fall décor and hay bales.

Clyde sighed. Fall already. The summer has just started.

Must get started on those sales.

What kind of sales? Nothing benefits me.

True, but do it for the customer Clyde.

Whatever, Serena.

Clyde moved to the Front Section where he worked the previous night. Most of the Beach/Summer stuff was already gone, as the signs for 75% off seemed to have sold the stuff down. Very good, Clyde thought. He opened the second set of entrance and exit doors and went out into the foyer. There was a bunch of summer and beach stuff here already. Clyde found his water bottle, took a sip of it, and went to work. He first went to the shelves and condensed down the sections into one wall. With the extra wall space, Clyde wheeled the cages out into the foyer and killed everything from the cages into the wall. Whatever couldn't fit into the wall, Clyde kept in the cage and set the cage in a spot in the foyer that would allow customers to see it and walk by it. Good enough right? Good for me. Clyde nodded and continued his work. When he finished moving the cage, he went back inside of the store after closing the second set of doors. It feel strange when doing this, as the second shift workers were still cleaning the store and pulling the drawers. There had always been a shortage of help around at Martins, but nothing was like this. There were only two cashiers, three people to clean the floor, and one person who carried keys. Supervisor? Maybe, but I haven't seen her before, so she must be new. I'm guessing only been here for a couple years or so. Ahh I see. Yeah, let's go. Clyde knew that he had space out in the foyer for the other Beach/Summer cages, so he brought them out to the foyer, condensed them the best that he could and when he was done, brought out the cage to the Front Section. Again, he had to open the second set of doors again, but that was beside the point. Clyde was not a fan of being the only one here on the overnight crew. Normally, well, on a normal night, there would be more people here helping on this stupid packet, but it was only Clyde and Brandon. Wherever he was, Clyde thought. The cages that were empty amounted to only two. Clyde filled one cage with fall décor, which consisted of a lot of wooden statues and figures. All dumped in a cage, which is what the packet wanted. The other cage Clyde put the hay bales in them, and the cage was filled to the top. Clyde sighed and looked at the work that he did. It surprisingly took him longer to do those two jobs, which Clyde was thankful, but also not at the same time.

Weird.

Clyde looked around and the silence in the store was deafening. The second shift were already hanging out the customer service desk. It was already close to ten. Shouldn't they be leaving by now? Clyde thought.

Then Brandon came out and talked to them.

Topic.

Figures.

Clyde was not invited to the topic, as he continued down the packet. The third and fourth things on the packet required him to take the rest of the Beach/Summer stuff and move it down to any section that could be filled. Easy enough, Clyde thought. What's the matter Clyde?

I have this feeling that something isn't right, but I can't place it.

I am getting this same feeling.

Clyde nodded.

Let's go to the back and get a rack of stuff to put out. I think they need more frames. That is what's next on the list.

Ok.

Clyde walked across the store and towards the backroom, where all the racks were kept. He searched through them, finding the rack that was labelled for Frames. Clyde realized that this was going to be a big job. There were four more racks of frames and what seemed like pictures and wall art. Great. Just fucking great, Clyde thought. Well, one rack at a time, right. Yes, one at a time. Clyde grabbed the first one and brought it out to the floor. Something didn't feel right.

There was no way that Brandon could have finished his topic. He takes way to long anyways. Another signal was that the music was off, and the silence was eerie. What is going on, Clyde? I have no idea. I'm scared. Me too. Clyde moved the rack off to the side, completely blocking a section off. Clyde slowly went towards the front of the store, then stopped in his tracks. How could he have not heard. Two cars crashed through the front doors. Armed men, probably about ten of them, armed with guns, had Brandon and all the second shift crew on their knees.

"Please, just take what you want and go." Brandon said.

He sounded scared. Good, Clyde thought. You aren't going to feel bad for him, Clyde?

No. He's an asshole to me anyways. Oh I see.

"Boss, we got two more!" A voice shouted.

Clyde backed away and hid behind a wall. He peeked out just enough to see the chaos that was happening in front of him. Two men brought in Jemma and Michelle. Jemma struggling violently, trying to get away. Clyde pulled out his iPhone. The time read 1am. I should be going home. And leave them here. That's says a lot about you, Clyde. What you want me to be a hero? You can be one. Right here, right now. No thanks. Clyde watched as Jemma and Michelle were put with the others.

"Tie them up. Take all the money and then kill them all."

To Clyde, that sounded like the leader of the gang. Surprisingly, no burglar alarms went off. Another man came through. He was a shorter build and held pliers in his hands.

"Everything is shut down. No one will know that we are here."

"Excellent Peter. Excellent. Help the others tie the rest of these guys and girls up. Then meet me in the back office."

Clyde watched as the leader looked at Jemma.

"I've always wanted a little girl, you know that Peter?"

"I've been aware of it, Cameron."

Peter and Cameron. I must make a note of that, Clyde thought. He watched as Cameron took Jemma and forced her towards the office, with Peter in tow behind him. Clyde rushed into the Arts and Crafts section, hiding behind the wall. He prayed that he wasn't spotted and when he moved his head out, he saw Jemma, Peter, and Cameron going into the office. Clyde could hear Brandon's screams in the front. They are torturing him for the access to the safe. I know, but fuck him. Clyde, you must put your differences aside. The man is dying. Well, so am I! Whatever Clyde. Just figure out how to get out of here.

I'm not leaving anyone behind, but I must plan this out.

One on ten. Most of them have guns. I only have a boxcutter and two extra blades.

That could work.

Kill them one by one. Rambo style?

Might be the only way that you are going to get out of this one alive, Clyde.

If that Peter guy cut the power, then the cameras must be off as well. I must get to him first, then everyone else. I'll save this Cameron guy for last.

Do it quick Clyde. I've never seen you kill or get angry.

Well, there's always a first time.

I want to witness this.

You are going to help me.

The screams up front stopped. Maybe Brandon gave in. That thought was gone when a gunshot rang in the store. Fuck, he's dead, Clyde thought.

Now what?

We need to get into the office, but I must do it my way.

Ok. You lead.

I was planning on it.

Clyde went to the other side of the first fall and peered around the corner. Another gunshot ran out, followed by a scream. They are killing everyone one by one, Clyde thought. He pulled away and took off his shoes, carrying them in his hands. If he were to run, then the echo from his shoes would echo in the room. The place was eerie without the music going on in the background, but Clyde didn't care. For the first time since he found The Hooks and Serena, Clyde was scared. Terrified even. He shook his head and jogged lightly through the next sections. He passed through Toys, Pets, Clearance, and another Summer section in the back. God knows why it's back here, Clyde thought. Serena was quiet as Clyde led. He crept along the wall of summer stuff, peered out, then pulled back behind the wall. Two men were coming down this way. They could not have heard me, Clyde thought. The footsteps of the men echoed on the floor as they got closer. Clyde hid behind the endcap section between Summer and Clearance. Clyde held his breath.

The footsteps stopped.

Clyde found the boxcutter and held it in his hand, gripping it until his hand was white. The footsteps continued and Clyde knew that they were going go head down the back walkway of the store. Moving silently, Clyde went into the Clearance section and crouched down. The footsteps continued, then stopped. Clyde heard guns loading. They found me this time, Clyde thought.

Then gunshots.

Clyde tried to hide himself behind the wall more, but he realized that they weren't shooting at him. Clyde moved to the other end of the wall and peered out. The two men were shooting up the Housewares section of the store. Glass sprayed everywhere as the men focused their weapons on the various mugs, plates, and cups. Jesus, Clyde thought. I guess they don't want anything from that section. This might be my chance to go. Clyde watched as the men continued down the back section, firing their guns. There are at least ten of them. Here are two. Where are the other eight? Clyde screwed up his face and went out onto the main walkway of the store. Many called it the racetrack. Others called it the walkway. Either way, Clyde moved at a slow pace and hid behind a bulk section of plastic storage containers. The sounds of the men echoed in the distance. I'm in the clear, Clyde thought. He moved through the walkway and crossed towards the food section, which was one of the largest sections in the store. The double doors that led into the backroom were near and Clyde entered them with ease. I must find a way to bring these guys down.

That was close Clyde. Don't scare me again please.

Serena was back.

I'm sorry if I scared you.

What are you going to do now.

Why don't you watch.

Clyde looked about the backroom. Racks of stuff that was supposed to be put out tonight lined both sides of the area. Clyde went over to the nearest one and noticed an apron that was on one of the top shelves. Clyde went towards the back of the rack and climbed it. The rack was a bit unsteady, and Clyde had to be very careful when being up here. The other racks were close to him, which was a good thing. The racks were not supposed to move, however, they did rock back and forth as Clyde stretched himself on the rack. He grabbed the apron. It was a sold green color, the ones used by cashiers or stockers. Clyde rummaged through the pockets and found a nametag.

Sarah.

I hate this bitch. I don't want to be any closer to her than I must be. In the other pockets, he found Sarah's boxcutter and blades. Clyde took them and put them with what he had. Then he heard a noise and Clyde was still. The double doors opened, and a man came through. Clyde held his breath. I'm dead this time. The man carried an M-16. For God sakes, Clyde thought. The man didn't even notice that Clyde was on top of the rack and continued to look around through the backroom. Then Clyde got an idea and he smiled. The apron was still in front of him, and Clyde inched forward on the rack. The man stopped. Clyde stopped. The man continued looking through the stuff, then proceeded to fire at some of the racks in front of him. Good, just a few more inches. Clyde moved, gripping the apron as tight as he could. The man continued to fire, the shells falling and the bullets spraying a whole rack of plastic toys. Clyde got to the end of the rack and waited for the man to back up. Then Clyde struck. He reached out with the front of the apron and wrapped the strap around the man's neck. The man, surprised, lashed out. When Clyde wrapped the strap on the man, he lifted himself and the man hung in the air. Clyde watched as the man struggled to get away, his arms and legs flailing. Clyde kept the pressure on the man, eventually choking him out. The man stopped moving and Clyde hauled the body on the top of the rack with him. Clyde searched through the man's body, finding a combat knife strapped to his leg. Clyde laid the man on the top of the rack and placed the apron on him.

He didn't like his first day.

In his head, he heard Serena laugh. Clyde slowly got down off the rack and picked up the M-16 and growled in disgust. There was only one clip left. The man wasted the bullets on a bunch of plastic toys and Clyde just shook his head at the wreckage. There were no more bullets on the man, so each one must have a certain amount of ammunition. I can use this to my advantage.

"Henry! Henry do you copy?"

It was a voice. Clyde went over to the rack again and looked through the man. The man had a small walkie on his person. Clyde switched the walkie off and pulled the man off the rack. With the body on the ground, Clyde hide it underneath one of the racks in the back. He took off the man's shoes and placed them somewhere else. They are going to be here soon. I must find another place to be, Clyde thought. He went through the backroom and found the storage area where the hangers were. The bin was only half full and it was large enough for a person to fit in. Footsteps echoed and Clyde hopped in, hoping that none of the men saw him.

"Where's Henry?"

Clyde recognized the voice of the Cameron guy and Clyde knew that he was pissed off.

"No clue boss. He went back here to take out some of the stuff and…."

The voice stopped. Footsteps.

"Cameron, there are shells here."

Fuck. I forgot to hide those, Clyde thought, shoving his fist into his mouth.

"He was here. Find him. I think there is one more worker here."

"You think so? We rounded up all of them and we can't ask the Brandon guy.."

"I don't give a shit about Brandon. We have another worker in here. Find this person and kill him or her. We already got the money, but we are waiting for George to bring the armored truck for the transport."

Transport? They are trapped here. This could also work to my advantage, Clyde thought. He waited for the footsteps to go away before peeking his head out of the bin. A single man was there, the one that Clyde assumed asked for the other guy named Henry. Clyde didn't know his name, but he knew that he had to get all these guys before the George guy showed up. Such generic names. They must all be part of the same club or something, Clyde thought. The man was looking around the racks and Clyde was tempted to step out of the bin, but he didn't want to risk the noise of the hangers that were below him. Clyde didn't know how long he was on them, but the slightest move could mean his death. Clyde's boy hurt from being in the bin for what seemed like an eternity. Clyde peered out and the man was still standing by the racks. Clyde's feet began to hurt. The hangers pressed against him on all sides and Clyde wanted to shift himself to be more comfortable, but the man was still there. The double doors opened, and the man left. Clyde took the opportunity to jump out of the bin and he stumbled because his body hurt. Clyde hid behind another set of racks, stumbling before he could crouch down again. The double doors opened, and the man came through the back again, armed with another M-16. Great, Clyde thought. He found the combat knife and gripped it. Clyde watched the man come closer to him through the racks. This man is so dumb, Clyde thought. Clyde moved towards the edge of the rack, staying completely still. The man turned and came down towards Clyde. The man stopped and looked down, noticing a single hanger on the floor. When the men bent down to pick it up, Clyde jumped out and dove the knife into the back of the man. The man tried to scream, but Clyde gripped the man's mouth shut with his hand. The M-16 dropped to the ground and a few bullets shot out. The sound echoed and Clyde stuck the knife deeper into the man, so the point of the knife stuck out of the man's chest. Bleeding and grunting, the man fell forward on the ground. Clyde ripped the knife out of the man's back and took the M-16. I have never fired one before, Clyde thought. Well, there is always a first time. Clyde sighed and knew that he had to get out of here. Clyde ran through the backroom and gunshots rang out. They found me, Clyde thought. Bullets bounced off the racks as three men fired at Clyde. Clyde ran into the other part of the backroom, where the furniture was. A single ladder led up to the roof and Clyde debated on going that way. His decision was forced when two more men came after him through another small backdoor. Clyde took the M-16 and fired it blindly. Two men fell down dead. The recoil of the gun almost forced Clyde on his ass and he stumbled backwards, hitting his head on the end of a rack. Shaking his head, Clyde forced himself up towards the small backdoor. Clyde bashed through it and closed it. Bullets hit the door and Clyde ran up towards the front. They know about me now, Clyde thought. A man appeared and fired at Clyde.

"Jesus!" Clyde shouted as he dived on the ground. Clyde slid and slammed against a wall of canned soups and other food items. The bullets hit the wall and it shook. Clyde moved as some of the cans exploded and fell off the wall, making a mess on the floor. The man came around the other side and Clyde hid behind the endcap. Clyde fumbled with the M-16, trying to get a clip into the gun. In frustration, Clyde threw it on the ground. I need you Serena.

Of course.

Clyde screwed up his face and went out to face the man. The man fired his gun, but Clyde stuck out his hand. The gun clicked and stopped. Clyde motioned his hand to the left and the gun flew out of the man's hand.

"What the fuck!" The man shouted.

Clyde shot out his hand and the man went flying across the store, bashing his head against the corner of an endcap section. Clyde gulped. The man was not moving, and Clyde went over to him. Blood pooled out from the man's head, as it was bashed in. God help me, Clyde thought. Clyde then heard footsteps. The three men, along with the guys Cameron and Peter, came out.

"We got you now, you little bitch!" One yelled.

Clyde faced them, his eyes full of hate and evil. The men began to cower, but then they rallied and fired their M-16's. Clyde held out his hand and the bullets fell to the ground. The men were in shock and Clyde kept on coming towards them. He pointed his hand to the ground and the floor shook. A wave of dirt rose from the ground and burst through the floor, taking the tile with it. The men tried to get away, but they were transfixed in the amazement. The mixture of dirt and tile crashed on them, killing all three instantly. Cameron and Peter, who stood in shock, ran towards the back office. Clyde then booked it, running after them.

Cameron got to the door first and locked it behind Peter. Peter tried to get to it, but Clyde got him. Clyde held out his hand and Peter levitated towards him.

"Don't kill me man! For God sakes!"

Clyde didn't care about Peter's screams. Peter struggled like an animal, flailing and thrashing.

"God sakes! Put me down man!"

"I'll never do it again man please man please man put me down..."

Clyde watched him struggle, then Peter was placed right into Clyde's right hand. Clyde squeezed with a strength that he had not known before. Peter's eyes bulged out of his head and Clyde kept on squeezing. Peter's screams slowly died out and soon, Clyde was squeezing a lifeless form. Clyde then tossed Peter's body with such strength, that Peter's dead body crashed through the door and broke it down. Clyde sighed. Cameron is next. He heard a scream coming from the office. Jemma! Clyde thought. He ran through the door and into the office.

"Stop it asshole!"

It was Cameron. He had Jemma in front of him, a knife blade at her throat. Clyde stopped where he was. Cameron smiled. Clyde got a good look at this guy. He was dressed in all black, with the only other color being his sandy brown hair. Clyde guessed that Cameron was in his forties. Jemma struggled against him, but it only seemed to turn Cameron on, and he pressed the blade closer to her.

"One more move out of you, buster, and she dies." Cameron said.

Clyde spat on the floor.

"Get bent." Clyde said.

Cameron laughed.

"I'll get bent with her. You seem to like her, so maybe if I get rid of her, then you, then my problems will go away." Cameron said.

"Why did you do this?" Clyde asked. He really wanted to know. Cameron kept his position against Jemma.

"We do all of the stores, mate. They give us what we want and then we give it to those who are starving. You know, the homeless and all that."

"No charity group that I know would carry M-16's." Clyde said.

Cameron screwed up his face.

"You know nothing of being poor kid. You know nothing of eating dirt for days on end, while others laughed at you and called you a disgrace to society." Cameron said, raising his voice.

Clyde knew about this all too well. He knew what it was like to be on your own, without any help. The only one who gave him help was Jeremy and in the last few years, Clyde could not think of any other close friend besides him. Clyde seemed to forget about the feud that he and Jemma were having. I intend to save her, whatever it takes. Clyde thought. Jemma tried to pull away from Cameron and he yanked her back so hard that she screamed.

"No!" Clyde shouted.

Cameron forced Jemma to her knees, holding her by her long ponytail. Cameron pointed a finger at Clyde.

"We have what we want, but I want you to do something special for me." Cameron said.

"What is it?" Clyde asked.
Cameron smiled.

"I knew that you would come along just nice. I want you to help me load the money into the truck, then..."

A phone rang. Cameron pulled out his phone.

"None of you fuckers move!" Cameron shouted.

Clyde watched as he put the phone on speaker. A ruff voice sounded through the phone.

"Cameron. Where the hell is everyone! I'm out front, crashed through the windows like we planned."

Clyde guessed that it was George.

"Bring the armored truck into the store as best as you can. I have another helper here." Cameron said.

He then clicked the phone off and forced Jemma to her feet. "Out! The both of you!" Cameron shouted.

Clyde walked out of the office and onto the salesfloor. Cameron guided himself and Jemma past the body of Peter and out where Clyde was standing.

CRRRRRSSSSHHHHHHHHHHHH

The armored truck smashed through the front windows and took down with it a few of the registers. Stuff went flying in all directions, along with glass and debris. A cloud of smoke rushed through the area. George stepped out of the truck. He was an older man and Clyde guessed that he was in his fifties, maybe early sixties. God Damn, Clyde thought.

"Come on, let's move!" Cameron said, shoving Clyde.

Clyde wanted to kill him so bad, but he had Jemma and he wanted to save her. Clyde went to the area where George was. He was already loading the tills into the truck. Cameron took Jemma, found some handcuffs, and cuffed her. Clyde was about to react when George grabbed him and pulled him away. There was a single register pole that stood, and Cameron fastened Jemma to it, so that her hands were cuffed over her head. Fuck, Clyde thought. Jemma struggled, but Cameron didn't seem to care. Instead of doing anything, Cameron decided to feel her up and Jemma screamed. Clyde grunted and groaned, trying to fight George, but George threw him against the side of the armored truck. Clyde saw stars, then got angry and pushed George from him. George, in shock, flew backwards and crashed into a register, smashing the whole thing. Clyde waited for George to get up, but he didn't stir.

George was dead.

"What the hell." Cameron said.

Clyde turned to face him.

"Face me. You should be able to win." Clyde said.

Cameron screwed up his face in anger, looked at Jemma, then Clyde.

"I'm going to screw you up, then I'll fuck your little friend before killing her."

"Go ahead." Clyde said.

Cameron went over to Jemma and sliced her throat with his knife, then put the knife into her chest. Cameron then charged for Clyde, not feeling any remorse for what he did. Clyde felt the

Energy inside of him. The anger and sadness washing over him like a wave, consuming his entire being. He put out his hand and Cameron stopped mid charge. Clyde lifted him up in the air.

"Put me down, freak!" Cameron shouted.

Clyde didn't listen and moved Cameron towards the armored truck.

"You want your money right?" Clyde asked.

Cameron struggled and flailed.

"Yes, a hundred times, yes!" Cameron shouted.

There was a rumble from the armored truck. All the tills appeared, then one by one the tops blew off. Money and coins swirled in the air.

"Then take it." Clyde said, gritting his teeth.

Cameron screamed. Clyde forced his mouth open by looking at him. Cameron's eyes went wide, as he couldn't believe what was happening. Then a constant stream of bills and coins entered in Cameron's mouth. He flailed and screamed in Clyde's grip, but Clyde was not letting him go. Clyde forced Cameron's hand's back with the Energy, then forced his head back and opened his mouth as far as it could go. More money streamed into Cameron and his body flailed. Clyde watched him gag and sputter, trying to get out of Clyde's invisible grip. Clyde focused harder and Cameron's jaws broke, but that didn't stop Clyde. Eventually, Cameron was dead, completely stuffed with the money that he was supposed to use. The stream of dollar bills and coins stopped. Clyde dropped Cameron's body to the ground, the coins and bills spilling out of him. Clyde tried to move his body, but he was weak. Cameron was completely stuffed full of money. There is nothing of him now, Clyde thought.

Jemma!

Clyde turned to see Jemma slumped over and bleeding. The knife was still in her chest and her shirt was covered in blood from the slash on her throat. Clyde went towards her, then fell on the floor, weak. Serena appeared and Clyde clawed his way to Jemma. Holding back tears, Clyde undid the cuffs that were around Jemma's wrists. Jemma's body fell on top of Clyde and Clyde moved out of the way. Clyde turned her body around and pulled the knife from her body. There was a movement and George, who Clyde thought was dead, stumbled up to his feet. Clyde ended his misery by throwing the knife. The knife sailed and hit George in the forehead. Clyde watched as the man fell, dead for good. Clyde then grabbed Jemma's body and held her close to him.

"Oh Jemma Jemma is going to be ok I'll get you out of here and you are going to be fine and we and we and we."

"Clyde."

Clyde looked and saw Serena standing there. She was dressed in a summer outfit now, with jean shorts, a solid color tank top, and sneakers. Clyde could see the outline of her sports bra underneath her top.

"Clyde, she's dead."

"She can't be dead she can't be. Come on man! You have to help me!"

Clyde was full on crying now. He had never cried for a girl that barely knew him, but he was crying and couldn't stop. His body hurt and he was weak from using his Energy. Serena came over to him and hugged him.

"Clyde. She's dead. No one could have survived that, and you know it. She's dead Clyde."

She kept repeating this over and over, but Clyde was not having it. He got up and hugged Serena.

"She's not dead!! Not dead! She isn't dead god Dammit! You have to help me!" Clyde shouted.

He pulled away from Serena and tried to revive Jemma. He smashed her chest with his hands, the blood imprinting on his palms and fingertips.

"Jemma! Jemma wake up!" Clyde shouted.

Serena stood there, shaking her head as Clyde continued. He got down and gave her mouth to mouth. Nothing. Clyde screamed at the top of his lungs, until there was no air in his system. He slumped backwards and cried, lying on his back on the floor. Serena looked down at him.

"Clyde. We have to bring her back."

Clyde wiped his eyes.

"Back? To the apartment." Clyde said.

Serena nodded. She held out a hand and helped him to his feet.

"We have to complete the experiment Clyde. This will be our chance to see if our theory works." Serena said.

Theory?

"Making the dead REAL CLYDE!! That is what we wanted to do in the first place!" Serena yelled.

Clyde waited until she was done. Serena was breathing heavy now, her face screwed up in anger, her eyes bulging out.

"THIS IS WHAT YOU WANTED RIGHT, CLYDE?!"

The yell sent Clyde back on the floor and he hit his head in the process. Shaking his head, he got back up, fighting more tears.

"Yes." Clyde said, weakly.

Serena calmed down.

"Fine, I'm going to get your car." Serena said.

"You can't drive! You've never driven before." Clyde said.

"Too bad. Wait here and I'll get your car. Where are your keys?"

"Glovebox. Car should be unlocked."

With that, Serena was gone. Clyde sighed and got back on the ground again. He grabbed Jemma's body and placed her in a sitting up position, leaning against the large, armored truck that was in the front of the store. Everyone was gone. Clyde just looked at the destruction that he had caused. Well, it was Serena after all. I should have never picked up The Hooks. Then everyone would have been alive. Doesn't matter. The attack would have happened regardless of what happened.

Clyde heard the screeching of wheels. His car came crashing through the other main front window and knocked over more of the registers. Serena stepped out of his car. She was wearing a racing outfit, with a number #01 on her back. Her hair was loose down her back. Her outfit was a solid white color, while stripes of blue and green ran down the sides. Serena tossed her helmet in the back seat and looked at Clyde.

"So you into changing outfits now?" Clyde asked.

"I like to be prepared for the occasion. Driving is not as bad as I thought." Serena said.

There was something about presence that calmed Clyde, like everything was going to be alright. Serena looked at him.

"Are you and Jemma going to come in the car?" Serena asked.

"Yeah. Help me out." Clyde said.

Both Clyde and Serena grabbed Jemma's dead body and placed it in the back of Clyde's car. Well, now everything is going to be stained. Just great, Clyde thought. Serena got into the driver's seat and Clyde in the passenger seat. Serena smiled.

"What's the matter Clyde? We are about to embark on our greatest adventure."

Clyde didn't respond. Serena launched the car in reverse and put it into the street.

The Experiment

It didn't take long for Serena and Clyde to get back to Brightcourt. Clyde realized that it was 4am. All of that took three hours of my life, Clyde thought. He looked at Serena. She was still in that racing outfit, focused on driving the little way. Thankfully there wasn't anyone around, as Serena was a terrible driver and Clyde guessed that she would have hit everything in her path if she could. What have I gotten myself into? Clyde thought again. He was surprised that Serena was not in his head, and this was a good opportunity to think for himself for once. Serena pulled into Clyde's parking spot and turned the car off.

"Hold on." Clyde said.

"What?" Serena asked.

"I'm going to go in and see if Jeremy is awake. I don't want him to be awake and see what we are doing." Clyde said.

Serena let out a sigh, then nodded.

"Ok. Just be careful ok."

She planted a kiss on his cheek. Clyde then stepped out of his car and went to the entrance of the complex. He descended the stairs and looked for any signs of life.

Nothing.

Jeremy and Alexandria must still be asleep. Clyde doubled back to the parking lot and Serena got out of the car. The two worked in silence and brought Jemma's body out of Clyde's car. Clyde opened the door by using the Energy and the door opened in silence.

"Let's put her on the table." Clyde said.

Serena only nodded and followed Clyde inside. Serena seemed to struggle with the lifting part, but Clyde managed to take Jemma's body and put it on the table. His shirt was stained red with Jemma's blood, and he took it off and got a new one. When Clyde returned, Serena was back in her fall outfit, this time wearing a set of thick glasses that brought out her eyes.

"Now what?" Clyde asked.

"We bring her to life, that's what." Serena said.

"How is your hold?" Clyde asked.

"I'm getting stronger, which is good. Clyde. You seem tired."

Clyde nodded warily. He was weary. There was something in him that tired him out.

"Was it the Energy?" Clyde asked.

"What?'

"Is it the Energy that is making me tired."

"It might be Clyde, but together we are going to be ok."

"Then let's do this." Clyde said.

Serena smiled and she disappeared.

In here.

Ok.

Serena was back in his head again.

Take off her clothes, Clyde. Everything must go or else we are going to get the cops on our tail.

Clyde nodded and proceeded to undress Jemma. He had never touched a dead girl before, so it was a strange experience for Clyde. One by one, Jemma's clothes were off, so that she was completely naked on the table. Clyde put her clothes in a pile near the sink.

Think of some ropes. Her wrists and ankles. We don't want her to get away when she's alive.

Just like that, ropes appeared in Clyde's hands. He tied each ankle to a leg of the table, spreading them out. He took both Jemma's wrists and tied them together. Clyde brought her wrists over Jemma's head, then tied the rope to the back of the other chair. As if on que, rocks appeared on the chairs, holding them down. Serena then appeared.

"It's time Clyde." Serena said.

"How are we going to do this?" Clyde asked.

"I'll be with you Clyde. Every step of the way. Use the Energy to make her alive." Serena said.

"Ok." Clyde nodded.

Clyde was afraid to admit that he feared doing this. What if it doesn't work? What if it was all for nothing? Clyde went over to Jemma and looked at her. Her body was so innocent and still tied on the table. Clyde sighed. He thought of her, the first moments when he met her. He thought of her first night, the night when he trained her. The time of when they both told Sarah to go fuck herself. The other day when it was just him and her on the sales-floor. He thought of the two leaving the backroom, Clyde smoking a cigarette.

A thump.

A gasp and a moan.

Clyde watched with amazement as Jemma's body filled up with life. Her chest heaved in and out. Her eyes were wide with shock. Another loud gasping breath, as if Jemma was underwater this whole time. Serena watched in earnest. She looked at Clyde.

"Come on, you can finish this." Serena said in his ear.

Clyde remembered Jemma driving away. Then the fight between him and Brandon. The remarks that he made towards her when he was using the Energy at work. Then the fight at the end. Clyde saw Jemma tied up at the pole, her hands cuffed over her head. The amounts of blood that spilled from her wounds were deafening and Clyde struggled to keep his thoughts straight.

"Clyde?"

It was Jemma's voice. She was alive. Clyde stopped and looked at Serena, who jumped for joy.

"We did it! We did it! We did it Clyde!" Serena shouted.

Serena then hugged Clyde and while Jemma was looking, Serena pulled Clyde close to her and kissed him. Clyde, overcome with a wave of mixed emotions, let Serena do what she wanted with him and returned the kiss. When Serena pulled away, the two looked at Jemma. She began to pull at the ropes.

"Can someone explain what is going on?" Jemma asked.

Clyde realized how beautiful she was and was thankful that Serena was not in his head. Clyde noticed that the slash on her throat and knife wound in her chest were both gone. A true mira-cle indeed, Clyde thought.

"Clyde. You know what has to happen now, right?" Serena said.

Clyde looked at her.

"What do you mean?" Clyde asked.

"Well, Jemma is alive, but how do we know that she is real? If she is real, then she can feel pain and pleasure." Serena said.

Oh no, Clyde thought.

"Clyde, you have to have sex with Jemma. That is going to be the only way that we will really know if this works." Serena said.

For the first time, Clyde almost threw up. Sex! With Jemma Sterling! He only wanted Serena. Clyde's throat became dry, and he began to sweat a bit.

"Serena... I...."

"You have to do this, Clyde!" Serena said, raising her voice.

Clyde shook his head. For the first time, he never wanted sex. What kind of man am I? Saying no to sex when its available! What the hell is going on with me.

"Clyde. You have to do this, no matter how uncomfortable it is." Serena said.

"And if I don't?" Clyde asked.

"Then this whole thing was for nothing, you fucking idiot." Serena said.

Clyde was taken aback by her remark.

"Serena. I just want you. You would be mad at me for doing this for years to come..." Clyde pleaded.

Serena shook her head.

"Clyde, I don't care. I want this done. For the sake of this experiment, sacrifices must be made. You have to do this." Serena said.

Clyde gulped. I can't believe this. Serena came over to him.

"Come on. Let me help you with these." Serena said.

Clyde let her undress him, first starting with his shirt, then his pants, and last his underwear.

"What's going on? Where am I? Clyde? Let me go!" Jemma shouted.

Clyde watched as she struggled now. Clyde stood there, naked and in front of Jemma Sterling, the one who he thought he loved. There was nothing to show for it. When Serena came close to him, it seemed like his body only wanted her and to test this, Serena stepped away. Clyde couldn't feel anything for Jemma. He watched her struggle against the ropes, the skin rubbing on the rope, creating burns on his wrists and ankles. Tiny droplets of blood seeped out and dropped to the floor. Clyde looked at Serena.

"Come on man! There has to be a better way..."

Serena shook her head.

"No Clyde! There isn't!"

Clyde let out a whimper and began to cry. Tears streamed down his face.

"And you say this was the girl that you loved! The one who you wanted in the beginning before you met me and now that you have her here, you refuse to take advantage of her! What man would not want to have a free piece of ass, especially like this when she is served to you on a golden platter. She's naked! She's tied down! Go and fuck her for Chrissake! Isn't this what you always wanted! Go Clyde!" Serena shouted.

She shoved him forwards and Clyde almost hit his face on the end of the table. Jemma struggled to get off the table, writhing in the ropes. To make her stop, Serena rechecked the ropes and tied them tighter.

"Clyde! Do it!" Serena shouted.

"Fine!" Clyde shouted.

Serena fell backwards, shocked. Jemma cried. Clyde cried. He got on top of the table and lay down on top of Jemma. Trying not to cry, he stroked her like he did with Serena. Nothing. Nothing grew and he knew it, He put his hand down and stroked. Nothing. Fuck!!! Clyde thought, screaming at himself. Jemma continued to cry, and Clyde tried. Nothing. With every pass, nothing. Jemma wasn't even wet.

There was no connection.

There was no love.

Clyde cried like he never cried before, Jemma's naked body stained with his tears. In a scream he launched himself off the table and crashed on the couch. Clyde got himself up, put his hands in his face, and cried.

"What the fuck is wrong with me!" Clyde shouted.

He felt Serena behind him and immediately, he grew. Rock hard. So hard that it hurt to move or touch. Serena smiled at him.

"You can't do it, Clyde. I know you can't. I knew that this was going to be too much for you." Serena said.

Clyde got himself together.

"There has to be another way." Clyde said.

Serena sighed.

"The only other way is to torture her Clyde. Do you want to do that?" Serena asked.

Clyde almost threw up. He felt his heart in his throat. Torture. Christ forgive me, Clyde thought.

"It might be the only other way Clyde." Serena said.

"How do you want to do it?" Clyde asked.

"The question is, are you going to do it?" Serena asked back.

Clyde nodded.

"I'll do it."

"You are sure."

"Positive. What will I do?" Clyde asked.

"Whatever you think of. The first thing that comes to mind when you want to hurt a beautiful girl that is helpless." Serena said.

Fuck. That could be a myriad of things, Clyde thought.

Then it came.

A couple buckets of water appeared next to the sink, followed by a generator with wires attached to it. A sponge was strapped to a wand.

Electricity.

"Good choice, Clyde." Serena said.

"Clyde! Let me go right now or I'll call my parents!" Jemma shouted.

Clyde and Serena watched the struggling beauty on the table and did nothing. Clyde sighed.

"Here goes nothing." Clyde said.

Clyde then went towards Jemma as she struggled to get away from him. Clyde went over near the sink and grabbed the buckets of water, one in each hand.

"Remember to dump them on her Clyde." Serena said.

Clyde brought over the buckets. Jemma looked at him, her

eyes piercing Clyde. Clyde tried to look away, but he was not able to get rid of her gaze.

"Don't think about Clyde. Just do it." Serena said.

Clyde got himself together. He took one bucket and dumped the water on Jemma. He watched as Jemma writhed, trying to get the water off her as it soaked her body. He took the other bucket and did the same thing, drowning Jemma in the water.

"Now hook her up." Serena said.

Clyde felt tears going down his face again and he wiped them away with a shaking hand. He went over to the generator and flipped on the switch. Clyde was thankful that the wand was already connected to the generator, so when it turned on, Clyde could feel the power coming through it. Great, Clyde thought. The wand was on an extension cord of sorts that seemed to go on forever. Jemma writhed.

"Please God no! please!" Jemma belted.

Clyde sighed.

"I'm sorry Jemma. It's for your own good."

Clyde brought up the wand.

"Stop!" Serena shouted.

Clyde turned to her and watched as she produced a gag.

"Open." Serena said.

Jemma refused, so Serena pinched her nose and placed the gag in Jemma's mouth. Clyde watched as Serena produced tape from the air and strapped the gag to Jemma's mouth.

"Bite on it, Jemma or else you will bite your tongue clean off. Clyde. Proceed." Serena said.

Clyde brought up the wand and then hovered it over Jemma's chest. She struggled.

Then Clyde brought it down.

Jemma's body seized as the electric current coursed through her. Clyde bit his lip so hard, that blood flowed from it. He held back screams and tears as he did this to the person that he thought he loved. She was supposed to be one, but I'm not so sure anymore. Clyde took the wand off and Jemma relaxed for a bit. Clyde then brought it down a few more times, with every time forcing the wand on Jemma a bit longer. He tried different parts of her body, mainly her chest, in between her legs, and even close to her head. On the fifth time, Jemma was not screaming anymore, rather, she was writhing in so much pain that Clyde was not caring. It's all part of the experiment, Clyde thought. He looked at Serena.

"I can't do it anymore, Serena." Clyde said.

"More, Clyde. More!" Serena said.

"Serena, Jemma is spent. She can't take much more." Clyde pleaded.

"One more time."

Clyde was crying again.

"I can't!"

"Do it! Stop being such a bitch!" Serena yelled.

Clyde screamed as he brought the wand down on Jemma. He held it between her chest and Jemma's body seized and writhed, trying to get out the bonds that held her to the table. After a few minutes, Jemma was not struggling anymore, and Clyde took the wand off her. In a rage, he threw the wand across the room. The object broke off the extension cord and slammed into the wall, disappearing into a cloud of dust. Clyde looked at the generator and that too, disappeared into dust.

"Clyde?" Serena asked.

Clyde turned to her, and Serena was launched towards him. He held her in an embrace and cried. Serena, stunned that she was being hugged by Clyde, hugged him back.

"I can't' do it anymore I can't I don't want too no more no more no more."

Serena rubbed his head and back with her hands.

"Clyde relax. It's ok." Serena said.

The two collapsed on the floor, leaning up against the back of the couch. Jemma slowly stirred from the table, moaning, and trying to get out of the ropes. Her words were muffled by the gag that was still in her mouth. Clyde then looked at Serena and kissed her. She returned the favor and they interlocked tongues. I can't believe it. A time like this, Clyde thought. Serena and Clyde both stopped before things got out of hand and the two of them stood up. Jemma was still alive. By God, it's a miracle, Clyde thought.

He looked at Serena.

"Don't you ever make me do that again!" Clyde shouted.

"I made you and pushed you to do it. If you didn't, then we would still be in this situation." Serena said.

Jemma said something, but it was muffled. Clyde looked at Serena.

"Now that she is alive, it proves our theory. We don't need The Hooks. The Power in them are weakening..."

"Clyde, this may be true, but we can't get rid of The Hooks yet. If The Hooks are gone, then the Power will need another host and it will find the nearest thing." Serena said.

This can't be good.

"It will find me. I'm the last thing that touched The Hooks." Serena nodded.

"Exactly. For you to be free of The Hooks, we will need them a bit longer than anticipated." Serena said.

"Clyde? Clyde bro, are you awake!"

Jeremy. Serena tried to disappear, but she couldn't.

"What the hell?" Serena asked.

"The Hooks. You said that their power was weakening, and you were becoming stronger. Does this mean you won't be able to disappear?" Clyde asked.

Serena was scared now.

"I don't know Clyde."

Serena buried herself in Clyde's chest. The door rapped again.

"I'm coming!" Clyde shouted.

"What about her?" Serena asked.

She pointed to Jemma, who was now fully awake and struggling to get out. Clyde sighed.

"There isn't much more we can do. Leave her there and you distract Jeremy." Serena said.

It was probably the only plan that they had. Now that Serena was not able to disappear, Clyde was expecting her to any moment. Nope, still real, Clyde thought. This is not going to be good at all. The door rapped for the third time and Clyde rummaged through his things for a set of clean clothes. When he put on his jeans he looked at the clock. 7:30am. Jesus, Clyde thought. Serena was dressed in other clothes too. She wore the same summer outfit as she did before and went over to where the door was. When Clyde opened the door, Serena was hidden from view. Jeremy was all dressed and ready to go for the day. He looked at Clyde.

"Clyde? Are you ok? I heard a lot of screaming in here." Jeremy said.

"I had the TV on, and I slept. It was one of those action movies." Clyde said.

"May I come in?" Jeremy asked.

"Why?" Clyde said, nervously.

"Because I own the building. I also want to check some of the piping."

"Why didn't you check it when I was at work?" Clyde asked.

Jeremy was silent. Clyde smiled.

"You were having sex with Alexandria, where you?" Clyde said.

Jeremy immediately became embarrassed, however, he kept himself cool.

"No. She was doing videos all night long and I couldn't sleep. I went down to the 99 on Bridge Street and spent some time at the bar before coming home."

Clyde immediately felt bad for assuming that Jeremy and Alexandria were having sex.

"Sorry. I just thought that you two were…"

"We did on the first few nights that she was here, but now its limited to every two nights or something like that. We don't like to do too much."

"Are you two going to get married?" Clyde asked.

"Already did. Signed the papers and got a priest to witness it all."

"Nice."

"In all seriousness, Clyde. I must come in and check the pipes, then I'll be out of your hair. What were you doing in here?" Jeremy asked.

Clyde obstructed his view.

"Just watching the TV. That's all Jeremy, I swear."

"Why is there a new table behind you?" Jeremy asked.

"I needed a new one." Clyde said, quickly.

"You brought that in yourself?" Jeremy said, raising an eyebrow.

"Yes."

"Who helped you, because it wasn't me."

"Jerry from work."

"You hate that guy."

"It was his and he didn't want it. He gave it to me for quite the deal."

"Clyde let me in."

"Jeremy my apartment is messy. You don't want to come in." Clyde said.

He stretched his arms and legs in the door, blocking Jeremy from going forward.

"Clyde, I don't give a shit what the apartment looks like. Let me in!" Jeremy said, irritated.

"No."

"Clyde.."

"No!"

Jeremy pushed Clyde and Clyde fell to the ground. Before Jeremy could do anything, Serena jumped on Jeremy from behind, wrapping her arms around his neck. Jeremy, stunned and confused, fell to the ground, the air knocked from his system. Clyde watched as Serena choked Jeremy out and soon, he was knocked out cold. Serena got off Jeremy and pulled Clyde to his feet.

"Where did you learn that?" Clyde asked.

"I didn't. I just tried and hoped for the best." Serena said, smiling.

God Dammit, Clyde thought.

"Close the door." Clyde said.

Serena closed the door as Clyde dragged Jeremy into the apartment. In no time, Jeremy was tied up with ropes and a piece of duct tape was put across his mouth. Jemma struggled on the table and Clyde looked at Serena.

"We now have two witnesses. One that was knocked out

and one that was brought back to life. What are we going to do. It's only a matter of time before the cops show up." Clyde said.

"Is there any place that we can go?" Serena asked.

Clyde knew of one place.

Quabbin Reservoir.

It was a vast open space, littered with islands and small towns. Forest would dot the place for miles. It wasn't the ideal place, but it would be a place where Clyde and Serena could hide out. And make love? Clyde thought. He knew that there wouldn't be much time for sex, but he was not going to let the opportunity slip away. If he could have it, he will.

"Quabbin Reservoir. That is where we will go." Clyde said.

"Why there?" Serena asked.

"It's out of the way. There are islands in the middle of it. Small towns. We can blend in, disappear. No one will find us."

"Except the cops."

Except the cops.

The words echoed through Clyde's mind. If there was one thing that Clyde could not stand, it was dealing with the Government. Pay taxes and they leave you alone, Clyde thought.

"Have you been there?" Serena asked.

"A few times. We can use the GPS on the phone." Clyde said.

"Will you drive?" Serena asked.

"I will."

"Good because clearly I can't drive."

"Well, you can't."

"Shut up Clyde."

Serena pushed him lightly and then the two hugged. I want to get with you so bad right now, but I can't. Jemma was still on the table, naked and Jeremy was tied up too. Clyde sighed and after planting a kiss on Serena's forehead, he went over to Jemma. At first, she struggled, but Clyde slowly untied her, but kept the gag on. He then thought of a new set of clothes, and they appeared in the air. Clyde hauled Jemma to her feet and dressed her, giving her a bra and underwear first, then a long, ragged shirt that stretched down to hang just above the knee caps. Clyde then forced her arms behind her and tied them up. When he sat Jemma down, he tied her legs and ankles together, and did the same thing to Jeremy. Serena looked over at Clyde.

"I'm going to clean up most of the mess before we go." Serena said.

Clyde noticed that she was talking about Jemma's blood-stained clothes, and he only nodded. Soon, the sink was running, and the water was a dark red color. Serena then made a clothes-line that stretched from the wall across the room. Clyde watched as Serena hung Jemma's clothes on the line to dry. Jeremy began to stir, and Clyde punched him in the face, knocking him back out.

"Back to sleep." Clyde said.

Jemma just watched all of this, her eyes fixed on Clyde. Clyde didn't feel any attachment or love towards Jemma. I brought her back to life and for what? I wanted her, but now, I only long for Serena. Serena then came over to Clyde and hugged him from behind.

"We did good, you and me. We proved out experiment works." Serena said.

"I know, but I want to see what else is in store for us." Clyde said.

They kissed quickly and Clyde turned on the TV, then flicked to the local news station.

Clyde almost had a stroke.

On the news it showed Martins in a complete disarray. Cops and News vans were all over the place. Cops had all Main Street locked down.

"In a surprising upstart, Martins, one of the largest retail chains in the country, has experienced a robbery. The suspects are still unknown as many of the workers are now dead. Store manager Charlie explains."

The screen cut to Charlie. He looked tired, as if he was asked to get up and out of bed.

"I have no words for this. I have no idea why this was caused or who would do this, but I hope and pray that our police department will found out who was responsible for this and bring them to justice. Justice has to be served."

Clyde could not believe that Charlie said any of this. His voice was somber, and Clyde had never seen this side of Charlie before. It was scary and Clyde only shook his head. Serena came over to Clyde, stood next to him, put her arm on his, and put her head on Clyde's shoulder.

"Now, we have to get out." Serena said.

"We can't take both Jemma and Jeremy. It would cause too much of a commotion." Clyde said, looking at her.

"Then what do you think we should do?" Serena asked.

Clyde sighed. For the first time, he had no idea what to do. He didn't want to hurt his best friend, but he also didn't want him to betray them to the authorities.

"Jeremy is a threat, and you know that. We have to finish him off." Serena said.

"No way. I can't kill my best friend."

"Then we have to buy his silence."

"Jeremy can't be bought. He will report us faster before you could send a text message." Clyde said.

"Then keep him tied up and the door locked."

"No. Jeremy has all the keys. Besides, Alexandria will come and find him."

"Then we are fucked." Serena said.

"Yup. Royally."

The two turned around. Jeremy was stirring, trying to get himself up off the floor. Clyde went over to him and loomed over him. Jeremy looked up at him.

"Can I trust you to keep quiet so I can explain?" Clyde asked.

Jeremy didn't move, just looked up at Clyde with his eyes. Clyde knew that he wanted to get out in the worst way, but there was no way that Clyde was going to let him out. How can I trust him? Do I do the same way as trusting Serena? How can I do this? Clyde thought. Other thoughts went through his head. Jeremy just looked at Clyde and Clyde got down on his level. He reached over and took off the gag. Jeremy let out a sigh of relief and breathed in some air.

"What the hell Clyde?" Jeremy asked.

"Want to know what is going on here?" Clyde asked.

"Of course I do! I'm your best friend remember! Or did you forget about that part."

Clyde slapped him.

"I'll always be your best friend, Jeremy, but don't make me have to hurt you."

Clyde knew that Jeremy wanted to rub the check where it hurt, but Jeremy just looked at Clyde with an evil look. Jemma was awake, but she too, stayed still. Clyde looked at both, then got up.

"I need to show you two something." Clyde said.

Serena came over and sat on the table, looking at Clyde. She wore a summer dress now, covered with flowers and other spring designs. The dress was just short enough so Clyde could see the outline of her panties. Great, Clyde thought. Serena only smiled as Clyde picked up The Hooks and brought them over to Jeremy and Jemma.

"Look. Jemma. These Hooks gave me powers. I was able to bring you back to life with the Power that I got from these Hooks. Jeremy. With these, I was able to do that and fix a bunch of stuff in the apartment. That table is one of the things that I made and brought in here. I didn't get it in by myself."

Jeremy couldn't believe it and laughed. Clyde screwed up his face.

"What's so funny!" Clyde said, voice raised.

"I can't believe that you would make up something so stupid. Come on Clyde, really. Untie me and let me go." Jeremy said.

Clyde didn't move. Jeremy sighed.

"It's all real, isn't. The powers and all." Jeremy said.

Clyde nodded.

"It is."

"I'm supposed to be dead. But I feel alive!" Jemma said.

Serena hopped off the table.

"The Hooks come with a deadly side effect. If Clyde's powers are revealed to the world, then everything will start to be undone, starting with the first thing that he made."

Jeremy looked at Clyde.

"What did you make?" Jeremy asked.

"I made another bedroom in the apartment around my bed." Clyde said.

"I don't see it." Jeremy said.

"That's because it is gone. The things that Clyde has Created are beginning to be undone. Soon, it will come for his other things." Serena said.

She looked at Jemma and Clyde knew what she meant. Jemma would only be alive for a certain amount of time.

Then she would die.

Great.

Just fucking great.

Jeremy gulped.

"So, Clyde. What else did you make?" Jeremy asked.

"I defended myself and killed those thugs that were found dead at Martins." Clyde said.

"Shit."

"I was the only one alive besides Serena. We know that the authorities are coming for us soon."

"Very soon." Serena said, pointing to the TV.

Mark Durn was on the TV now, making a speech.

"I was elected your new Sheriff and leader of the Casper City Police Department. As my first act of new sheriff we will lockdown the city at night and smoke out this Martin Murder. A reward has been setup by the State and so far, the pot has reach 50 Million Dollars for the capture of what appears to be a local boy..."

The news showed footage of Clyde. Impossible! I guess when Peter cut the power, he didn't turn off the cameras. On the news station, it showed Clyde using his powers inside of the building. Clyde felt anger well up inside him and the TV Remote was in his hands. As the TV switched back to Marks point of view, the remote sailed through the air and broke the TV, splitting it in half. Serena stayed on the table, while Jemma and Jeremy stayed put. Clyde looked at Serena.

"We have to go." Clyde said.

"But Clyde..." Serena started.

Clyde rounded on her and grabbed her by the shoulders,

shaking her.

"I said, we have to go!" Clyde said raising his voice.

That is when Clyde went down, screaming. He smashed his head on the corner of the table. Jeremy jumped to his feet and pushed Serena out of the way. Clyde shook his head and charged blindly. Jeremy tried to hold him, but Clyde's weight sent the two of them over the couch. Clyde was on top of Jeremy, wildly punching him with a force that was not his own. God Damn, Clyde thought. Jeremy grabbed him and threw him off. Clyde rolled on the ground. Jeremy tried to get to the door, but Clyde stretched out his hand and pulled him back using the Energy. Jeremy struggled, but Clyde yanked him back. The two collided with each other and Jeremy landed on top of Clyde. Struggling, Clyde threw Jeremy off him and got back to punching him. Jeremy screamed as Clyde attacked him, but he eventually got the best of Clyde and threw him off. Clyde rolled on the floor, but like a cat, got back up and charged. I can't believe it. I'm fighting my best friend. It didn't matter. Clyde knocked Jeremy down and soon a knife was in Clyde's hand. Jeremy stopped.

"Wait a minute man, we can work this out." Jeremy said.

Clyde watched as Jeremy backed up against the wall. Clyde came towards him.

"You would betray your best friend for money! Is that what this is all about!" Clyde shouted.

"You aren't yourself man! I believe you now!" Jeremy wailed.

"I know you believe me Jeremy, but I need your loyalty."

It was the same line that Serena used to break Clyde. He was now using it to break Jeremy, to buy his silence. Clyde knew that this was only going to make things worse, but the anger inside him had consumed him now.

There was no going back.

Clyde rushed for Jeremy and brought the knife down in Jeremy's arm. Jeremy screamed, but Clyde held him with force. The knife was in Jeremy's left arm and using the blade, Clyde carved: MONEY OVER FRIENDS into Jeremy's left arm. Jeremy screamed and wailed, but Clyde held onto him. When the whole thing was done, Clyde threw the knife at the wall, and it disappeared into a cloud of dust. Jemma struggled to get up, but Serena went over and hauled her to her knees. Clyde walked away from Jeremy, as he was crying now and looking at his arm. Jeremy screamed again as the words carved on his arm began to sizzle and burn, permanently keeping them on his arm. Clyde looked at Jeremy.

"I'm sorry man." Clyde said.

Jeremy tried to get up, but he fell back down again, his body weak from the fighting and the blood loss. Clyde looked at Serena.

"Get Jemma in the car. We leave in a few minutes." Clyde said.

Jeremy jumped for Clyde, but he moved out of the way as Jeremy landed flat on the floor.

"I won't let you take her Clyde." Jeremy said.

Clyde laughed.

"Who's going to stop me. Definitely not you." Clyde said.

He kicked Jeremy in the face, sending him rolling to the side. Jeremy lay on his back, struggling to get up from the blow.

"It didn't have to be this way Jeremy, but you are making it very hard for me." Clyde said.

Jeremy spat.

"Fuck you and your Hooks!" Jeremy shouted.

Clyde shrugged.

"The Hooks came to me. I had nothing to do with it." Clyde said.

Jemma struggled as Serena brought her towards the door.

"I'll put her in the back and knock her out." Serena said.

Clyde nodded.

"Good. I'll get The Hooks before we leave." Clyde said.

Jeremy tried to make another effort to get at Clyde, but Clyde easily moved out of the way. He brought his foot on Jeremy's chest and Jeremy gasped for air. Clyde got down on the floor.

"You know, Alexandria will find you and she will heal you, but I swear to God, if I find out that you are coming after me for money, I'll make sure to use the Energy to kill you both. Is that understood?"

Clyde noticed that Jeremy was knocked out and he left the apartment, locking the door.

The Reservoir

Clyde joined up with Serena in his car. In the back seat, Jemma lay down, completely unconscious to what was going on. Clyde hopped into the driver seat and noticed that Serena was back in her racing outfit. It must be hot wearing that, Clyde thought. I'm thankful that Serena is not in my thoughts anymore. It was really annoying having her nag in my head. Clyde started up the car and quickly pulled out of the parking lot. Clyde went the speed limit, as to avoid an confrontation with the police. Main Street was crawling with the authorities, so Clyde took a detour out on Braxton Avenue, then back onto Main Street. Clyde knew that he couldn't go back home.

I'm on my own now.

Serena just looked at him and placed a hand on his leg.

"Hey, I'm trying to drive." Clyde said.

Serena smiled.

"I know that, but maybe later..."

Clyde smiled.

"Later. Let's just focus on getting the fuck out of here, ok." Clyde said.

Serena nodded.

"Ok."

Driving through Casper was no easy task. There was always traffic during all hours of the day. No matter how much anyone tried to beat it, there was always traffic. The commotion at Martins didn't make anything better. Clyde drove the speed limit until he was sure that the cops were far behind him. In the back seat, Jemma lay there, trying to get her bonds removed, but it was no use. What about Jeremy? Will he turn me in? Clyde thought. I can't imagine my best friend turning on me in that way. Clyde was not sure what Jeremy was going to do. If he does turn me in, then he is going to have a world full of hurt coming towards him. Serena's hand moved away from Clyde's leg and Clyde watched for a second as she curled up in the passenger seat. Serena is real. God Damn, she is real now, Clyde thought. I never thought that I would ever live to see her be an actual person. He recalled the first time he was in bed with her, how she smelled so good, and how good the sex was. Maybe tonight, when the other one is tied up or something, Clyde thought. Casper was not a city of large buildings. It was more of streets and streets of houses, with block upon block of homes. Most of the yards were of decent size, however, Casper reminded Clyde much like the other cities in Massachusetts; loads of houses squeezed together, with not much space in between them. Most of the houses were duplexes, while another half of the structures were triple decker apartments. The structures of Casper varied in size and stature, however, the one thing that all of it had in common was that it housed the people that lived here. Not much of a place to call home, Clyde thought. He was only here in Casper because his parents were. If they weren't such assholes, I wouldn't be in this stupid city.

Clyde hated the city. He hated the traffic, the streets, the people, etc.

Clyde hated everything.

Except for Serena.

For the first time in Clyde's life, he was excited to leave Casper.

The only thing that he was not looking forward to was getting to the Reservoir. Clyde had only been there a few times. The place that Clyde was really going to was a town called New Salem. It occupied a good amount of land and Clyde would get onto one of the islands from that town, then head south itself. I hope that this all works, Clyde thought. He had never hidden on an island before, never one that was in the middle of the Reservoir. God help me, Clyde thought. The drive through Casper seemed to get better as Clyde moved away from the city and into the countryside. Well, it feels like countryside to me, Clyde thought. Serena was knocked out cold, sleeping. So was Jemma. Clyde looked through the rearview mirror to see that she was not moving anymore. Good. She's going to need all the strength that she needs, Clyde thought. This is such a good time to think. Serena is not in my thoughts anymore and for the first time, I can finally think for myself. Clyde found his way out of Casper, going down Main Street, until he passed through Leominster. He then went down on Mechanic

Street, going on the Leominster Connector to merge onto US-Route 2, which would take him West towards New Salem. Clyde was now driving at an average speed, going a bit above the speed limit like the other cars around him. Clyde had only been this way one time and he didn't remember it being so crowded. Everyone was leaving Casper for the weekend, so it would explain why the drive was slow going. Clyde saw the exit signs for Fitchburg, and he passed right by it, not even thinking of getting off the exits. Serena stirred in her seat. Clyde drove with his left hand and with his right, placed it on Serena's leg.

"Aren't you supposed to be driving?" Serena asked yawning.

"I'll be fine. We have a ways to go yet, so go back to sleep." Clyde said.

"It's hard to do that when you are touching me." Serena said, smiling.

Clyde then focused on the road and continued the drive. There were exit signs for Westminster, which Clyde blew right past. Not what I want, Clyde thought. More cars and trucks were around on Route 2 and Clyde began to get a bit nervous. He was used to driving in Casper, where many drivers would just go onto different streets and move on. This was something different and Clyde began to feel uneasy. The signs for Gardner came up and Clyde got caught in a snag. The holdup. An accident with a truck and a small car. The accident itself was not bad, as Clyde found out that the people involved were ok, however, everyone wanted to see what the issue was, therefore, they all slowed down to look at the scene. Serena watched the entire thing and just sighed.

"I can't believe people."

She said this after Clyde got past the accident, continuing his way through Gardner, and then passing the signs for Templeton. Why even go here, Clyde thought. On both sides of Route 2 were trees and it seemed that Clyde was driving further away from the civilized world that he once knew. I won't be going back to work, Clyde thought. It just hit him now that he would never be working at Martin's again. There would be no way that they would let me back in. No fucking way. I destroyed the store and killed people. No way would I go back.

There was no turning back now.

Clyde passed through Gardner, then took Exit 71, heading south towards New Salem. The landscape was completely different. Jemma stirred in the back, but she just laid in the backseat. Serena watched with Clyde as the landscape changed around them. The town of New Salem was what Clyde remembered; it was quaint, with a few scattered houses and businesses. Not many cars were around, which was a good thing. The drive through the town itself was boring. Even though the landscape was beautiful, for Clyde, it was almost like nothing was going on out here. He had been so used to the city life of Casper, that any place out in the countryside was foreign to him. Strange on how quiet it is, Clyde thought. He continued to drive, making sure that he was doing the speed limit or just barely over it. I don't want to miss the turn, Clyde thought. He knew that he had to get off soon, and he got off at Shutesbury Road. He continued for a bit, then took a right on Vaughn Road, and went down the road. Trees closed in on them now, with very few houses here. Clyde turned onto Underhill Road and went all the way down it. He made sure to go slow, as the road was narrow. Only a two more cars passed his way and Clyde thought that he was going to have a heart attack. With every car, Clyde imagined a police officer, hunting him down to bring him back to Casper and lock him up in Casper State Prison.

That wasn't the case.

Clyde went off to the right and went all the way to the end of Underhill Road. There was nothing here. Underhill Road went back in the other direction and went God knows where. Clyde put the car in park. Serena stepped out of the car, then went to drag Jemma out. Jemma was still tied up and gagged and she didn't make any noise or fuss about. Serena then forced her up against the back of Clyde's car while Clyde looked around the place. The three of them were surrounded by thick forest, with no way of telling where they were. Across the way, was an island, then a bigger island. Clyde knew it all too well.

It was Russ Mountain.

Clyde had been here only the few times that he came out

here. He knew that the area was abandoned, except for the wild animals of course. They will never find me here, Clyde thought. It will only be a matter of time before Mark comes out to find me or if Jeremy turns me in. Either way, I'm fucked, Clyde thought.

"Now what?" Serena asked.

"Where are The Hooks? Set Jemma down and get our stuff." Clyde said.

Serena forced Jemma to sit on the ground while she opened the door and got their belongings. Clyde went over to the edge of the road, where it dropped off and it was just water. Russ Pond was the small body of water that stretched between here and the island that had Russ Mountain on it. To the North, was Dead Pond, and then beyond that was the rest of the Quabbin Reservoir. It's a good place to hide, Clyde thought. He stretched out his hand and opened his palms. The water began to ripple and the ground shook. Jemma let out a muffled scream, but Serena held her still. A large rock came up through the water. Then another. And another. Soon a rock bridge formed, making a bridge that connected the edge of the road to Russ Mountain.

"Come on, we have to go." Clyde said, urging the girls.

Serena grabbed their belongings and forced Jemma to her feet. Clyde grabbed Jemma and dragged her along the bridge of rocks. When the three reached the other side, Clyde motioned with his hand and the bridge disappeared. Serena looked at Clyde.

"What about the car?" Serena asked.

Clyde looked at it and pointed at it with his hand. The car began to shake, and it turned towards the water. Slowly, it moved forwards until it was submerged into the water and then it slowly sank.

"Now we will never leave." Serena said.

"You got that right. Come on." Clyde said.

Clyde decided to take the gag out of Jemma's mouth, on the condition that she wouldn't scream or try to get away. Jemma only agreed, as it would be one less thing that was inside of her mouth. Clyde led the way, with Jemma behind him and Serena in the back. Russ Mountain was not a big mountain and when the trio got to the top, it was a less impressive view. Trees blocked their way, however, they knew that water was all around them. They were completely alone and in the forest. Clyde looked at them.

"We will Create something here for us." Clyde said.

"Wouldn't that force them to come here?" Serena asked.

"I don't care if they come for us. We have the Energy. We can take them on." Clyde said.

Serena noticed that his eyes were wild. His appearance was unkept. Clyde's hair was longer, with dark circles under his eyes. Clyde was not who he was before, and this was scary for Serena to accept.

"Would it be best to make a small camp?" Jemma asked.

Clyde looked at her. It was the first time that she spoke, and Clyde was shocked. He sighed.

"I would want to, but I want a fortress, something that we can defend if they decide to come this way." Clyde said.

"Then make it." Serena said.

Clyde nodded.

"Ok, stand back."

Serena and Jemma backed away. The summit of Russ Mountain was mostly covered with trees, with a small clearing that the three stood in. Clyde just had to imagine the fortress. The ground shook. Trees disappeared. Gray battlements began to spread out, forming a large square. A keep formed, along with two towers in the front. A set of double doors appeared in the front, along with a gatehouse and two more large towers. The fortress rose out of the ground, like it had been hidden inside of Russ Mountain the entire time.

It had not.

Clyde Created it.

The fortress levitated in the air for a few seconds and when Clyde brought down his hand, the structure slowly came to the ground, then settled into place. When the ground shook, Clyde fell at the same time, as if he was attached to what he had Created. What the hell, Clyde thought. The fortress loomed over them. It was a square fortress, with the Keep built into the back wall. The front of the fortress faced the southern end of Russ Mountain, making the Keep face North and the two side walls faced East and

West respectively. Serena came over to Clyde and helped him to his feet.

"Come on. We need to get inside." Serena said.

Jemma looked like she was about to argue, but didn't. Clyde stumbled for a bit, his body feeling a bit weak. He shook his head and straightened out. The three went inside of the fortress as the double doors opened for them automatically, then closed behind them. The courtyard was decently sized, with enough room for the three of them. Jemma and Serena brought all the clothes and belongings into the Keep. The door to it was at end of the courtyard. The first floor of the Keep was a dining hall, where the three had plenty of space. A series of large tables were scattered, along with chairs to sit at them. Off to the left, was a kitchen space for food. Off to the right, was a door that led to the stairs that led to the top floors of the Keep. The three went up the stairs in silence. The second floor of the Keep contained a living room space, along with more tables and chairs to sit at. A bar area was off in the back corner, along with storage spaces for food and drinks. Serena and Jemma put the belongings in this room, while Clyde checked out the last floor of the Keep. It was a large bedroom, with a large bed and all the furnishings. A couch with a side table was off in the corner, while two chairs were in the other. This is for me and Serena, Clyde thought. Jemma would have to find a place to sleep. Unless I put her somewhere? Clyde thought. I can't believe that I have Jemma Sterling as a prisoner of mine. I have no idea what to do with her.

For the first time in his life, Clyde was not sure what to do with Jemma. I've always dreamed of having her as mine, but now that she is, what the hell do I do with her?" It doesn't make any sense to me. The door creaked and Clyde jumped.

"It's only me."

Serena entered the room. She was wearing her fall clothes.

"The wind from the water makes it cold." Serena said.

Clyde nodded.

"Indeed. This is where the two of us will be sleeping." Clyde said.

"You're so thoughtful, Clyde." Serena said, smiling.

Jemma appeared in the room.

"Clyde? Where am I going to go?" Jemma asked.

"Why do you care where you go? You can't go anywhere." Clyde said.

Jemma shrugged.

"Well, I want to know. You were the one who brought me back to life and brought me here. I don't want to be here, but there is nothing that I can do about it." Jemma said.

Clyde could tell that she was irritated about the situation, but Clyde couldn't risk being found out. If Jeremy went to Mark, then we are fucked. If we have two witnesses going to Mark, then we are still fucked.

Either way, we are fucked.

That was the look that Serena flashed Clyde. We have a prisoner, do something with her.

Clyde knew that this is what she was thinking. What to do with Jemma Sterling? Clyde thought. I can't bring myself to have sex with her. I already tried that, and it didn't go well. I can make her a slave, maker her do what we want. Clyde then smiled.

"I know what to do with you, Jemma Sterling. You will wait on us hand and foot. If you refuse to do what we say, then you won't eat. You can sleep on the floor, at the foot of this bed." Clyde said pointing to the bed.

Serena smiled. Jemma was not pleased.

"That's it! That's all you are going to do with me?" Jemma asked.

Clyde nodded.

"Yup and as my first request, I want you to unpack all our clothes and belongings, then prepare us some food. I think that there is stuff in the kitchen. There should be a fridge, sink, and some food in there." Clyde said.

Jemma only nodded and got to work. Serena looked at him.

"Is this a modernized fortress? Does that mean that there is a shower and stuff?" Serena asked.

Clyde noticed that her eyes were bright, but he knew she saw the wildness and his haggard appearance. Clyde nodded.

"Yes. I thought of the modern necessities."

Serena planted a kiss on his cheek.

"Thank you. Together we will overcome this."

"I hope to God we do." Clyde said.

Clyde and Serena lounged around as Jemma did all the work. Jemma unpacked all the clothes, separated everything, then began to make lunch. It was around that time when the three ate a chicken salad, fixed up with vegetables, cheese, and dressing. The three of them were happy and ate in silence.

"Are you happy, your highness?" Jemma asked.

Clyde looked at her and furrowed his brow.

"I'm not a king." Clyde said.

"You are technically a king. You do have a castle." Jemma said.

"A king without a wife." Clyde said, taking a bite of chicken.

"You have plenty of options." Jemma said.

This sent Clyde over the edge, and he shot out his hand. A chain came from the back wall, and it wrapped itself around Jemma, then pulled her to the other side of the room.

"I think you can think about what you have done." Clyde said.

Jemma tried to pull the chain off her neck, but it held on tight. After a while, she stopped struggling. Serena got up and put all the plates away, leaving Jemma and Clyde alone. Clyde looked at her.

"Are you going to be a good girl?" Clyde asked.

Jemma scoffed.

"Depends on what your definition of a 'good girl' is."

"I guess not. Stay over there. I don't need you." Clyde said.

"Funny. You needed me before. Now suddenly, you don't want me. Typical guys. They only want sex, the leave the girl on the side of the road, pregnant and by herself."

"That's not true." Clyde said, raising his voice.

"You know it's true and you know it Clyde." Jemma said.

"Shut up!" Clyde shouted.

"No! Not until you admit it's true!"

"Fuck you!"

"You tried and couldn't get in me!"

"Take that back! I was forced to. It wasn't love!"

Jemma was taken aback and began to cry, trying to get the chain off her neck. Then two more chains came out of the wall, each one attached to her wrists and pulled her hands over her head. Jemma fell back, forced into a sitting position. Clyde looked at her. She's helpless and scared. Serena came back into the room and smiled.

"I can see that you made accommodations for our friend." Serena said.

"More like enemy." Clyde remarked.

"You both can fuck yourselves!" Jemma spat.

"Whatever." Serena said.

Clyde got up.

"I'm going out on the walls to look. Care to walk with me?" Clyde asked.

"What about Jemma?" Serena asked.

Clyde looked at Jemma, then Serena.

"She isn't going anywhere." Clyde said.

Jemma struggled.

"You are just going to leave me here?" Jemma asked.

Clyde nodded.

"Yup, until you can be a 'good girl'. We'll be back." Clyde said.

Jemma let out a wail, then sobbed as Serena and Clyde went out onto the walls. The third floor of the Keep also contained a hallway that led to a back staircase that led down to the walls. The walls went around the fortress and the battlements were thick enough to block anything. I hope that this is the case, Clyde thought. There was a firing step that was under the battlements and in each of the towers, there were arrow slits to fire through. I can't believe that I Created all of this, Clyde thought. I can't believe that all of this is happening to me. I wish that I never found The Hooks. I wish that my life was just the same as it was before. It was easy going to work, getting paid, dealing with the everyday bullshit. It was easy. Serena found his hand as the two walked around the fortress. They could her crying on the third floor of the

Keep.

"What are we going to do with her Clyde?" Serena asked.

The two stopped on one of the firing steps, looking out towards the Reservoir. Clyde sighed.

"I have no idea, Serena. We can't let her go and we can't kill her. By now, Mark must be on his way to come find us. Alexandria must have found Jeremy and he is probably spilling his guts all over to the press and the authorities. They will come one way or the other." Clyde said.

"What will we do? Only you and I have The Energy to deal with them." Serena said.

"We can Create some help." Clyde said.

Serena's mouth dropped.

"Like an army?" Serena asked.

Clyde nodded.

"I can't think of any other way." Clyde said.

"You do realize then that would set us up with war with the Massachusetts State Police Department right." Serena said.

"I don't give a damn. They want a war, they will get a war, a war that they won't fucking believe." Clyde said.

He was breathing heavy now, his other fist closed. Serena looked at him.

"Clyde? Are you ok? You don't have to get this upset."

Clyde calmed down.

"Sorry. I haven't been myself lately and I'm angry and all that and....."

Serena stopped him by kissing him.

"Clyde. It's ok." Serena whispered in his ear.

"Ok. Thanks." Clyde said.

Serena then hugged Clyde, holding him tight. The two finished their walk around the walls. The sun was slowly setting. When the two got back to the bedroom, Jemma was asleep, her neck and wrists still chained to the wall. Clyde waved his hand and the chains disappeared. Jemma startled herself and woke up.

"Get us some supper please." Clyde said.

Jemma only nodded and left, heading down the stairs towards the kitchen. Clyde looked at Serena.

"When she's asleep, we can have some time for ourselves."
Clyde said.

Serena nodded.

"That would be nice. Can't have sex all the time. Need a
break occasionally."

"True."

Jemma came in with supper a few minutes later. She had
cooked chicken, rice, and vegetables. The three ate in silence
again and Clyde knew that Jemma was not happy about her situa-
tion, however, Clyde was not going to feel sorry for her. The night
was setting in and Clyde was tired. When he was done, he passed
his plate to Jemma.

"I'm taking a shower." Clyde said.

That left Serena and Jemma in the same room. The shower
was down the hall, in a room right before the set of stairs that led
to the walls. Clyde took a pair of pajamas and went in. He stripped
down and got into the shower. The door opened and Clyde felt
hands on him. It was Serena. She was naked and her warm body
pressed against his. He turned and kissed her while the water ran
down on both.

Clyde and Serena stepped out of the shower in their paja-
mas. Jemma got up and used the shower as well, while the other
two climbed into the large bed that was in the room. When Jemma
came back, Clyde sat up, while Serena was on her side, asleep.

"You can sleep on the floor or on the couch. I don't care."
Clyde said.

"You aren't going to torture me, Clyde?" Jemma asked.

Torture. It was the one thing that Clyde couldn't get out of
his mind. There was the urge to tie her up, strip her naked, and do
whatever he wanted to her, however, there was another urge that
pulled at Clyde harder than anything else.

Just leave her alone. You have Serena.

Clyde looked at Serena. It didn't take her long to fall asleep
next to him and Clyde let out a sigh.

"No, I won't hurt you anymore." Clyde said.

"You promise?" Jemma asked, hands on her hips.

Clyde put his hands up.

"On my honor, if there is any left." Clyde said.

Jemma nodded.

"Then, I'll sleep on the couch. You know that Jeremy is going to come for you and me."

Clyde nodded.

"I know. I hope he gets here soon."

"Good night Clyde." Jemma said, going on the couch.

"Good night." Clyde said.

He watched as Jemma slept on her side, placing a pillow under her head. Clyde then lay back down and wrapped his right arm over Serena, pulling her close to him. He planted a kiss on her cheek, then whispered.

"Good night Serena."

Serena smiled.

"Good night Clyde."

Clyde put his right hand under her shirt, touching her right tit, then fell asleep as the two were intertwined with each other in the sheets.

The next morning, Clyde woke up with Serena on top of him. She was naked and he found that his hands were wrapped around her, holding her close to him. Did we? Clyde thought. No, there was no way that we did. Jemma would have heard us the entire time. Clyde slowly rolled Serena off him and placed her head on a pillow. There was no way. Clyde looked down and realized that he was naked. He leaned over the side of the bed and found his clothes on the floor. Then we must have? Clyde thought. Clyde heard laughter and looked up. It was Jemma. She was already dressed and held Clyde's underwear in her hands.

"What the fuck?" Clyde asked.

"While you two were asleep, I stripped you both and placed Serena on top of you. I thought it was funny." Jemma said.

Clyde sat up in the bed, cracking a small smile.

"It was good. Make us breakfast please." Clyde said.

"Whatever you wish." Jemma said.

She threw his underwear across the room and Clyde watched as it fell to the ground. Jemma left the room, closing the door just loud enough for Serena to awaken. She stirred and let out a morning moan. Clyde kissed her on the forehead, then Serena turned around looking at him.

"Did we..." Serena asked.

Clyde shook his head.

"No. Jemma thought it would be funny to strip us naked in the night and make it look like we did." Clyde said.

Serena nodded.

"She's funny, that one."

"I didn't find it funny." Clyde said.

Serena came close to him and kissed him on the lips.

"What? You wanted the real thing?" Serena asked.

Clyde nodded. There was a part of him that wanted Serena right now, but another part that refrained from the activity. Jemma was here. The only way that they could spend some time would be...

Clyde then got the idea. He slowly got out of bed and put his pajamas on. Grabbing Serena's pajama's, Clyde threw them at her, and Serena got dressed. Clyde and Serena went down to the second level of the Keep. They figured that they should start using the other rooms that they had. Jemma was on the second floor, making breakfast that consisted of pancakes, bacon, and scrambled eggs. Jemma was shocked when both Clyde and Serena came into the room.

"We are going to eat here today." Clyde said.

Jemma nodded.

"That's fine with me." Jemma said.

The three of them gathered at the table and ate breakfast. Water, juice, and coffee were the only drink options for the three of them. The three ate in silence. The food was very good, better than anything that Clyde had back in Casper. From the second floor, they watched as the rays of the sun reflected of the water of the Reservoir. Today is a new day, Clyde thought. This might be the last day that we have peace. They must be getting close to us by now. They must have sent out the reward and gathered everyone available to go after Clyde. Jeremy and Alexandria must be with them. There is no doubt about that. It would only be a matter of time before they would show up.

I will be ready.

The fortress was useless without an army and that is what he and Serena were going to try to do, which was make an army of some sort. Without it, there wouldn't be a point in holing up on Russ Mountain. Clyde knew that the place was deserted and out of the way, but it wouldn't stop the authorities from finding where he was holing up. When breakfast was done, Jemma cleared the dishes, leaving Clyde and Serena alone. The two got up, went back upstairs, and got dressed for the day. They took a shower together and when they were done, both were ready for the day. Serena wore her a fall outfit, as it was still cold. The weather outside was clear, however, the wind blew across the Reservoir, making the inside of the fortress a bit cold. For the first time, Clyde wore a long sleeve shirt, with a pair of jeans, socks, and his sneakers. After he got dressed, he found a razor in the drawer, and he shaved himself clean. Serena had to do a double take.

"Wow. You are stunning, Clyde." Serena said.

Clyde smiled.

"Thanks. You aren't looking too bad yourself." Clyde said.

Serena blushed. Clyde was not wrong. Her fall outfit was stunning. Her clothes conformed to her body, so that when Serena moved, it was as if she glided across the floor. Serena wrapped her arms around Clyde and hugged him from behind.

"I love you." Serena said.

"I love you too." Clyde said.

When the two got out of the bathroom, Clyde looked for Jemma. That's weird, she usually goes in the restroom when we are out. Serena thought the same thing.

"Clyde? Where did Jemma go?" Serena asked.

"I thought she was on the second floor." Clyde said.

The two went down the stairs. No one was here. The dishes from breakfast were gone, so this meant that Jemma brought them down. Clyde and Serena ran down the stairs to the first floor of the Keep. The exit door was wide open.

"Clyde?" Serena asked.

He was running now.

"I'm going after her. Stay here!"

Clyde crashed through the exit door, forcing it wide open. Jemma went through the double doors at full speed. Clyde cut across the courtyard and went out into the woods of Russ Mountain. Jemma was fast, zigzagging down the mountain. She ran through the undergrowth, stumbling through bushes and tripping on rocks. It didn't matter to Clyde. It made it easier for him to follow her. The slope was steep, and Clyde had to adjust his pacing, but he continued to run after Jemma. Jemma then tripped and fell forwards, rolling down the hill. When she landed on the ground, Clyde jumped on top of her, pinning her down. Jemma punched Clyde, scratching his cheek with her nails. Screaming, Clyde pulled away, feeling the blood drip down his face. Jemma got up and ran towards the shore, hoping to swim across Russ Pond and hopefully, to get out of here. Jemma jumped in the water as Clyde stumbled after her. He was out of breath and out of shape. I wasn't meant for running, Clyde thought. He stopped at the shore, catching his breath by bending over and putting his hands on his knees. Jemma continued to swim across the water, getting further away from Clyde. When Clyde got himself together, he stretched out his hand, thinking about the Energy. It pounded through him like waves crashing on the shore. Jemma tried to swim away from Clyde, but she was pulled back. The water rose with a wave, and it carried Jemma back to the shore where Clyde stood. The water crashed on the shore and slammed Jemma on the ground. Coughing and sputtering, Jemma tried to get up and back into the water, but Clyde grabbed her by the hair and hauled her to her knees. When she faced him, Clyde slapped her. Jemma cried.

"Why Jemma? Why!" Clyde shouted.

"I thought I could get away." Jemma sobbed.

Clyde slapped her again and Jemma fell to the ground, crying. Clyde looked at his hand. It was red from hitting her. Did I hit her that hard? Clyde thought. He then heard rustling across the way. Jemma got up, looked, and hid behind Clyde.

Across the way, on the other shore, stood Mark, Jeremy, and Alexandria. Behind them, hundreds of men, women, and children, all armed with various weapons. There were guns among them, along with other weapons. Great. Clyde noticed that there were also lots of police officers. Some of them even had K-9 Dogs with them at their heels, sitting and waiting for the command to strike.

"Isn't this a surprise."

Mark's voice echoed across the water.

"I knew that we would find you here. Come closer and we can talk." Mark said.

Serena crashed in behind Clyde as Clyde went towards them. Jemma and Serena stood their uneasily while Clyde went to the edge of the shore. The rock bridge that was under Russ Pond came out of the water and Clyde walked about halfway, while Mark walked the other half. The two stood on the bridge, while the others gasped in amazement. Clyde could hear the murmurs that went through the crowd of people.

"What do you want?" Clyde said, looking at Mark.

"I want justice and I want answers." Mark said.

"For what?"

"What were you doing at Martins?"

"What is there to tell? I was attacked and I defended myself. Is there anything else that you want to know?" Clyde asked.

"I want to know why you ran away."

"I ran away because I would have been blamed for murders that were not my fault." Clyde said.

"That's why you killed those people?" Mark asked.

"You would have done the same if you were in my position."

"Would I?"

"What do you mean?"

"Would I take someone's girl and keep her hostage here?"

Clyde watched as a man and a women appeared out of the crowd. Jemma tried to run towards them, but Serena held her back.

"Let me daughter go!"

It was Jemma's parents. Both were across the water.

"Mom! Dad!" Jemma screamed.

Mark smiled.

"See. I'm not like you Clyde. Hand over yourself and the

girl. If you do, then I'm willing to drop the charges against you and leave you alone." Mark said.

Clyde looked at Jemma, then Serena, then back at Mark.

"You are going to have to come get her. I'm not letting her go." Clyde said.

"We can worth this out." Mark pleaded.

"There isn't nothing to work out. I won't go to jail for crimes that I haven't committed. This is now war." Clyde said.

In a quick movement, Clyde motioned his hand down. Mark scrambled back to the other shore as the rock bridge disappeared. Clyde just made it to the shore himself when the last rock went under the water.

"This isn't over Clyde! We will get you!" Mark shouted.

Clyde ran as fast as he could towards the fortress. Gunshots rang out and bullets sailed across the water. Serena and Jemma, confused and afraid, followed Clyde. Clyde made zigzag motions up Russ Mountain and when he reached the fortress, opened the double doors. Serena and Jemma entered the courtyard. Clyde was pacing back and forth. The girls could see that he was slowly losing his mind. Clyde shook his head and muttered stuff that didn't make any sense.

"Clyde? What are you going to do?" Serena asked.

Clyde looked at her, eyes wide and wild.

"We are going to stay here until they leave. They know that they can't get us here. They know that the walls are too thick..."

"Clyde. We are outnumbered. We have to surrender." Jemma said.

Clyde went over to her and grabbed her shoulders.

"We can't surrender Jemma. If we do, then everything that we have is lost." Clyde said.

"I don't want this Clyde. I never wanted this. I just want to go home!" Jemma screamed.

Clyde hit her and Jemma fell to the ground.

"You are home, you stupid bitch!" Clyde shouted.

Serena just stood there. I don't like this Clyde. He's gone nuts. Clyde looked at Serena.

"Get her in the Keep. I have some work to do." Clyde said.

Serena nodded and led Jemma to the Keep. Serena came back out and witnessed what Clyde was doing. Both hands were outstretched, palms wide. Clyde pointed his hands to the dirt ground that was the courtyard. The ground rumbled and a head appeared. Soon, the entire courtyard was full of medieval knights made of dirt. The knights carried guns, bows, arrows, and other weapons. Clyde smiled.

"My friends. We have work to do."

Excessive Force

Serena counted more knights than she had in her life. Clyde had created ten-thousand Dirt Knights. It was midday and the Reservoir was deathly quiet. Clyde then Created some armor for himself, along with a bow, arrows, and a sword. He's going to fight just like them. Brutal, Serena thought. Clyde looked at Serena. She's scared of me now. She wants nothing to do with me anymore, Clyde thought. He went over to her to hug her, but Serena pulled away.

"I don't want to distract you from what you have to do." Serena said.

Clyde nodded.

"Understandable. Are you going to help me with the defense?" Clyde asked.

Serena shook her head.

"No."

Clyde nodded.

"Fine."

The Dirt Knights stood shoulder to shoulder. The fortress was just big enough to have all of them inside of it. Serena went into the Keep and locked the door behind her. Clyde looked out on the Eastern Wall. The Dirt Knights were ready to do what Clyde commanded. On the other side of Russ Pond, Clyde could see Mark, Jeremy, Alexandria, and the enemy forces. They outnumber us three to one. Clyde thought. A sizable force, but Clyde was confident. Dirt can't be shot through, only blown up. I hope that they don't have explosives. If they do, I'm fucked. Clyde thought.

The sun was at its highest peak in the clear sky and the heat bore down on Clyde and his forces. Mark hadn't made a move in hours, which was strange. Most of his forces seemed to just be on the shore. Clyde knew that something was up, but he was not going to react and play into Mark's games. Let Mark make the first move, Clyde thought. Clyde then went to the Southern Wall and looked down through the trees.

Movement.

Ahh, there you are, Clyde thought. The Dirt Knights saw it too and nocked arrows into their bows. About half of his forces were on the walls, all of them equipped with bows, arrows, and swords. Clyde made a motion with his hands and barrels appeared on the walls, filled with arrows for his forces. Clyde went over to the firing step, then ducked down and hid behind the battlement. Clyde peered out and looked down. As soon as the first head of the enemy appeared, an arrow sailed and hit the man in the neck.

The battle had begun.

The enemy forces charged out and fired at the Knights. Being made of dirt, the knights absorbed the bullets and fired arrows. The arrows sailed in all directions, hitting their targets. Clyde was delighted that his forces couldn't get hurt. The Knights were in full view of the enemy and no matter how many bullets they shot, nothing happened to them. The enemy hid behind trees and rocks, firing as many bullets as possible. Clyde witnessed a few of the Knights die. So many bullets will kill them, Clyde thought. When one Knight died, one from the courtyard would move and replace it, so that the ranks were always full. A few more Knights died, and more replaced them. Clyde nocked an arrow into his bow and fired, killing a women with a hunting rifle. He fired his bow, bringing down target after target. Then fighting started on the Eastern Wall, where Jeremy and Alexandria were leading the fight. The fight was more of a skirmish, as arrows and bullets sailed in all directions. Some found their targets, others didn't.

"Mark your targets before firing!"

Clyde could hear Jeremy barking out orders. Since when did he become a boss, Clyde thought. He unleashed his bow again and a man went down, arrow in his neck. The Knights were not dwindling, however, the number was going down a bit. Clyde only had to think, and more Knights appeared out of dirt, ready to serve. I can hold out here for ages, Clyde thought. He leaned up against the battlement, hiding from the battle. The Knights were doing the heavy lifting for him. It's what they are there for, Clyde. Thought. So far, Mark had only pressed two walls. As far as Clyde knew, he was in a good position. The enemy was not pressuring many of the walls. This is what Clyde thought that Mark was going to do, but so far, this was not the case. He could hide and let Mark fight it out with his forces. I don't have to be here. I don't have to die here, Clyde thought. His Knights would do all the work.

And that is what was exactly happening. Some groups of Knights stood by the double doors, as if the enemy were going to try to get inside the courtyard.

Nothing.

Clyde was not sure to take Mark's stupidity for a weakness or strength. Clyde went over to the Eastern Wall. The Knights continued to fire arrows and the enemy forces fired bullets back. Clyde noticed that there were not as many as before. He's pulling back somewhere. Mark must be using his numbers to test the strength of my Knights, Clyde thought. It didn't matter what Mark was doing. I know that I'm winning the fight, Clyde thought. His Knights were doing well, firing back with bows and arrows at the citizens and police officers that were under Mark's protection. Something itched at Clyde, and he turned around. Facing the Western Wall, a whole row of bows came towards the fortress. Beach landing, Clyde thought. In front of the enemy forces in the boats, were Jeremy and Alexandria. Son of a Bitch, Clyde thought. He went over to the Western Wall.

"Fire!!! Bring them down!!!" Clyde screamed.

The Knights obeyed and unleashed volley after volley of arrows into the enemy forces. Groups of the enemy went down, arrows in their chests, necks, and heads. When the enemy got in range, bullets sailed in their direction. A few Knights were destroyed in the process, but more from the courtyard came up to take their place. Clyde ducked down, nocked his bow, and fired at the enemy. He brought down a man that was close to Jeremy and he watched as his friend jumped back, scared out of his mind. I hope that they all go away, Clyde thought. I'm beginning to get a bit nervous now. The enemy pressed against three walls now, spreading out in skirmish lines, firing bullets at the Knights. The Knights did their job and when one exploded into clouds of dirt, another would replace it. Clyde only had to look at the courtyard and more Knights manifested themselves. The Energy coursed through Clyde like it had never before. So this is what Power feels like, Clyde thought. His energy level was through the roof and Clyde had this feeling that he could be like this forever. There is nothing stopping me now.

He looked down from the battlement on the Western Wall. Jeremy and Alexandria were now in cover, firing guns. They hate me because they don't know what this is. None of them do. None of them know what it is like with the Energy that I have. None of them know what it is like to have the power to Create what you want and live with the consequences, Clyde thought. Mark could have avoided this, all of it. The bloodshed was all for nothing. If I had the Energy to undo all of this, I would, but because Mark asked for this, I won't do it. I won't give in to what he wants. The enemy forces had surrounded three sides of the fortress, effectively fighting. Clyde noticed that more of the Knights were slowly dying. The courtyard was still full of them, and they climbed the stairs to fill in the gaps. I hope that Mark pulls back his forces because they must be tiring out by now, Clyde thought. He looked over the battlement again on the Western Wall. All the boats landed on the shore and wave after wave of enemy forces marched up, firing guns at the Dirt Knights that held the fortress. The fire fight between the Knights and the enemy forces was slowing down, as the enemy hid behind trees and rocks. Clyde then walked towards the Keep. The Knights were doing a great job holding back enemy. Mark will never get inside this fortress. His forces are too weak, and they won't be able to do anything. Clyde entered the Keep and went up to the second floor. Jemma and Serena were sitting at the table, watching the battle unfold below them. Both girls looked at Clyde as he entered.

"Anything to report?" Serena asked.

Clyde shook his head.

"Not much. The Knights are holding back Mark's forces. Before long, he will eventually call off the attack." Clyde said.

Serena stood up.

"Do you think that he will really give up Clyde? He outnumbers us three to one and the attack doesn't seem to be stopping anytime soon."

"If the attack goes through the night, then I will be shocked. He is just wasting his time. The Dirt Knights keep coming back when one dies, so he is in a losing battle anyways." Clyde said.

"Then why don't you just let me go? If you know that you are going to win, there is no need for the bloodshed." Jemma said. Clyde looked at her.

"I can't let you go, Jemma. If I let you go, then that will be playing into his hand, and I can't have that. I want Mark to suffer for what he has caused. He caused this, so he should pay the consequences for his actions." Clyde said.

"You are one selfish bastard." Jemma spat.

"Good. I'm a bastard that brought you back to life and treated you ok." Clyde said.

Jemma just stuck her tongue out and Clyde ignored her. Down below, the battle raged on for the fortress. Clyde noticed that the Knights were not replacing each other on the walls anymore. He went closer to the window and found out why. The Knights braced themselves against the double doors.

"They're trying to get in." Jemma said.

"Not if I can help it." Clyde said.

Without other word, he rushed out of the Keep and into the courtyard. On the walls, the Knights were engaged in hand-to-hand combat. Clyde could see the ends of ladders. Damn it all, Clyde thought. The enemy were swarmed on the walls, fighting the Knights with whatever they had. The Knights were having an easy time with the wall fight, however, Clyde was concerned about the enemy getting inside of the fortress. Clyde got close to the double doors. The Knights were up against it, holding it back. Clyde peered through the cracks of the doors. The enemy weren't trying to break it down.

They were going to blow it up.

Clyde ran away from the door and that sent a signal to the Knights to fall back into the courtyard. The Knights on the walls did the same thing and the enemy were confused.

It was too late.

The explosions rocked the Russ Mountain and shook the ground. Stone and wood flew in all directions. Knights that were not away from the blast evaporated. Clyde pointed his hand to the ground and rank upon rank of Dirt Knights appeared.

"CHARGE!!!!!" Clyde shouted.

The Knights, led by Clyde, charged forward and Clyde noticed that he had a real sword in his hand. He swung it and the first person that was closest was cut in half. The Knights charged against the enemy like a wave crashing on the shore, and soon the courtyard was one mess of a combat fight. The enemy still came on the walls, but they charged down into the courtyard to fight. Clyde signaled for some Knights to retake both Eastern and Western Walls and his forces did with ease. Clyde chopped down two enemies that came for him at once and the battle raged on. He looked back to see Serena and Jemma looking through the window, horrified at what was going on outside. A group of Knights protected the door to the Keep, cutting down anyone who tried to get inside. More enemy forces came through the breached front entrance of the Keep and they began to outnumber Clyde's forces. More Knights came from the ground and joined the fight, pushing more of the enemy back. There was now a fine battle line in the courtyard and Clyde wished that he had made the fortress a bit bigger than what it was. Oh well. Just going to have to deal with it, Clyde thought. He pulled his sword out of the chest of a man and looked up. Mark was on the Eastern Wall, fighting with a group of Knights and it didn't take him long to win the engagement. Clyde saw him, created more Knights, then ran towards him. Mark was not aware of Clyde's presence, until Mark grabbed a sword from the ground. Clyde swung and Mark turned around just in time, deflecting the blow. Mark's eyes went wide, and Clyde pushed on Mark, pressing him up against the battlements.

"Give up Clyde! I'm taking you in and bringing justice to those that you killed!" Mark shouted.

"Avenging the murders of murders is not going to change anything, Mark." Clyde said with gritted teeth.

"Then I'm going to take you in and charge you for murdering thousands of innocents."

"With a Power that you once had!" Clyde shouted.

Mark pushed Clyde away and hung his sword at his side.

"How do you know?" Mark asked.

"Serena told me." Clyde said.

Mark sighed.

"I knew that she would tell you."

"You knew Serena?" Clyde asked.

"Serena came to me when I had The Hooks. She promised me the same thing that she said to you, that if you helped her become Real, then The Hooks would lose its hold on the both of you." Mark said.

"She did say those things to me. What happened? Why did you give up The Hooks so easily. You could have had Power like no one else, like me." Clyde said.

Mark shook his head.

"I gave up The Hooks because I wanted my freedom. I wanted to be me again. Serena however, refused my freedom, said that I was bound to The Hooks. So what I did was killed myself so The Hooks could release the hold on me. My wife at the time resurrected me with the same power that I once had, and I began a new life. I knew that in that moment, that I had to find those Hooks and destroy them, so that others would not go through what I went through. When I found out that you had them, I knew that you weren't going to be easy to take down, and when you murdered those thugs, I knew that you were the one."

Mark looked at Clyde, holding the sword.

"And that I why that I've come to kill you Clyde. For both our sakes. Everything that you have done will all be gone and none of this would have ever happened. I will remember it, but I'll take what is left of myself, resurrect myself, and start a new life. No one will know or remember you because you will be dead." Mark said.

"I can't let that happen. The Hooks are mine!" Clyde shouted.

He charged for Mark and the two engaged in a sword duel. Down below, the Knights were slightly winning against Mark's forces, but Clyde knew that they would not be able to hold onto

forever. A group of Knights were on top of the Keep, firing guns
and bows down at the enemy forces. Clyde noticed that some
of the Knights were also on the second floor of the Keep, firing
through the windows. The enemy had no answer for this and took
the shots. Men, women, and teens fell dead in the onslaught that
occurred. Mark swung his sword. Clyde ducked and swung back.
Mark jumped back as Clyde brought the sword down. Mark land-
ed a left hook and Clyde fell backwards. Mark brought his sword
down. Clyde dodged and lashed his foot out, landing a hit to Mark
in the chest. Gasping for air, Mark fell. Growling, Mark charged
for Clyde, who backed up towards the stairs leading to the top
of the Keep. Mark chased after him. The two-sword dueled up
the stairs, each taking a fencing stance. The swords danced with
each other, the ring of metal on metal echoed in their ears. The
two reached the top of the Keep and continued their fight. Down
below, the Knights took back both Eastern and Western walls,
but the courtyard was still a tossup. Clyde was shocked that he
was just as good with a sword as Mark. The two had been fighting
for some time and Mark was not showing signs of backing down.
Clyde swung again and this time, his sword cut through Marks'
thigh. Stunned, Mark fell back. The gash on his thigh was a red
waterfall. Mark fell back and leaned up against the battlement.
Clyde brought his sword down and crushed it against the battle-
ment, holding it there. He then pulled back and swung at Mark's
sword. The sword went in the other direction and Clyde swung
again, this time sending the sword out of Mark's hand. Mark held
up his hand, backing away from Clyde.

"Don't kill me!" Mark shouted.

Clyde smiled as his inched forward.

"I won't kill you Mark." Clyde said.

"You won't?" Mark asked, confused.

Clyde dropped his sword.

"You're not worth it." Clyde said.

He spat on Mark, then grabbed him and hauled him to his
feet. Mark was shocked that Clyde had the strength to pick him
up. Clyde moved close to the edge of the battlement and held Mark
out, so that his feet dangled in the air.

"Oh, Jesus man don't drop me don't drop me. Oh no man."
Clyde didn't listen to Mark.

"Oh God help me help me help me please not please no! I'll be good!"

Clyde pulled him close.

"Remember when I told you that you weren't worth it? I meant that it wasn't worth it for me to kill you yet. If you survive, I'll eventually kill you if the fall from the Keep doesn't." Clyde said.

Mark struggled and Clyde threw Mark off the top of the Keep. Mark flailed his hands in the air, hoping to grab onto something, but he was thrown too far. Clyde watched from the top of the Keep as Mark fell. Mark slammed to the ground and didn't stir. Clyde knew that his forces saw this and one by one, they scattered from the fortress. The Dirt Knights cheered and went onto the walls. Arrows flew into the backs of the fleeing enemies, and many fell dead trying to escape. Clyde watched the chaos from the top of the Keep. The heavy forest and terrain did not make the retreat easy for the enemy and Clyde laughed as they died. I have never seen such a large, disorganized group in my life, Clyde thought. He just laughed harder and harder as men, women, and teenagers died trying to escape. Clyde doubled over, his laugh echoing from the top of the Keep. The Dirt Knights were not laughing, but they were all cheering. Clyde recovered himself from laughing, wiping the tears from his eyes. His face was all red from the laughter and he looked over the battlement. The enemy forces were gone, however, Clyde knew that this battle was far from over. Sighing, Clyde got up. A wave of tiredness came over him and he struggled to stay on his feet. Clyde fell forward and crawled towards the stairs. When he tried to stand, he fell back down again and began his descent down the stairs, sitting on his bum and slowly sliding down. Clyde's legs felt like jelly, and he did not want to take the chance of standing and falling face first down the stairs. When Clyde got down the stairs, he went over and stood on the Eastern Wall. The Dirt Knights all turned around and cheered when Clyde leaned up against the battlement, then were silent when Clyde waved his hand.

"They will be back. We must rebuild the fortress and pre-
pare for another assault. They might come in the night, so we
need every Knight to help pitch in for this. The war is not over
yet. Get going and protect this fortress." Clyde said.

The Knights went back to work, helping rebuild the front
wall, gatehouse, and the gate. They set up a perimeter, lining all
the walls with Knights armed with bows. Anything that moved
close to the fortress, would be shot on sight, regardless of if it
was an animal or not. Clyde gave them instructions to finish the
fortress and to keep it safe. The Knights, even though that they
didn't talk, were good about following orders and directions.
Order is what I want, Clyde thought. Clyde slowly went over to
the Western Wall and looked down. Mark's body was nowhere to
be found. So he is still alive. Wounded, but alive. Clyde thought.
I don't want to face him again, but if I must, then I will. The guy
can't die, but there must be a way where his curse can be lifted so
that he can finally die in peace, Clyde thought. Shaking his head,
he went into the Keep, struggling to stay on his feet. Serena and
Jemma ran down to greet him and Clyde fell forwards, his body
weak from the fight. Serena pushed Jemma out of the way and
grabbed Clyde, hauling him to his feet. Jemma shook her head.

"I can see that you know how to attend to him the most."
Jemma scoffed.

Serena stuck her tongue out and brought Clyde up to the
third floor of the Keep.

"This isn't over." Serena said, raising her voice.

Jemma got up and sighed. Whatever bitch, Jemma thought.
She then went over and grabbed a sharp knife. Serena pushed
open the door and she and Clyde stumbled through the door. Sere-
na hauled Clyde and laid him on the bed. Clyde was completely on
his back, and he dropped his sword somewhere in the Keep. What
the hell is happening to me? Clyde thought. He had been weak
before without The Hooks, but this was worse. Much worse. I hate
this, Clyde thought, and he groaned. Serena grabbed his legs and
swung them around, so Clyde's legs were on the bed. Serena came
over and pulled Clyde close to the pillow, lifted his head, and laid
it on the pillow. Sighing, Serena gave him a kiss on the forehead.

"Please relax." Serena said.

That was easy for Serena to say.

Clyde couldn't relax. In fact, he almost jumped off the bed, eyes wide.

"Serena!" Clyde shouted.

He launched himself forward, grabbed her and pulled her onto the bed. The knife that Jemma had just missed her, and it dug into Clyde's leg. Screaming, Clyde launched his leg to the side and hit Jemma, sending her backwards towards the door. Serena was in shock and Clyde screamed as he tried to get the knife out. It was deep in his leg, right underneath the knee-cap. Jemma struggled to get to her feet. Clyde bit his lip so hard that blood streamed from his lips. He grasped the knife.

Then pulled.

The pain went through Clyde like a shockwave and when he finally got the knife out, Jemma launched for him, grabbing the knife with her hands. The two struggled for the knife. Clyde still bit his lip, the blood slowly dripping down his shirt. Sweat ran down both sides of his head. His body was tired, but Clyde's mind was fully alert. She's gonna fucking kill me, Clyde thought. After bringing her back, the one that I used to love is now going to kill me. Serena stirred on the floor as Clyde and Jemma fought over the knife. The blade pointed towards Clyde's chest, inching closer with every second. Clyde never realized how strong Jemma was. She isn't strong. You are just weak. The blade came closer and soon, it touched Clyde's chest. Clyde breathed in and out rapidly, trying to get the blade from him. Jemma smiled as she put pressure on the knife. Clyde couldn't hold it anymore. His arms were sleepy and losing strength. Then the tip of the blade touched Clyde and went into his chest. Clyde screamed until his voice was hoarse, struggling and arching his back in pain. Jemma put more pressure and the knife went further into Clyde. In pain, Clyde lashed out and tackled Jemma. Jemma and Clyde fell to the ground, with the knife going completely through Clyde now, the blade sticking out of his back. Screaming, Clyde punched Jemma in the side of the head. Clyde got off Jemma and yanked the knife out. Blood came from Clyde's shirt, but he was not dead. Jemma,

surprised that her plan didn't work, ran for the door of the Keep.
Serena leaned up against the post of the bed and Clyde followed
Jemma, the knife still in his hand. Clyde stumbled through the
hallway and saw Jemma go up the stairs. He threw the knife,
but it missed, and Clyde cursed like a sailor. Clyde held onto the
wall with his hand, with the other hand holding the hole in his
chest. The blood seeped through his fingers, but again, Clyde was
shocked that he was not dead. Clyde went up the stairs and got to
the top of the Keep. Jemma was there. Clyde noticed that her right
hand was on the side of her head. The wound was deep enough to
draw blood and Jemma tried to cover it the best that she could.
She held up her hands.

"Clyde please…..." Jemma started.

Clyde stepped forwards, then leaned up against the battle-
ment.

"I'm sorry Jemma." Clyde said.

"Clyde no!" Jemma screamed.

There was no place for Jemma to back up to. If she tried
to run through the fortress, the Dirt Knights would have stopped
her. Clyde inched forward, leaning on the battlement. Jemma then
launched herself forward. The two fell with screams. Clyde got
the best of Jemma and slammed the side of her head with a punch.
Clyde then got his hands under Jemma and pushed her off him.
Jemma staggered back, holding onto the battlement. Clyde got up
and with his hands, pushed her off the top of the Keep. Jemma
flailed as she fell, trying to get a hold. Clyde watched as she fell
and slammed onto the ground.

Silence.

The Dirt Knights looked from the top of the Western Wall,
looking down. Clyde leaned on the battlement, still holding his
chest. Jemma didn't stir. She's dead, Clyde thought. For the first
time in a while, Clyde cried. There was a time when I loved her,
but now, I'm just so consumed by Serena, that I don't even feel
anything for her. Was that why I couldn't have sex with her when
she was tied down? Clyde thought. He shook his head and made
his way down the stairs, towards the third floor where Serena
was. Clyde stumbled through the door and Serena caught him.

"Come on, let's get you to bed." Serena said.

Her voice was so soft, so innocent and Clyde weakly nodded. The weakness of his body was so great, that he let himself be carried by Serena.

Hours passed and Clyde woke up in the bed, lying on his side. The shade's in the room were down, signaling that it was nighttime. His clothes were changed into comfy pajamas. In front of him, was Serena, dressed in pajamas and sleeping on her side. Clyde's right hand was across her chest. Clyde could feel Serena's breathing, her chest rising with every breath. He shifted in the bed and Serena turned around and faced him. The two kissed.

"How?" Clyde asked, weakly.

Serena put her fingers to his lips.

"Relax, Clyde. I healed you with my Energy." Serena said.

"Thank mhhhhhhmmm." Clyde said.

It was supposed to be a thank you, but Serena kissed Clyde again, muffling his words.

Clyde then drifted to sleep.

Clyde woke up the next morning with Serena next to him. They were still in their pajama's and still in a spooning position. Serena stirred and turned to face Clyde.

"Good morning." Serena said, smiling.

"Morning." Clyde said.

The two kissed and Serena went back into her position.

"You and I are still so tired this morning." Serena said.

"Yes, very." Clyde said.

"How did you do it?" Serena asked.

"How did I do what?"

"Kill Jemma."

Clyde kissed Serena's neck. She shifted.

"I pushed her off the Keep. She's dead." Clyde said.

"Do you feel any regret?" Serena asked.

Regret? Why regret?"

"What do you mean Serena?"

"You loved her once, so do you feel guilty that you killed

her?"

Clyde shook his head.

"No. I feel nothing."

"Why?"

"Because I don't. I love you."

Serena turned to face Clyde again.

"Have I broken you?" Serena asked.

"You have. I only want you." Clyde said.

Serena wrapped her arms around Clyde, pulling him close for a hug.

"I love you too, Clyde." Serena said.

A shout echoed outside. Clyde kissed Serena on the forehead, then got out of the bed. He went over and pulled up the shade. The Dirt Knights had completely rebuilt the fortress, but they were all lined up on the walls. Clyde noticed that they were not fighting. Serena came up next to Clyde.

"What's going on?" Serena asked.

"No idea." Clyde said, shaking his head.

"We should go find out." Serena said.

"We should get dressed, shower, eat, then find out." Clyde said.

"In that order?" Serena asked, smiling.

"I guess so. Have another order?" Clyde asked.

The two grabbed their clothes and showered together. It was a quick shower and soon, the two were downstairs, eating a quick breakfast that Serena made. Clyde wouldn't have called it made, because Serena just thought of cooked food, and it appeared on plates in front of the two of them. After breakfast, another shout echoed, and Clyde and Serena went onto the Western Wall. Down below, was Mark. He looks the same, Clyde thought. Mark looked the same as he was yesterday before the fight. He was right, he can't die, Clyde thought. I am going to change that.

"Good morning Clyde. How are you?" Mark asked.

"I feel better now that I'm awake." Clyde said.

Mark shook his head.

"You know, you can always come down and we can talk it over, Clyde."

"I won't come down to answer for murders that weren't my fault."

"We know that Clyde, but you what we had to do last night?" Mark asked.

"I'm itching to find out." Clyde said.

That brought a snicker from Serena. Mark looked at both, then continued.

"We had a funeral for your friend, Clyde. It was nice of you to throw her off the top of the Keep...."

How did he know? Clyde thought. His eyes were wide in surprise.

"What, you didn't think that I wouldn't have noticed Clyde. I was already alive when you threw her off. I was watching in the bushes, waiting for the end. It was like watching a TV episode where you want to know what is next, but you must wait a week or whatever for the next one. The only thing is Clyde, is that I didn't have to wait a week. I saw the ending and saw Jemma plummet to the ground. Her parents were devastated and then I realized that they could join her, so I killed them and buried all three of them in one spot. You can see it from the top of the Keep..."

"You sick bastard!" Clyde shouted.

"You can come down, Clyde. If you do, we can end this and all of it will go away. I just need you to die, so that I can take the Energy that you have so I can live. No hard feelings. I'll resurrect you and Serena and you guys can live happily ever after or whatever the fuck you guys want to do, but I just want you and your Energy. Is that so hard to ask?" Mark said.

"Yup. You aren't getting it." Clyde said.

"A man of few words Clyde."

"I'm a man of action. Come and get me. You did it before and you can do it again." Clyde spat.

Mark then turned away, huffing, and walking behind the lines of his forces. Clyde noticed that he had more help this time. The bodies of those that Clyde's forces killed yesterday were still piled up along the outside of the walls. It's going to be the same thing, Clyde thought. Same battle everyday until I give up. The fortress would hold any assault, but if Mark was going to keep brining people here, sooner or later, I won't have the Energy to make more of the Knights to hold the fortress. A bullet went over Clyde's head, and he got down behind the battlement. The second assault for the fortress had begun and the enemy crashed against the walls like a wave. This time, they brought plenty of ladders and soon, they were climbing the walls like ants, flowing onto the walls. The Dirt Knights managed to get off a few shots of arrows, however, they had to switch to their swords to fight against the enemy forces that swarmed over the wall.

"Bring the fortress down! I want Clyde alive!"

Mark's voice echoed over the fighting. Clyde went towards the Keep and locked himself in. The Knights were outnumbered, and many were dropping. Clyde didn't even have to do anything. More Knights sprang from the ground, filling up the courtyard with more forces. Clyde was surprised that Mark hadn't decided to blow up the fortress gate like he did the first time. Serena came over to Clyde and the two went up to the third floor of the Keep. From the window, they watched the battle rage below. This is not good, Clyde thought. Mark must have brought in more reinforcements. That's impossible. All these towns out here have no one, so how could have Mark brought in more people to fight for him. Clyde thought. Serena wrapped her arms around him, hugging him from behind.

"They won't win you know." Serena said.

Clyde nodded.

"I know they won't win." Clyde said.

"Mark will always come for you. He won't rest until he can have your Energy and The Hooks. His curse will never be broken. It will always exist if you are alive. He will never stop hunting you and will eventually find you." Serena said.

"I know."

"Will you let him kill you so his curse can be broken?" Serena asked.

"No. He's going to have to try harder than this to break his curse." Clyde said.

Serena nodded, then placed her head on Clyde's shoulder.

"We should go and help them fight. Maybe Mark will leave

if we join in." Serena said.

"I'm not too sure about that." Clyde said.

The door flung open as a bomb went off, destroying the entire left side of the Keep. Clyde and Serena were thrown to the floor in the blast. Clyde saw stars and his ears were ringing. Rubble and debris blew into the room in clouds. Clyde struggled to get up, but he staggered and fell to the ground. His vision was hazy, and Clyde tried to see what was in front of him. Another explosion went off and more clouds drifted through. Coughing, Clyde put his hand to his mouth and tried to keep the dust out of his mouth. With his hazy vision, Clyde saw Serena being grabbed and carried out of the room.

"Clyde!!!!" Serena screamed.

His ears stopped ringing and Serena's screams echoed in Clyde's ears. It was so strong, that Clyde put his hands to his ears to block out the voice. Screaming, Clyde got himself up, but was tackled to the ground by an enemy. Using his strength, Clyde tossed the man off him. The man rolled and Clyde got himself up to face as enemies poured into the room. Clyde faced them and shot out his hand. The enemies shot back and slammed against the wall. Clyde levitated one man and tossed him out the window, crashing into his comrades below. Clyde walked through the broken room and staggered to the broken doorway. He leaned on it with his right hand and watched as Serena was carried down the stairs towards the courtyard. Gathering up his strength, Clyde ran down the stairway. He tripped on one of the middle stairs and fell face forward. Serena's screams echoed as Clyde chased after her.

"Clyde!!! Clyde!!!"

"I'm coming!" Clyde shouted.

His voice was hoarse. His body was beginning to weaken. Not again you son of a bitch, Clyde thought. Clyde shot a blast from his hand, sending a group of enemies flying in all directions. The courtyard and wall fight had become a free-for-all. There was no proper battle line or formation or anything. The Dirt Knights were fighting for their lives. Clyde did not care about the fortress or his forces. I know that they are going to win the fight anyways. More Dirt Knights appeared, charging against Mark's forces. Clyde rushed off the walls and made his way through the courtyard. Mark held onto Serena now. He had her thrown over his shoulder like she was a sack of potatoes. Serena's hands were tied behind her, as well as her ankles. She struggled in Mark's grip, but it seemed that Mark did not care about her hitting her. Clyde went out of the fortress and chased Mark and Serena down the slope of Russ Mountain. Clyde's lungs were on fire, his breathing heavy. Clyde's body felt weaker, and his eyes began to blur. Don't you dare, you bastard! Clyde yelled at himself. In a desperate effort, Clyde shot out a blast and it felled a tree in front of Mark. Startled, Mark stopped on his feet, falling forwards. Serena launched over the tree sliding down the slope. Mark got up, just in time for Clyde to deliver a right hook, sending him sprawling over the tree. Mark was about to react when Clyde jumped him and yanked him to his feet. Mark tried to get away, but Clyde's strength matched his and Mark was tossed back over the tree, sliding on the ground. Mark got back up and he charged at Clyde. Clyde took a blow to the chest, only to bring both fists down on Mark's back, sending him to the ground. Mark coughed and Clyde pressed down on Mark, forcing his head into the ground. Mark tried to get away from Clyde, but Clyde would not let up. His anger was too much, and Mark flailed, until he landed a good kick in Clyde's back. In pain, Clyde rolled off Mark and he ran down the slope. Serena struggled to get up, however, Mark hauled her to her feet and forced her down the slope. Clyde rubbed the area of his back where he was kicked by Mark and then chased after Mark down the slope. Clyde then fell forward. The fortress exploded, the Eastern Wall destroyed by the blast. Rocks flew in the air and crushed members of both armies. It's all over now, Clyde thought. He struggled to get to his feet and chased after Mark down the slope. As he got closer to the shore, Clyde watched as Serena was given to Alexandria, who took Serena on a boat to ferry her to the other side. Mark jumped into the boat. Clyde was out in the open for seconds as bullets flew towards him. Clyde rolled out of the way and hid behind a group of boulders. The bullets ricocheted off the boulders as Clyde hid behind them. Crawling, Clyde moved to another set of boulders, then stood up and hid behind a tree. A whole line of enemies were on the shore, armed with weapons and ready to fire at Clyde. The bullets stopped and that is when Clyde made his attack. He shot a blast and sent the enemies into the water. The enemies flailed in the water and Clyde realized what he was doing.

He was drowning them.

Clyde had no idea that he was even doing this, however, Clyde noticed that the enemies slowly came up to the surface of the water, not moving at all. The Energy is getting stronger, Clyde thought. God Damn.

"Clyde."

Clyde looked and noticed that Jeremy was across from him. Alexandria was too. She must have went from the boat and back in that span of time. Clyde looked across the shore to see Serena being taken away in a truck, where Mark got into the back seat with her. He better not touch her or he's dead, Clyde thought.

"Clyde."

It was Jeremy's voice again, snapping him back to the present. Clyde looked at him.

"Jeremy."

"It doesn't have to end like this Clyde. Just hand over The Hooks and Mark will give you Serena back." Jeremy said.

"Is that what he told you?" Clyde asked.

Jeremy was confused. Clearly not, Clyde thought. He took a step forward.

"Mark is not who he seems, Jeremy. You better step aside and let me on that boat. I'm going after Serena, and I don't care who is in my way." Clyde said, raising his voice.

Another explosion rocked Russ Mountain, the final explosion. The fortress was no more, nothing but a pile of rubble now. The survivors cheered, however, there was not much to show for their victory. Clyde was still alive and kicking. I can kill all of them with the Energy by myself, Clyde thought. Then I would be extremely tired. That was the only downside to using the Energy. The tiredness was expansive. Jeremy took a step forwards.

"I won't let you get on the boat, Clyde." Jeremy said.

"Come on, Jeremy. You know that you can't win against

me." Clyde said, smiling.

"What's to say that I haven't gotten better since the last time you saw me?" Jeremy asked.

"Then I guess we are going to have to test this theory." Clyde said.

By now, the remaining survivors of Mark's forces came, and they formed a ring of sorts around Clyde and Jeremy.

"FIGHT FIGHT FIGHT."

The words echoed through Clyde's ears, but it was not for long as Jeremy lunged for him. The two friends grappled with each other. Clyde rolled on the ground with Jeremy, letting him get on top. A couple punches later and Clyde shot Jeremy off him, sending him flying and Jeremy smashed against a tree. Dazed, Clyde got to his feet and Jeremy charged again. Clyde shot out his hand and hit him in the chest. Jeremy wheezed and fell to the ground. A kick in the back from Clyde forced a scream out of Jeremy. When anyone moved, all Clyde had to do was point his hand, his palm stretched out.

"One move and I blast to you to hell." Clyde said.

They stood still, except for Jeremy who got up again. Clyde rounded on him and nailed him in the head with a kick. Jeremy was down for the count, dazed and seeing stars. Blood dripped from the wound on his head. Alexandria ran to him and began to minister to him. Clyde rubbed his hands together, as if he was just getting started. The Energy coursed through him like never. For the first time in weeks, Clyde felt more alive, more alert. Clyde looked at the remaining survivors. Should I kill them, or should I let them go? Clyde thought. If I let them go, then they will tell everyone about me. If I kill them, then Mark will get even more upset.

They must die.

Clyde made a swift motion with his hand. All the weapons that the survivors carried were whisked away from them. Clyde levitated the guns in the air and pointed them at their previous owners. They all got down on their knees and begged for their lives, bowing, and scraping at Clyde's feet. Clyde paid no attention to them, and all the guns went off, killing all the survivors.

When they tried to run in different directions and hide, the bullets followed them. No one was safe. Clyde then tossed the weapons into the water. It was during the massacre, that Jeremy got onto the boat and escaped. Alexandria ran after the boat, as she pushed it into the water. Clyde saw this and as Alexandria jumped into the boat, Clyde yanked her back with the Energy.

"No!" Jeremy shouted.

"Jeremy!!!" Alexandria shouted.

Clyde levitated her in the air and Alexandria struggled. Eventually, she was next to Clyde, with unseen forces strapping her wrists and ankles together. Clyde smiled and he stroked Alexandria's hair.

"How about we make a deal? Alexandria in exchange for Serena and my freedom. You won't hear from me again." Clyde said.

Jeremy was stuck in a hard position. On the one hand, he followed Mark's orders to the exact letter. On the other hand, Alexandria was his first and only love. She was girl that he wanted to marry. He will break, Clyde thought. Jeremy would be stupid to give her up. I'll take Serena and no one else will get hurt. Jeremy stood there in the boat. It hadn't gone very far, and Clyde could tell that Jeremy was debating on getting back onto the shore.

"You swear that she won't be hurt?" Jeremy asked.

"I give you my word. I just want Serena back." Clyde said.

"Then I want The Hooks and Alexandria. Then we can work on getting Serena back." Jeremy said.

Clyde shook his head.

"No, only my deal stands. I need The Hooks."

"What you need is some help, Clyde. The Hooks and Alexandria for Serena."

"No Deal."

Jeremy sighed.

"Then I can't help you!"

"God Damn you, Jeremy!"

Jeremy was silent. Clyde continued. He felt some tears coming.

"You were my friend! My only friend, the one who was like a brother to me, and this is how you treat me! You were supposed

The Doom of Casper

   ` Clyde left Jeremy moaning next to Alexandria. The day was half over and soon, night would crawl into place. Clyde shot a fireball into the air, and it floated above him to give him some light. The sun slowly set, and it reflected across the Reservoir. The fortress was nothing but a large pile of rocks and wood. Amongst the wreckage, Clyde searched for The Hooks. He could feel the spiritual pull that dragged on him. Clyde noticed that he would get more energy when he was closer to The Hooks and would be tired when he was further away. The Hooks were under one of the doors from the Keep. Clyde pushed the shattered wooden door out of the way to reveal The Hooks. The set looked like the first time that Clyde had gotten them, unused and untouched. Even through all the mess, The Hooks remained. Amazing, Clyde thought. Clyde grabbed The Hooks and held them tight, as if the objects were a stuffed animal. I missed you two, Clyde thought. The Energy coursed through him like never before. Clyde felt like he didn't need to sleep or eat anymore. Jeremy still sobbed next to Alexandria and Clyde only shook his head. Weak, Clyde thought. He waved his hand and the rubble formed into a spacious cave, with a firepit in the center, along with string lights that lined both sides of the cave. Two beds formed on each end, along with an end table, lamp, and a storage chest. To add the final touch, a round door appeared in front of the cave. Clyde slid the door to the left and right, testing the function of it. Clyde then went down to Jeremy.

    "Are you coming or what?" Clyde asked.

    Jeremy looked up at him, tears streaming down his face.

    "How can you be like this?" Jeremy asked.

    "Be like what?" Clyde asked, raising his voice.

    "How can you be so civil, when someone just fucking died." Jeremy said, standing up.

    Clyde sighed.

    "I never knew Alexandria, so I don't care."

    "So that's your response? I didn't know her, so I don't give a shit."

"Yup." Clyde nodded.

"You are more selfish than anything else."

"Then go and fire me. Now do you want to be out here with her or no?" Clyde asked.

Jeremy sighed.

"I don't know what to think."

"Then stay out here for all I care. I'm going inside." Clyde said.

"Inside that cave that you just made?" Jeremy asked.

"Where else am I going to go?" Clyde asked, throwing up his hands.

He walked away, rolled the door to the right, and stepped into the cave. As Clyde closed the door, he could hear Jeremy going back to cry over Alexandria. Angry, Clyde combusted the other bed and materials. If he doesn't want my kindness, then he won't get it, Clyde thought. Clyde then ate a small piece of chicken and drank some water. I guess that will hold me until tomorrow, Clyde thought. Clyde crawled into the bed, switched off the lights, and went to sleep.

Outside, Jeremy tried to get into the cave, however, he found a spot on the ground and slept.

The next morning, Clyde woke up to find Jeremy on the ground, sleeping in front of the cave. He must have tried to come inside last night, Clyde thought. Doesn't matter, he can fuck himself. I offered to help him, but he refused. Clyde just sighed and went outside. The sun slowly rose over the horizon, the sun's rays reflecting off the water. Clyde climbed a high pile of rubble to look over the water of the Reservoir. Out there, Serena is waiting for you, Clyde thought. I must get her back. Mark is going to pay for taking her, Clyde thought. There was a part of him that just wanted to go back to way things were. The other part of Clyde wanted revenge on Mark for what he did. He destroyed your fortress, took your girl, ripped apart your friendship with your best friend. Are you really going to let him get away with all of that? These thoughts echoed in Clyde's head. Clyde turned around to see Jeremy getting up from the ground. He rubbed his eyes and looked at Clyde.

"How long have you been up?" Jeremy asked.

"Long enough to see that you were sleeping out here all night." Clyde said.

"Well, I would have gone in, but the door was closed."

"It wasn't locked, Jeremy." Clyde said.

Clyde went down the rubble pile and towards the cave. Jeremy sighed and followed him.

"Are you going to have breakfast?" Jeremy asked.

Clyde shook his head.

"Nope. I'm not hungry."

"I am."

"That's too bad for you. Go and find something in the woods." Clyde said.

Jeremy flipped Clyde off as he walked away through the small forest on Russ Mountain. Clyde shook it off and went into the cave. Clyde was going to eat, but he didn't want Jeremy to have any of his food. Clyde whipped up some scrambled eggs and bacon. He ate the food quickly, so that Jeremy wouldn't barge in and ask for some. When Clyde was done eating, he grabbed The Hooks, and stepped out of the cave. Today we must go back to Casper, Clyde thought. I'm not sure how far Jeremy is going to go with this. Do I really trust him enough to take me back to Mark? How much does he really love Alexandria? If he wants her so bad, then he better not pull any tricks. Jeremy came out with a rabbit, a fat one. Clyde leaned up against the outside wall of the cave and watched as Jeremy prepared his food. Man, we have really gone far downhill, Clyde thought. He watched his friend make a small fire, skin the rabbit, and eat it. From Jeremy's facial expressions, Clyde could tell that he hated eating the rabbit, however, Clyde was not going to give in. You wanted this, Clyde thought. He shook his head and slowly slid down the wall, so that when Clyde landed on the ground, his legs were outstretched. Jeremy just looked at him, his mouth moving and teeth crunching on the rabbit meat. Jeremy spat out a bone.

"Are you going to wait for me?" Jeremy asked.

"I wouldn't be a good friend if I left you by yourself." Clyde said.

"Did you eat?" Jeremy asked.

"None of your business."

"Whatever." Jeremy said, taking another bite of the rabbit. Clyde sighed.

"I don't want to go back to Casper, but I have no choice. Your friend Mark..."

"Stop calling Mark my friend. He isn't. You are." Jeremy said.

"You haven't been much of a friend to me, Jeremy." Clyde said.

"What the hell is that supposed to mean? Just because you have powers that I don't understand, that doesn't mean that I'm not your friend." Jeremy said.

"You were going to tell everyone my secret, but I guess Mark told you all about it, about the Energy, and what he plans to do to me when he sees me." Clyde said.

"Mark never told me what he had planned. If I had known, I would have helped you Clyde, and you know that." Jeremy said.

"It doesn't matter now, Jeremy. Mark has Serena and I'm going to do whatever it takes to get her back." Clyde said.

"Wouldn't going back to Casper be playing into Mark's plan to get you?" Jeremy asked.

"It doesn't matter what Mark is planning. I'm going to disrupt it." Clyde said, standing up.

Jeremy finished off his rabbit and followed Clyde down the slope of Russ Mountain. Back to Casper we go, Clyde thought. He felt like he was at the Quabbin Reservoir for what seemed like an eternity. The reality was that Clyde was here on Russ Mountain for a short time, at least two days. When Clyde got to the shore, the bridge of rocks that he previously made, rose from the water. Jeremy followed Clyde across the bridge and when the two reached the other shore, the bridge disappeared under the water. For safe keeping, Clyde thought. I don't think I will ever come back here, but there is always the chance that I could. There was no one around in New Salem, as the sleepy citizens were still inside their houses. Hopefully it stays this way, Clyde thought. We won't be able to make it back to Casper on foot. Clyde only had to think and soon, the ground parted ways. Jeremy stood back in shock, as a brand-new GMC Canyon Denali appeared out of the ground. The vehicle itself was onyx black and seemed to have all the new features. Clyde found that the keys of the truck were in his pocket. The specially designed key fob was new to Clyde and all he had to do was point. The doors opened automatically.

"Beautiful." Clyde said.

Jeremy followed Clyde as he hopped into the drivers seat. The truck roared to life and the journey back to Casper was underway. Driving through New Salem was not challenge, as no one was one the road currently. Getting onto the highway was another story. The morning traffic rush began, and Clyde was thankful that he stayed in the right lane. Clyde drove slightly above the speed limit, however, he let other drivers merge onto the highway and would follow the signs that were posted. Casper was not long of a drive and Clyde estimated that they would arrive in Casper in the afternoon.

"Get comfortable for a bit." Clyde said.

"Long drive?" Jeremy asked.

Traffic seemed to build up ahead. "Yup." Clyde said.

The ride from New Salem to Casper was rough. Route 202 seemed to be packed for whatever reason. Maybe everyone is going to the Cape or something? Clyde thought. It was that time of the year for going down that way. I've never been there. When Clyde got onto US-Route 2, which 202 formed into, the traffic was steady. It was not bumper to bumper as before, as many were getting off the highway to head to work. Good, keep them over there, Clyde thought. Jeremy was asleep in the passenger seat. Clyde noticed that they had forgotten about the body of Alexandria. It might be a good thing that we didn't bring her along. If the police stopped us, then there would be a lot of explaining to do, Clyde thought. There was also the chance, that if Jeremy was really helping Clyde, then Clyde would have to return to resurrect Alexandria back to life. I hate playing God, Clyde thought.

I did it once with Jemma and she hated me. She absolutely

hated me and wanted me dead. She didn't love me like I thought she would. Serena.

Serena.

Clyde could not get Serena out of his head. It is strange that she is not inside my head. It is strange that she is Real now.

It's strange.

All so strange.

The signs for Gardner and Templeton flew past Clyde as he drove. In the rearview mirror, the flashing lights for a police car approached him. Shit, Clyde thought. What could I have possibly done now. Clyde acknowledged the police officer and pulled over in the breakdown lane on the highway. The officer shortly followed, parked his car, then came over to Clyde. When the officer got close, Clyde rolled down his window.

"What can I do for you officer?" Clyde asked, keeping his hands on ten and two at the wheel.

"Can I see your license and registration?"

"Of course."

Clyde handed over the paperwork. The officer took it and read it, then handed it back to Clyde.

"The license and registration are in order, but there is one problem."

"What is it?" Clyde asked.

"The vehicle has no plates."

Clyde furrowed his brow. No plates, Clyde thought.

"No plates?" Clyde asked.

"Yeah, no plates." The officer said.

Clyde unstrapped himself and got out of the truck. The officer was right. The truck did not have a front or back plates. Then Clyde knew what to say next.

"That's right, no plates because I was on my way to get them today." Clyde said.

The officer did not seemed convinced about Clyde's story, then he just nodded.

"Well, I'll hold you to it. Make sure you get those plates soon. Another officer like myself might not be so nice."

With that, the officer left Clyde standing outside of the

truck. When Clyde knew that he was gone, he thought of a random number combination and soon, the plates were on the front and back of the truck.

A red Massachusetts plate.

Now no one will question me again. Clyde thought. There was a single drawback that Clyde realized when he got back into the truck. The officer knew that the truck didn't have plates. Clyde also knew that the officer probably took pictures of the truck before entering the information into the computer. Clyde was now known by the police as someone driving without plates. This could be very bad, Clyde thought. As he started the truck to life, he tried not to think about the what ifs or what could happen. It doesn't matter now, Clyde thought. He merged back onto the highway and found signs to get onto the Leominster Connector and into Leominster. As he got off the connector, Clyde was on Mechanic, then Main Street, heading north towards Casper. Clyde noticed that at the middle of the day, no cars were out. Strange, Clyde thought. It was always packed at this time of day. Main Street stretched north into Casper. Clyde was right about the city being deserted. Clyde drove through the various neighborhoods to find cars parked in driveways. Trash bins lined every corner of the houses. The silence was killing Clyde and he stopped his truck in the middle of the road. Further up, was Mark. Serena, Clyde saw her tied up to a flagpole that was in front of Martins. Around Mark and Serena, were citizens, however, Clyde noticed that they were different than the ones he had seen before. These citizens were haggard in appearance, almost as if they were the undead themselves.

They can't be Clyde thought.

There was no way that Mark killed all the citizens of Casper, then raised them as zombies. It was outrageous and Clyde agreed, however, there was something that told Clyde that he could have been right. Another thing told Clyde that he needed to run, to forget Serena. Clyde shook his head. No, I need to save her. I need to get her back. Jeremy woke up in the passenger seat.

"Are we here?" Jeremy asked.

"We are." Clyde said.

Jeremy noticed that Clyde was looking out through the windshield of the truck.

"What is the matter?" Jeremy asked.

"Mark killed all the citizens and made them into something else. I don't know what it is, but it is not good, I can tell you that." Clyde said.

Jeremy gulped. Clyde continued.

"They have Serena tied to a flagpole in front of Martins. I need you to free her and bring her back to the truck. I'm going to see if I can fight Mark's whatever's." Clyde said.

"Alright. I'll go see what I can do."

"Ok, just go. I have a plan. Make sure no one sees you and Jeremy, good luck." Clyde said.

Jeremy nodded and got out of the truck. Clyde shortly followed. Main Street was completely deserted, with the only vehicle on the road being Clyde's GMC Truck. Clyde turned off the vehicle and gave the key fob to Jeremy. Then Jeremy went off on foot, going through the thick neighborhood alleys towards Martins. Clyde had The Hooks with him. He didn't need them, however, he felt safer with him on his person. A rope appeared in the air and Clyde tied The Hooks together, then tied them to his jean belt. With every step, The Hooks slammed his thighs.

"Clyde."

The booming voice echoed inside of Clyde, and he fell, pressing his hands to his ears.

"CLYDE!!"

The voice was Marks.

"Yes I can talk into your head. You should have never come back. You should have surrendered when you got the chance. Now the entire city of Casper will face the consequences. They are coming for you Clyde, the Mirrored. They are all cursed, just like you and I, and they are coming for you. Only the Energy can beat them, Clyde, so use it wisely."

As Mark's voice finished, the first large group of Mirrored showed up. They were the ugliest things that Clyde had ever seen. Most of them were all charred bodies. Walking, charred bodies, with burnt skin that fell off like snowflakes when touched. Small clouds of ashes came from them as they moved. Mirrored then charged for Clyde, but he was ready for it. A shockwave came from the ground and sent the enemy backwards, crashing into houses and cars. Horns went off and alarms sounded. The battle for Casper had begun. Clyde ran up Main Street, heading towards Martins. Mirrored appeared out of the alley's and homes, jumping off roofs and crashing through windows. Clyde had never shot so many blasts in his life. With each blast, the Mirrored were killed or knocked back. There were so many of them and Clyde knew that Mark was only making more of them. Wave after wave came from Martins. It must be Mark's base of operations. Where it all started. Clyde knew that he had to do something to stop the Mirrored. The ground shook. The Mirrored stopped. Clyde focused, then screamed at the top of his lungs. The road behind and in front of him began to crack. The crack stretched up and down Main Street. The ground shook violently, almost knocking Clyde off balance, but he recovered. One by one, buildings fell straight into the ground. The earthquake was massive, that the Mirrored ran in waves back to Martins. The entire city of Casper shook and one by one, fell into the ground.

"This city will sink with you and me Mark!!!" Clyde shouted.

At Martins' Mark struggled as Clyde's voice shattered his eardrums. The earthquake sent up large clouds of dust and debris as the ground swallowed the city whole. Houses, businesses, and everything else was taken by the earthquake. The only thing that remained was Martins and the surrounding area, along with a little island that Clyde stood on. When Clyde looked up, the entire city of Casper was reduced to a pile of rubble. Thousands of people swarmed below, trying to get back up the slope, but it was no use. Clyde had trapped everyone in the large crater that was below him. Casper was no more. Clyde then shot his hand downward. It broke the tiny spire that held the island and Clyde floated towards Martins. The Energy coursed through him now. Clyde jumped off the island as it crashed through the front of Martins. Mark got up, only to be kicked by Clyde, then tossed off to the right. Mark slammed through the other front window and disappeared into the store. Serena struggled against the flagpole and Clyde ran to her. Clyde wanted her so bad, but he knew that he had to get her out first. Clyde cut the ropes that held Serena and removed the gag that was across her mouth. The two kissed, but it was cut short as Mark grabbed Serena.

"Don't move!" Mark shouted.

A knife pressed against Serena's neck. Clyde growled.

"Again! What is this Mark? And endless loop. Look around. You saw what I can do. Hand her over." Clyde said.

Mark was shocked.

"Hand her over!" Clyde shouted.

That scared Mark and he dropped the knife. Serena got away, turned around, and nailed Mark in the chest. Coughing, Mark fell back and hit his head on the flagpole.

"Come on, I'll lower you down." Clyde said.

"Ok." Serena said.

Clyde looked down below. The foundation underneath Martins held up the entire building, creating the store an island in the crater. It was straight drop below, about forty feet or so. The ruins of the entire city littered the bottom of the crater. No one could have survived that, Clyde thought. A rope and harness appeared in the air. Clyde caught it and strapped the harness to Serena. So intimate. Focus damn it! Clyde thought. He took the rope and wrapped it around his waist.

"Ok, nice and slow." Clyde said.

Serena gripped the rope with her hands and slowly went over the cliff. Clyde dug his heels in as Serena slowly drifted down. Clyde was shocked that he could hold her weight, however, he knew that all the strength was not his. The Energy. It still coursed through Clyde. The Hooks leaned up against his thigh. Clyde looked over the edge. Serena was halfway down, almost at the bottom of the crater. Clyde dug in his heels more and gave Serena slack. She went down further. Clyde looked back. Mark slowly got up. He had a large lump on his head and staggered towards Clyde.

"You're dead!" Mark shouted.

He charged Clyde, holding the knife in his hand. Fuck! Clyde thought. Clyde dug I his heels and turned to the side to take Mark's charge. Instead of knocking the knife from Mark's hand, the knife lodged itself into Clyde's shoulder blade. Screaming, Clyde almost let go of the rope. The rope went taut as Clyde punched Mark with his left hand. Mark staggered back, surprised by the blow. Below, Serena screamed as she held onto the rope. Clyde watched as she got closer to the bottom of the crater. She only had ten feet to go until she reached the bottom. Clyde went in for another swing and hit Mark in the chest, then in the jaw again. His right shoulder and arm were useless. The knife must have hit the nerve in Clyde's arm, as he struggled to even lift it. Blood seeped from the knife wound, dripping down Clyde's arm. He looked over the edge of the cliff and Serena got to the bottom. She took the harness off herself and was taken by Jeremy. Serena screamed, but Jeremy calmed her down. Clyde was glad that the two were ok with each other and watched as Jeremy shook the key fob in his hand. I hope he finds the GMC ok, Clyde thought. Clyde braced for another charge as Mark slammed into him. He's gonna push me off the cliff. Clyde turned around now, bracing his heels, and pressing his hands on Marks' chest, pushing him back. Dirt and debris fell from Clyde's feet kicking back, hoping that Mark's strength would wane.

It didn't.

The two pushed on each other, however, Clyde struggled. The rope was still tied around his waist. Even though Serena was not on the other end of the rope, Clyde knew that he had the disadvantage. Screaming, Clyde shoved Mark away. Mark fell backwards and slammed his back on the ground. In shock, Mark struggled to get up. Clyde took this opportunity to untie the rope from his waist and charge for Mark. Clyde got on top of him and wrapped the rope around his neck. Mark laughed as Clyde choked him.

"You know how this ends Clyde. It will always be an endless cycle. I'll die, yes, but I'll come back and hunt you down until you had over those Hooks." Mark said.

Clyde tried to choke Mark harder, but even with the rope completely around his neck and at its tightest, Mark still talked to Clyde.

"You think you are hero because you have the Energy? I'll

show you what real Energy can do." Mark said.

Clyde was hit in the chest by an invisible blast. He shot off Mark and now hung on the edge of the cliff. Mark slowly stood up, his hand outstretched. Clyde struggled to hold onto the edge of the cliff. He looked down below to see Jeremy and Serena waiting for him in the GMC Truck. At least it survived. Mark stood over Clyde now.

"You see Clyde, nothing good comes out of trying to beat someone who can't die." Mark said.

Clyde tried to pull himself up, but he couldn't. Sweat rolled down his face and arms, seeping to his fingers. Blood from his shoulder wound still dripped slowly and his shoulder throbbed with every heartbeat. Mark then placed his foot on Clyde's right hand, pressing down. The pressure caused Clyde to scream, but he stayed where he was. I'm not going to let go! Clyde thought, but the pain surged through him like electricity and there was the temptation to let go. Mark let his foot up, then squatted down on Clyde's level.

"Give me The Hooks Clyde. Give me your Energy so I can finally reverse the curse." Mark said.

"You can't kill me, Mark. You need me." Clyde said.

"That's true." Mark said.

Clyde then was yanked up by the Energy. He could feel it around him, binding his arms and legs to his sides. Mark slowly walked away as Clyde drifted up towards him. Mark then set Clyde down and the Energy left him. Mark stood in front of Martins.

"I can't kill you Clyde, but I want to fight a worthy opponent, so face me with the Energy. Show me that you are a true adversary." Mark said.

"I won't fight you Mark. Just leave me alone." Clyde said.

Mark laughed.

"You won't fight me? After all this time, you won't fight me at all. Have you become weak since the fortress? Why won't you fight me? Can't you see that you and I are cut from the same thread, Clyde? We are one in the same. You and I have the Energy, the Power to change the world. When has anyone in the history of the world been able to create whatever they desire by thinking about it? That's right, no one has because you and I are the only ones. Help me reverse my curse, so that we can live together in peace. That's all I want, Clyde. I'm tired of running, tired of starting a new life repeatedly because of my foolishness and my recklessness. All I need is to destroy the lover of one more person, then I can be free..."

The lover of one more person. Serena. That's why he wants me! Clyde thought. He furrowed his brow. Mark smiled.

"So you've finally figured out why I need you." Mark said.

"I won't let you kill me or Serena, just so that you can get your life back. You don't deserve your life for the mistakes that you made."

Mark screwed up his face in anger.

"You will help me Clyde, whether you like it or not!"

Mark shot out his hand. A blast came from it. Clyde threw up his hands and the blast shot off to the left. Mark fired again and Clyde again deflected. Mark smiled.

"Good. Use the Energy!" Mark shouted.

The two fired at each other, with Clyde getting angrier by the second. He screamed as shot both hands out. Mark did the same. A vortex of Energy appeared in between them. Lighting crackled from the vortex as Clyde and Mark pushed on each other. The Energy was strong, stronger than what Clyde had imagined. He dug his heels in and pushed Mark towards the front of Martins. Mark was in shock, and he pushed back. Clyde swung himself around and whipped Mark with the vortex. Mark sailed in the air and crashed onto the ground. Taking the time to breath, Clyde grabbed the knife out of his shoulder. The pain did not bother him one bit as he threw the knife on the ground. Mark caught him off guard with a blast that Clyde took to the chest. Clyde sailed in the air and slid on ground, stopping short of the edge of the cliff. Staggering, Clyde got up to deflect another blast from Mark. The two fired back and forth, each getting good hits on the other. Mark was sent backwards, but he recovered, and it was Clyde that hung on the edge of the cliff again. Clyde began to get tired, his eyes slowly slitted. Not now, Clyde thought. The Energy still coursed through him, but Clyde knew what Mark was already thinking.

Clyde's tiring out.

Clyde pushed himself back over the cliff and fought against Mark. Another vortex formed and this time, Clyde controlled it better than before. Mark was in shock and the lighting that came from the vortex shocked his chest. Mark screamed as he tried to hold onto the vortex, but it was in vain, and he let go. The blast sent both backwards and hanging onto the edge of the cliff. Clyde was the first one to get back on. Sighing, he took the rope, made a harness, and tried to go down the cliff. Then The Hooks moved. Mark had an outstretched hand and tried to pull The Hooks from Clyde with the Energy. The Hooks pulled Clyde towards Mark. Now they were outstretched, the rope on Clyde's jeans went taut. Clyde used the Energy to try to pull The Hooks back to him, however, Clyde was beginning to weaken. The Hooks were not on his side anymore. They were right in front of him, however, they were out of reach. Clyde tried to reach forwards with his hands, grabbing at them and missing every time. Mark pressed the issue more and the Energy began to drag Clyde towards Mark. Clyde dug his heels in and fought against Mark. It was the biggest game of tug-o-war that Clyde had experienced.

And Mark was winning.

I can't let him win, Clyde thought. He used his strength to get back at Mark, however, it was no use. Mark sent a large push of Energy. The rope snapped and The Hooks were separated. Spread even more apart, Clyde felt dizzy. His head hurt, his chest tightened. Not this again. Clyde thought. His vision was blurrier, and he knew that it would only be a matter of time before Mark got the upper hand. Mark tried harder. The rope snapped, but something remarkable happened. One Hook flew into Mark's hand, the other into Clyde's. Energy came back to Clyde, but only just enough to combat Mark. Mark blasted Clyde into Martins, crashing through the window and into the ruined store. Martins was dark on the inside. The ruined store had product all over the floor. Every register was destroyed, and Clyde slowly got up. Mark stood in the doorway, the light from the outside reflecting his shadow. Clyde got up and hid himself among one of the shelves. Clyde was in the candle section. Great, Clyde thought. He held his single Hook tight in his hand, so tight that he thought that his hand would explode because of the pressure that he was exerting on it.

"Come out Clyde!" Mark shouted.

Let him find me, Clyde thought.

"Come out, or I'll make you come out!" Mark shouted.

The shelves in the store began to shake and move. Product fell off, like the store was having an earthquake. Clyde watched as the shelves and walls of product levitated in the air, then one by one, were thrown to the side. The crashing of walls into other walls was deafening and Clyde covered his ears to try to block the noise.

It was impossible.

Mark made the noise seep through Clyde's fingers, and he pressed them harder into his head, trying to block the noise of glass breaking and walls screeching. Clyde then screamed and launched out from one of the shelves. Surprised, Mark lost his focus. Clyde saw the opportunity to levitate a wall and send it crashing into Mark. Mark was shocked as he launched forwards, knocked by a wall of toys and beach gadgets. Clyde then took another wall and dropped it on the other one, just to piss Mark off. Well it did the job, as Mark emerged. The two walls went in opposite directions and Clyde ducked behind a cage as debris flew in all directions. Clyde stood up to face Mark and was caught in the Energy. Mark pulled Clyde towards him.

"Give me the Hook!" Mark shouted.

"Fuck you!" Clyde shouted back.

Clyde got out of Mark's grip and fought back. The Energy slammed into each other, two invisible forces fighting against each other. Clyde was beginning to get tired again. Mark was stronger of the two and slowly pushed Clyde back. He stopped pushing on Clyde and flipped a cage over. Clyde tried to stop the cage as it came down towards him by putting his hands up. The cage just floated over Clyde, slowly dropping on him. Clyde couldn't hold it any more and let the cage fall on him. God Dammit, Clyde thought. The cage forced Clyde to sit on the floor and in the process, he let go of the single Hook that he carried. Mark came over to and grabbed the Hook.

"All you had to do was give it to me." Mark said.

Clyde gripped the bars of the cage.

"You won't get away with this." Clyde said.

Mark smiled.

"We will see."

Groups of Mirrored appeared in Martins. One of them, who Clyde knew as a leader, came up to Mark.

"Get Serena and Jeremy. Bring them here." Mark said.

The Mirrored just nodded and went off on their mission. Clyde saw hundreds, maybe thousands of them now in Martins. Mark looked at Clyde.

"There is no escape Clyde. Soon, you will help me lift my curse. Soon, I will be a free man, one who can do what he pleases for once." Mark said.

"I'll never help you." Clyde said.

"That's too bad, Clyde, because you will help me, no matter what. Regardless on what you think, you will help me. Even if I must force you, you will end up helping me in the end." Mark said. The Mirrored came back with Serena and Jeremy. Both of Clyde's friends were tied up and placed in another cage in a similar position to what Clyde was in. Mark spent some time redoing the salesfloor of Martins, moving the walls and shelves to where he wanted. He couldn't care less about the product. Clyde watched as walls blocked the holes in the walls. Lights appeared on the ceiling, brightening the room. From the debris, Mark made a stone alter, with restraint points for ankles and wrists. I'm probably going on that, Clyde thought. Mark then made another stone alter. Then another. Three of them.

We are all dead now, Clyde thought.

Mirrored were all around them now, waiting on Mark's orders. Just like Mark, they couldn't die. Mark then stood on a stone circle with a podium in front of it.

"It is time, my friends, to reverse our curse." Mark said.

The Price of Attachment

The Mirrored cheered and Clyde tried to block out the noise. Mark made it specific so that the noise would echo loud in Clyde's ears. Mirrored were all over the ruined salesfloor of Martins. Some of them lay on the ground, others stood in groups in various corners. Clyde pressed his hands on the top of the cage, trying to push it up and over his head. He was successful. The cage lifted, however, it was only for a moment. A nearby Mirrored jumped on top of the cage, forcing it back down. Clyde was shocked by the movement, and he fell on his back, cursing. The Mirrored let out a hissing noise, a mixture of a laugh and a scream. Clyde shook his head and stuck his tongue out at the creature.

"Piss off." Clyde said.

The Mirrored looked down at Clyde through the bars of the cage, the charred face pressing against the bars. Clyde looked in the other direction, paying no heed to the creature that prevented him from escaping. Even if I did get out, it would be no use, Clyde thought. Mark had possession of both Hooks, therefore, his Energy was unstoppable. Clyde's body felt groggy, as if he was injected with a vaccine or something. His eyes were heavy, his vision blurry, and his body was warm. Clyde's head pounded with every heartbeat that slammed his chest. Not again, Clyde thought. I felt like this already one time, I don't need to feel the same way all over again. Despite how Clyde was feeling, there was one thing that he had to do.

I must get out here.

I need to get Serena and Jeremy out of here too. I brought both into this mess, I should be the one to fix it and bring them to safety. There is only one problem. How can I? Mark has all of us in his grip. As far as I know, no help would be coming to get us at all. We are all trapped in Mark's grip. With the Energy, he can do whatever he wants with us.

We are his playthings.

Clyde gulped and almost threw up at the thought of being poked and prodded. He felt like Jemma, naked and tied down, with nowhere to go. Mark paced up and down. The Mirrored followed his every move, their charred faces and black eyes watching him move. What is he waiting for? Clyde thought. He has all three of us. Why not do it now? Clyde thought too soon. Mark approached Clyde's cave.

"It's time." Mark said.

The Mirrored-on top of Clyde's cage moved. Clyde watched as the cage above him floated in the air.

Then Clyde ran.

Mirrored chased after him. Clyde knew that it was hopeless. He got to the front door of Martins before being tackled from behind. The Mirrored scratched and felt Clyde, ripping his clothes to hold him down. Clyde screamed as the nails from the creatures scratched his skin, making marks and drawing blood. Blood flowed from the little cuts, dripping down Clyde's' arms and legs.

"Bring him to the front alter please." Mark said.

The Mirrored hauled Clyde over as he screamed. Clyde flailed. He had never struggled in his life, however, there was always a first. The Mirrored brought Clyde to the stone alter. Clyde's shirt was taken off him, exposing his chest. His jeans were kept on as Clyde was thrown onto the alter. Clyde screamed in pain. His wrists and ankles were placed in the restraints. Mark stood over him, watching Clyde try to get away.

"Comfortable?" Mark asked.

Clyde spat in Mark's face. Mark wiped it off as Clyde tried to get out of the restraints. Clyde then slowed down, his body beginning to feel weak again. Mark motioned for the walls that blocked the windows to be moved, letting in the setting sunlight. The Mirrored backed away for a bit, then came closer to Mark, as he stood at the podium again.

"Tonight, the curse will be lifted. Tonight, I will change the course of history. I will be free of the bond that these Hooks have on me."

Mark held up the Hooks and the Mirrored hissed, as if they were a holy relic. Mark showed the creatures The Hooks, waving it in front of them.

"Tonight. I shall kill one more lover, then another. Soon,

the curse will allow me to live a normal life, a blessed life without any death. I'll be able to be a man again, however, I won't be bound to The Hooks. I'll be able to hold The Energy on my own. For the first time in recorded history, we will have a man with Energy in the modern world, a modern wizard will be created!"

The Mirrored cheered with their strange sounds. Clyde tried to get the noise out of his head, but it tortured him. Mark had bound him to it, torturing him through sound. Brilliant, Clyde thought. When the cheer was done, Clyde relaxed and tried to get the restraints loose. It was no good. Mark looked around the room.

"Bring out the other two, get them ready." Mark said.

The Mirrored went over to the other cage, who took out Serena and Jeremy.

"Leave them alone!" Clyde shouted.

Mark turned to him and pointed a finger at Clyde. Clyde seized and screamed. He looked on his chest and saw a burn mark appear. Clyde struggled violently as the mark went down the middle of his chest, then stopped. Clyde couldn't scream anymore. He struggled to fill his lungs with air and flailed on the alter.

"Not another word." Mark said.

Clyde nodded. I understand but you can go fuck yourself, Clyde thought. Mark smiled.

"I'm glad that we understand each other." Mark said.

Serena and Jeremy tried to get away, however, they were restrained to the other stone alters near Clyde. All three of them, tied down and at the mercy of Mark. He's going to torture us one by one, then kill us. Our deaths will give him enough Energy to break free of his curse. What was his curse in the beginning? Was it to kill lovers because he was not loved in return? I want to know how to stop this man before he ruins us all, Clyde thought. The situation is desperate. No one is coming for us and when he is done, Mark will probably level Martins with the rest of the crater, to make it look like that the entire city was hit by a large earthquake and nothing else.

There was only one problem with Mark doing that.

I was the earthquake. I created this mess. Clyde looked off

to the right to see Serena. She struggled to get out of the re-
straints, but eventually stopped. Jeremy had not moved since he
was restrained down. Clyde looked up at Mark, who stood over
him.

"We will now begin." Mark said.

Clyde struggled to get away, but he couldn't. He was
trapped. His friends were trapped. Clyde watched as Mark went
over to Serena. She screamed as he touched her, but Clyde
couldn't tell if he was torturing her or not.

"Leave her alone!" Clyde shouted.

He struggled violently, so much that he could feel some
of the restraints waning. Mark turned over to him and waved
as hand. Clyde felt weak. A massive headache pounded in his
head, banging against his temples. Sweat poured down his face
and his movements were sluggish. Despite this, Clyde fought
on. Mark was surprised and waved another hand. Clyde coughed
and choked, phlegm and mucus erupting from his mouth. Clyde
struggled to breath, as his mouth was filled from the stuff. Clyde
tried to throw up, but he couldn't. The phlegm and mucus swirled
around in his mouth, causing him to choke and sputter every-
where. Mark watched with angst. Clyde still struggled and then he
finally threw up. The throw up landed all over Mark, who tried to
shake it off, but couldn't. A steady stream of it came from Clyde
and when he stopped, Mark was covered head to toe in mucus and
phlegm. In a rage, Mark fought against the stuff that covered him,
however, Clyde noticed something. Mark was trapped it in. Clyde
felt the Energy in him, just a tiny bit, however, it was enough for
him to cause this damage to Mark. Mark used his Energy to burn
off the stuff that covered him. Fire came from his eyes and hands,
burning the new like stuff away. While Mark was doing this, Clyde
struggled in the restraints and got his ankles, then his wrists
freed. Mark was too busy to notice, and he screamed in a rage.

"It's finally time! Enough of this!" Mark shouted.

Mark produced a knife and held it over Serena. Serena
screamed and Mark brought it down halfway, then stopped. A
noise came from the outside. Everyone heard it. Mark went right
past Clyde, ignoring the fact that he could have been free. The

Mirrored joined Mark in seeing what came towards them. Mark's face dropped.

A swarm of Boeing AH-64 Apache Attack Helicopters came towards them, bearing the symbol of the United States Army. Mark noticed that on the outsides of the crater, were US Soldiers, in various land vehicles, support vehicles, and so much more.

Mark screwed up his face in anger.

"Get them!" Mark shouted.

In a steady stream, the Mirrored ran out from Martins and down into the crater, where the battle would take place. When Mark moved out of the way, Clyde noticed the helicopters. So help at last, Clyde thought. Mark went over to Serena, made sure that she was tied down and had the knife in his hand.

"You first, then your friends!" Mark shouted.

This was Clyde's chance. He jumped off the alter and knocked Mark to the side. The knife went off to the right and disappeared into the darkness. Mark threw Clyde off him and delivered a right hook. Clyde fell and landed on top of Serena, Mark grabbed Clyde and threw him back onto the alter, slamming his back. Screaming for air, Clyde delivered a left hook into Mark's jaw. Clyde's hand hurt from the impact as Mark was thrown off him. Serena and Jeremy struggled to get out of the restraints, trying to assist Clyde. Mark landed a kick into Clyde after he got up from the alter. Clyde slowly gained his Energy back, however, he was still weak compared to Mark. Mark placed his hand on the ground. A firepit appeared out of the ground, with a roaring fire in it already. Mark held The Hooks over the pit.

"If I can't kill you or her, then I can kill you both. I'll come back. The curse hasn't been lifted." Mark said.

Clyde screamed as he ran towards Mark. Mark was about to let The Hooks go, but Clyde got to him first. An anger exploded inside of Clyde, something that he was not sure where it came from. Mark dropped The Hooks as the two grappled on the ground. Jeremy got out of his restraints, then went over to Serena to free her.

"Come on, we have to go." Jeremy said.

"What about Clyde?" Serena asked.

"We have to safe ourselves." Jeremy said.

Serena knew that this was not what she wanted, however, she knew that Jeremy was right. Clyde got the upper hand in the battle and pushed Mark to the ground, before delivering a kick to his chest and head. Blood flowed from Clyde and Mark's wounds, however, both were not ready to give up just yet. Clyde charged and Mark moved out of the way. Mark grabbed The Hooks and threw them into the firepit. Clyde stopped short and began to scream. His toes began to burn slowly. The pain was unbearable. Mark laughed as Clyde struggled to get close to him. The fire climbed up his legs and Clyde tripped. Mark stood over him, nothing affecting him at all.

"It's over Clyde." Mark said.

Mark tried to get away, but couldn't. What? Clyde thought. He looked at Serena, who had her outstretched hand. Mark tried to get away, but the Energy wrapped around him, preventing him from moving. Clyde smiled. The fire slowly overtook him, and he screamed, however, Mark was going through the same thing. I guess we are both going to die. None of us will ever use The Hooks again. As Clyde's body burned, he saw Serena standing there, eyes full of tears.

"Clyde!!!!!" Serena shouted.

It was the last thing that Clyde hear before his entire world went black. Mark was in complete disbelief. The curse had to have been lifted. Why am I dying? Mark thought. He would never finish his thought. His screams echoed as the fire consumed him from the legs upward and he became nothing but a pile of ashes where he stood. Where Clyde had been was all ashes as well. Both piles met in the middle, mixing in with each other. No one would have ever known that they were there, however, there was only one issue.

Two witnessed their deaths.

And those same two descended down to the bottom of the crater.

Of the decades of service that Riley Sellers had done for the United States Army, this was the first ever instance in which an entire city caved in on itself. Riley had served in the Army since he was eighteen. He started off in an Infantry Unit that had long since perished in combat. Riley was not interested in girls, women, or a relationship, so he made a career out of the Army. When he returned from his first tour in '86, he buried both his parents, sold their house, and lived off the savings that his parents had. Riley had nothing to lose.

Other than my life.

Now in 2021, Riley was one of the youngest promoted Generals of the United States Army, having been promoted last year at 54. It was because of his service and undying loyalty to his country that everyone knew that he was right for the job. Riley did not disappoint. When President Carmen Mooney called him on the phone about Casper, Riley knew that he would be in for one of the biggest military operations in Military History. The phone rang and Riley picked it up.

"Yes, Mr. President?" Riley asked.

"Have you reached Casper?"

"We are over it now Commander, however, the situation has changed."

"How so?"

"We have unidentified enemies coming at our troops sir. Do I have permission to engage?" Riley asked.

"Permission to engage the enemy. Bring them all down, General Sellers, and extract the survivors immediately."

Riley was about to respond when he looked down below. Two blobs descended from a large island in the center of the crater.

"General?"

"We have two survivors I sight, sir. I think that's all we have."

"Engage the enemy and extract the survivors. Return to Washington when your mission is complete."

"Will do, sir."

The phone clicked off and Riley sighed. He ran a hand across his bald head, wishing that he had his long blonde hair. I lost it all on the job, Riley thought.

Serena looked at the two piles of ashes. Clyde and Mark were gone, the Energy consumed them both. Fighting back tears, Serena found The Hooks amongst Mark's ashes.

"We better go."

Serena looked at Jeremy. It was the first time that he spoke since getting free. Serena held The Hooks in her hands. The Energy coursed through her, and she felt different. I can't explain why I feel this way. Is it because I am real? Serena thought. Jeremy led her outside of Martins. The same rope that Clyde used earlier was still there. Jeremy wrapped the rope around himself and handed the slack to Serena.

"Take it." Jeremy said.

"Ok." Serena said.

She wrapped the rope around her waist, turned around, and slowly began the descent down the crater. Serena held onto The Hooks as tight as she could. With her other hand, Serena slowly lowered herself down. Thankfully, the Mirrored were down in the crater and not on the island where Jeremy was. Serena looked up to see him standing near the edge of the cliff, heels dug in. Jeremy fed the rope as Serena lowered herself down. She got about halfway when she turned and noticed the helicopters. The Military, Serena thought. When Clyde brought down the entire city, he should have known that something like this was going to happen. I wish Clyde told me about his plan.

Now I will never know.

Clyde is dead.

For now, Serena thought. A smile spread across her face. I'll go with the plan, but I don't want Jeremy to know. The less he knows, the better, Serena thought. She continued to lower herself until she got to the bottom of the crater. The crater was now a mess. The Mirrored were gathered in a long line. The Apache Helicopters fired at the creatures from above, however, the Mirrored took the blasts, then charged. The US Military charged down all sides of the crater, surrounding the Mirrored. The Mirrored created a large U-shaped formation and let the soldiers charge for them, It was a bloodbath. Jeremy must be impatient, Serena thought. She hurried down the rest of the way until she reached the bottom. From the top, Jeremy watched as Serena hit the bottom of the crater. Jeremy took the rope from his waist and wrapped it around the flagpole. He then made himself a harness and lowered himself down the cliff. Above, the Apache Helicopters flew in all directions, firing at the Mirrored. The Mirrored were not invincible to bullets, so they died instantly. Charred flesh and skin flew in all directions as the helicopters and the soldiers on the ground, blasted the creatures into oblivion. The Mirrored excelled when they got close to the soldiers, charging them, and flinging them off to the side like ragdolls. Some of the Mirrored ripped open the soldiers, tearing them apart with their hands. The soldiers formed ranks and opened fire with M-16s, Ak-47s, and other high-powered weapons. They advanced slowly as they fired. The Mirrored did not seem to give up, as many of them continued to appear. The Helicopters flew all around the crater, trying to find the source of where these creatures were coming from. Serena waited for Jeremy to reach the bottom of the cliff. Serena was surprised that he made it down as fast as he did. When Jeremy got to the bottom, he undid his harness and grabbed Serena's hand.

"We got to go." Jeremy said.

"You're hurting my hand." Serena said.

Jeremy didn't seem to care and dragged her towards the US Military. The soldiers had the upper hand in the fight now, slowly pushing the Mirrored back further away from them. The constant firing from the guns and the blasts from the Helicopters echoed in their ears. The soldiers saw them.

"We got survivors! I repeat we got survivors!"

"Get those two out of here immediately!"

"Copy that."

The soldiers ran towards Jeremy and Serena. The Mirrored chased after them, however, the soldiers formed around the two and fired. Bullets ripped apart the Mirrored. The creatures exploded into pieces of charred flesh and skin. Their screams were just as scary, as the soldiers had never experienced this before. Jeremy and Serena were escorted to a helicopter that landed. Inside, were more soldiers, and an older man. He was completely bald and dressed in a military uniform. The pins that lined one side of his uniform told Jeremy and Serena that this man was either an officer or a general. He man wore a pair of sunglasses, that when removed, showed light blue eyes. The man held out a hand.

"General Riley Sellers. You two must be the only survivors left."

"I'm Jeremy and this is Serena." Jeremy said.

"Nice to meet you both. We have lots to discuss." Riley said.

He turned to the pilot.

"All right, wrap it up and let's get out of here." Riley said.

The helicopter slowly rose into the air. All around, the Mirrored were scattered, dead on the crater floor. The soldiers were slowly pulling back, as there was nothing left for them to do. Riley looked at the island that held the ruins of Martins.

"That must be where those creatures are coming from." Riley said.

"You have to take us back there." Serena said.

Riley looked at her.

"Are you serious?" riley asked.

"I left something that was important." Serena said.

Riley watched as in her hands appeared two jars.

"What do you need?" Riley asked.

"Ashes."

"Ashes?" Jeremy asked.

"I need Clyde's ashes before you blow up the place." Serena said.

"Why didn't you get it when we were up there?" Jeremy asked.

"There is no time to argue. Take us over there." Riley snapped.

The pilot drove the helicopter over towards Martins. The vehicle hovered over it just enough so Serena could jump off and get back on. Serena let herself go down. Jeremy sighed and followed her.

"You don't have to come with me." Serena said.

"I owe something to Clyde. I know that you don't like me

but the least I can do for my friend is there for you." Jeremy said.

"Whatever." Serena snorted.

She went into Martins. Jeremy followed. Serena looked around for the ashes of Clyde and Mark. I can't let him see that I'm taking both piles of ashes, but Jeremy must have figured it out already, Serena thought. Serena found the ashes. They had not moved since both Clyde and Mark died. Strange, Serena thought. The ashes had not mixed in together, which was a good sign. Serena stood and looked at the piles. I can't remember which one was Clyde's or not. She then sighed and scooped up the furthest pile. This one must be Clyde's, Serena thought. She didn't have to scoop up the ashes at all. The ashes went into the jar all by themselves. Jeremy stood in amazement. There was no wonder why Clyde loved this girl, Jeremy thought. Serena closed the lid on the jar and handed it to Jeremy, as if she knew that he was standing there. The ashes did the same thing in the other jar. Serena just shook her head as she did this.

"Come on!"

It was Riley's voice, shouting over the whirring of the helicopter. Serena and Jeremy left without saying a word. The two left Martin's and got back into the helicopter. The pilot took off and the Apache Helicopters all flew in a formation back to Washington, D.C. Serena and Jeremy sat in two of the seats, facing forwards, while Riley sat in a seat across from them. Serena held onto the jars, one in her hand and the other in between her legs. I'm not going to let these drop, Serena thought. She held Clyde's ashes in her hands. Soon, I'll be with you again. Mark's ashes, which was the jar in between her legs, she could care less about. I don't need you, Serena thought. He caused us nothing but trouble this entire time. Riley looked at Serena.

"I'm going to assume that you won't tell me why you need those jars until we get back to Washington." Riley said.

"That's right. Classified." Serena said.

Riley leaned back in his seat.

"You two were the only survivors of the attack on Casper, which will no doubt go into the history books. Why don't you two explain to me what went on at Casper or is that classified too?"

Riley asked.

"Do you want the long or the short version?" Jeremy asked.

Riley's interest was piqued.

"Either one. It's still a long way until we get to Washington." Riley said.

Jeremy looked at Serena.

"Don't look at me for permission. I don't give a fuck what you do." Serena said.

"Nice language for a lady." Riley said.

Serena gave Riley a dirty look and for the first time in the military, Riley was scared for his life.

Jeremy leaned back in his seat.

"It started with those." Jeremy said.

Riley looked. Serena had The Hooks stuffed in her pocket, the tops of the hooks stood out.

"Really?" Riley asked.

Jeremy nodded.

"Yup."

"It also started with a guy named Clyde."

Behind them, the island that held onto Martins exploded and crashed into the crater. Riley leaned back and listened to the story as Jeremy told it from the very beginning.

Hello and Goodbye

Serena and Jeremy were the stars of the mainstream media for weeks on end. Riley listened to the story firsthand from Jeremy, who also got to meet President Carmen Mooney when they landed in Washington, D.C. Serena had never been in any other city other than Casper. Jeremy was used to the hustle and bustle of city life, so he had an easier time to adjust. Riley showed them to a hotel, where the two of them each had a room, paid for by the US Government. Over the next few days, reporters from all over the country came to them, asking and prodding them for questions. Jeremy didn't hesitate to take the opportunity to become famous and he took this opportunity seriously. On the other hand, Serena, hid from the world. During the weeks that she and Jeremy were in D.C, she only came out for comments when Riley and President Mooney came out. Other than that, Serena was shut inside of her hotel room. The first two nights, she stayed in the shower, running the hot water to such a high temperature, that she couldn't feel her skin anymore. Jeremy tried multiple times to reach out to Serena, however, she shut him off. He's not like Clyde. He's nothing like Clyde and I don't want anything to do with him, Serena thought. Serena was such a recluse, that she did not even know that Jeremy went home by the end of the second week in D.C. The media must have had enough of him, Serena thought. She watched from the hotel window as a car took Jeremy away and drove him back to the airport so he could fly back to Massachusetts. Not like he is going back to anything, Serena thought. The summer heat in D.C. was unbearable at this time of year, so Serena wore a lose fitting top, with a pair of shorts, panties, and a sport bra. All of this she made. The Hooks were on the nightstand next to the bed that she slept on. The hotel room that she had was of decent size, with two large beds, a TV, a couch, a mini fridge, a counter, and a small kitchen. The bathroom contained the sink and the shower, where Serena spent a lot of time recently. I might as well spend my entire life in the shower, Serena thought.

But I can't.

I must get out of this and fulfill the promise that I made to Clyde.

A knock rapped at the door. Serena jumped in surprise.

"Serena?"

It was Riley. The General had been one of the focuses of the mainstream media since they arrived. The door opened and Riley came in.

"What?" Serena asked.

"I just wanted to inform you that Jeremy is gone." Riley said.

"I saw."

Riley was taken aback by her response, and she sat on one of the beds. Serena turned and looked at him.

"What do you want?" Serena asked.

"Well, do you have a place to go?" Riley asked.

"Why are you asking me? Are you kicking me out?"

"Well.... Not really but..."

"Just say that you are kicking me out, dammit!" Serena shouted.

Riley put his hands up.

"Christ, you don't have to be so pushy. Yes, we are kicking you out, but we want to know if you have any family or place to go..."

"I don't have any family. I'm by myself. All I knew was Casper, but that is all gone now." Serena said.

Riley nodded.

"You have until tomorrow morning to leave. The first flight out of D.C. to Boston will be yours." Riley said.

"So that's all you wanted to tell me?" Serena asked.

"Yup." Riley nodded.

"I guess the media didn't believe you or Jeremy." Serena said.

"How do you know?" Riley asked.

"Classified." Serena said.

"Makes sense." Riley nodded.

The thing was, Serena knew that Riley knew that she could

read minds. The Energy was strong in Serena. It filled up her body like nothing else had. She hadn't eaten in days, however, the Energy provides, and Serena was not complaining about it. Riley got up off the bed.

"Well, I'll leave you to pack your things. You have until tomorrow morning." Riley said.

"Whatever." Serena said, facing the window.

She stayed like that until the door closed and she was certain that Riley was out of the hotel room. Serena then went into the bathroom, took off her clothes, turned the water on, and cried. The hot water ran over her as her tears mixed with the water that came over her. I hate this, Serena thought. She stayed in the shower for a long time and after a while, she turned the water off. Serena just stood in the bathroom, naked and looking at herself. Serena often looked at the door, waiting for Clyde to walk in. I miss him so much, Serena thought. She then went out of the room and made some food. A box of pizza appeared, along with soda. Serena closed all the window shades and put the 'Do Not Disturb' sign on the front door.

Serena then locked the door.

The pizza was gone in seconds, as hunger took over Serena. Sure she hadn't eaten in days, however, there was only so much that she could take without eating. Serena downed the soda in mere seconds, then threw the cup against the wall. The cup disappeared into a gray like mist. The pizza box did the same. Serena propped herself up on the other bed and flicked on the TV. She didn't want to flip through the channels, so she just kept the mainstream news on. The newscaster talked about Casper and what was to be done with the city. Serena watched as the TV focused on the large crater where the city used to be. The fleet of construction vehicles road around the entire area, filling in the crater with dirt and stone. All paid for by the United States Government, Serena thought. The news jumped to lines of people applying for jobs. A lot of people were eager to do something, so this was one of the ways to get people to work. Crowds of people formed assembly lines to pick up all the trash. Environmental groups were especially keen on the effort.

"We want to turn this space into a large forest." Said one.

Serena shook her head. Crazies, Serena thought.

Dumpsters lined the top of the crater, as makeshift ramps were created to allow the trash to be brought out. They had only done one section of Casper. The city itself was huge. It's going to take them some time until they finish, Serena thought. The news jumped to President Mooney. He was one of the youngest Presidents to be elected or that is what Riley told Serena. I don't know who to believe anymore, Serena thought.

"The Casper Crater will be filled over the course of a few years. We will never know what caused this or why it happened, however, members of Congress would like to create this area a National Park. There is enough land here to make it and many would like it..."

Serena toned out the voice of Mooney. Whatever, Serena thought. She curled herself up in her bed. She didn't even bother to put on any clothes. Not like anyone is going to come into the room anyways, Serena thought. She flicked off the TV, then went to bed.

Serena woke up early the next morning. A similar outfit appeared on her, this time with a different colored shirt, shorts, and underwear. Serena didn't bother to shower. I've had enough of the water to create my own pond, Serena thought. Silently, she packed up her things. The Hooks, which were on her nightstand, were the last things that she grabbed. The jars with the ashes of Clyde and Mark were placed in her carry-on bag. Serena only had the carry on. Her other clothes she could make whenever she wanted. Riley was surprisingly in front of her hotel room door. Serena peered through the peephole, saw him, and unlocked the door.

"Morning." Riley said.

He handed Serena her plane tickets.

"I'll drive you to the airport." Riley said.

Serena took the tickets.

"There's no need. I can drive myself." Serena said.

"I insist I drive." Riley said.

"I can't convince you to leave me alone, huh?" Serena said.

"Nope."

"You have a strange way of duty, General." Serena said.

"Come." Riley said.

Serena stepped out of her hotel room and followed Riley. The sun slowly rose over the horizon as Riley waved over a car for them. It was a four door Sedan and Serena had no idea what it was. Serena got into the back of the car. Riley did the same, however, he sat in the drivers seat. A couple of bodyguards came with Riley and sat in the other seats of the car. The drive to the airport was silent. The roads of D.C were crowded, as construction was going on this time of year. Riley got to the airport, which was the Ronald Reagan Washington National Airport. The sedan stopped in the drop off lane. The doors opened and Serena stepped out. Riley held out a hand.

"It was good to meet you, Serena. I hope all is well in the future." Riley said.

Serena shook Riley's hand.

"Thanks for putting up with me. It was good to meet you too." Serena said.

"Until next time?"

Serena nodded.

"Until next time."

Serena could tell that something was bothering Riley, however, she did not want to press the issue. Serena then walked into the airport. When she turned around, Riley and his crew were gone, as if they had never been out in the first place. Sighing, Serena made her way through the airport. She passed through security without any issues. Thankfully it is not crowded right now, Serena thought. I hate crowds. Serena found the gate and boarded her plane on the flight back to Logan International Airport in Boston. I've never been to Boston before. I hope that it is not like Casper, Serena thought. Her seat on the plane was towards the back, with a window seat. Riley must have thought that I wanted to see what was going on, Serena thought. The other two seats in her row were empty, which was a good thing. It didn't take long for everyone else to arrive on the flight and when the flight attendant was sure that everyone was here, the plane was cleared for liftoff. Serena looked out the window and watched as the world got smaller and smaller. She leaned in the seat and drifted off to sleep.

Serena jolted awake.

"Miss? We are here."

The flight attendant looked down on Serena.

"I'm sorry. I'll leave." Serena said.

The flight attendant left Serena. She got up and looked around. No one else was on the plane. It's just me, Serena thought. I must have been extremely tired. Serena grabbed her carry on and walked off the boarding bridge, towards the main lobby. She had never been to Boston Logan International Airport before, and Serena was impressed at the size of the place. Crowds moved in both directions, carrying dragging suitcases behind them. Children stayed close to their parents as groups boarded planes. Seats were lined front and back in large waiting areas, with little places to eat and shop in between the large walkways. Serena was just in amazement, and she found a seat to sit in. I'm so alone, Serena thought. She opened her bag. The ashes of both Clyde and Mark were there. I must dump Mark's somewhere. I don't need his. Serena thought. I only want Clyde. If he was here, then he would show me around and where to go. He's gone for now. So you are going to have to do it all on your own, Serena thought. She guessed that it was midday, as the crowds were heavy walking up and down the main walkways. Serena sighed, then got off her seat. Serena moved in the same direction of a crowd exiting the airport. Once when I get outside, I'll have no idea what to do, Serena thought. She knew no one. Except Jeremy but he was lone gone by now and I highly doubt that he would ever return to see me. I was such an asshole to him, so I don't expect him to be here, Serena thought. She got outside of the airport. Taxis, busses, and cars ran through the various lanes. Some were stopped to drop off passengers. Others were waiting to pickup people. Serena looked around. She had no idea where to go or what to do, so she found a bench further down to sit at. I can't go back into the airport and awkwardly wait. That would just be suspicious. Serena then heard a horn go off. A truck came up through the drop off lane.

It can't be.

Clyde's GMC truck was there, waiting for her. Serena went over to the truck and noticed that no one was in the drivers seat. Serena opened the driver's side door to reveal the key-fob. A note was next to it. Serena picked it up. The note read:

SERENA,

I KNOW THAT YOU DON'T LIKE ME, BUT I COULDN'T LEAVE YOU HIGH AND DRY. RILEY CALLED ME THIS MORNING AND LET ME KNOW THAT YOU LEFT, SO I ASKED A FAVOR AT THE AIRPORT TO HAVE THIS LEFT TO YOU. DON'T WORRY ABOUT THE PAPERWORK FOR THE TRUCK, I PAID FOR EVERYTHING. IF YOU DO COME BACK TO CASPER, I'LL BE WORKING WITH THE CONSTRUCTION CREWS TO HELP FILL IN THE CRATER. I KNOW THAT YOU LOVED CLYDE, MY BEST FRIEND. IF YOU ARE GOING TO BURY HIM, THEN I WOULD LIKE TO BE THERE. HE PROMISED ME SOMETHING THAT HE WOULD DO FOR ME IF I LED HIM BACK TO YOU. HOPE TO SEE YOU SOON. BEST WISHES

JEREMY

Serena couldn't believe it. Clyde, you have some strange friends. I have a feeling that he likes me, Serena thought. Push that out of your head! You are for Clyde and that's all the feelings that you have! Serena turned the note over, and it gave instructions to get to Casper or where Casper used to be. Sighing, Serena got into the GMC, plugged in the directions, and drove out of Boston. Serena was surprised that she was able to drive, as she had never driven before. This Real Life is going to be hard to get used to, Serena thought. The streets of Boston were always crowded, and Serena had a tough time finding her way through the city. She learned that it was all about being in the right lane, at the right possible time. It's a bit annoying, Serena thought. Serena drove on 1-90, heading out of Boston. The traffic was heavy at this time, as many were leaving the airport, having arrived back home. Serena knew enough to stay in the right lane and let all the other drivers pass by her. Some of them flipped her off, as she was going slow. Serena ignored them. You don't know how much

I want to flip your entire vehicle off the road, Serena thought. The Energy coursed through her, and she just ignored the other drivers. I know where I am going. I don't have to explain anything to anyone else, Serena thought. As Serena got away from Boston, the traffic let up a bit, however, she could see another snag of traffic up ahead. Great, Serena thought. After driving for a few more miles, Serena took exit 123A, heading onto 95 North towards Waltham. I've near heard of any of these places. The voice for the GPS was a female voice and Serena only shook her head. Of course Clyde would have a female voice. He never listened to me anyways, Serena thought. It took Serena a long time to get onto I-95, as the traffic to get onto the highway itself was terrible. By the time Serena got onto the highway, she was about to get hit with a truck that refused to yield. Serena slammed on the brake and put her hand on the horn. The guy, who was an older man, just looked at Serena and shrugged. Serena waited for the truck to move before getting onto the highway. The last thing I want is to cause an accident. A car was gracious enough to let Serena in and she moved onto the highway with ease. The traffic seemed to let up a bit after getting onto I-95, however, there was another snag, then another section that was open. Thank goodness I'm getting off soon, Serena thought. Serena then took exit 45B to get onto MA-2, heading towards Casper. Again, there was traffic that blocked the way when getting onto another highway, however, after that, the traffic was gone. The landscape changed around Serena. Instead of a heavily populated area, Serena was looking at a sparsely populated area. Trees and rocks were on both sides of the highway. Very little homes were close to the highway. I wonder why anyone would want to live out here, Serena thought. There was nothing around. I must be in the wrong state, Serena thought.

Nope.

She was in the right state, however, she was in an area that had no people around. This is going to be interesting, Serena thought. The directions on the GPS just told her to stay on this road, until they got to the Abbot Ave Exit. It won't be much of an exit now, Serena thought. The GPS was programmed to still have the directions to Casper when the city was still around. Serena sighed. The highway continued onwards. The signs for towns that Serena never knew passed by her on her side of the highway. On the other side, cars drove in the opposite direction. Why would you ever go back there? Serena thought. She shook her head and continued. Serena passed the signs for another highway, listed as 495. I don't want to go up there. I don't even know where I am going, Serena thought. She passed by the sign and continued. The voice for the GPS echoed, however, Serena ignored it and just looked at the map that moved on the screen near her. Technology is so great, Serena thought. Serena passed the signs for Harvard, Littleton, Devens, and Shirley. Never heard of these places before, Serena thought. The sign for Leominster came up and soon, the GPS told Serena to take the Abbot Ave exit.

There was only one problem.

That exit did not exist anymore.

Serena instead pulled into a large parking lot full of cars, trucks, and other vehicles. The city of Casper was just a large crater. A road ran from the parking lot into a large makeshift town that was created for the workers. Serena noticed that it was a massive trailer park. Lines of workers, flooded into the crater, hauling out garbage and cleaning the bottom of the crater. Makeshift ramps allowed the workers to go in and out of the crater. Fleets of construction vehicles dumped dirt and stone into the crater, trying to fill the space.

"It's just like the news." Serena said.

It was the first time that she talked out loud and her voice cracked. A car beeped behind her, and Serena moved the truck into a nearby parking spot. Another lot was on the other side of the trailer park, which was full. Another large section of trailers were stretched out on the other side of the crater, all connected by a road. This place is its own town, Serena thought. There was a large wooden structure that stat at the center of this makeshift area. Lines of people were standing outside it. They must be looking for jobs, Serena thought. She put the truck into park. The heat suddenly got to her, so she kept the truck running because the A/C was on. Now this was going to be the hard part, Serena thought.

I need to find Jeremy.

If he was here, then where am I going to find him? And how can I? Serena thought. Sighing, she started the truck again. I'm just going to have to drive around until I find him, Serena thought. At first, the idea was good, however, Serena noticed that more cars were coming onto the road. The road that was built was not built like a highway. It was just a two-lane road, made from dirt. Serena waited for a line of cars to pass by her, then she jumped into traffic. The road connected to the other trailer park at a T-Intersection. The road off to the left of her, stretched out for another trailer park, then two parking lots across from each other. Great, Serena thought. Serena went off to the right, off towards the other trailer park that was out of the way. Many of these trailer parks were all made the same, with paths that connected all of them together. Another large wooden building was here, with more people that were lined up to get a job. I can't believe that they are hiring all these people to help. A parking lot was on the left, however, Serena had to drive though the trailer park to get to it. She drove through it, allowing the other cars to drive by her. As she drove, Serena slowed down the truck. Jeremy was standing in the parking lot. Serena stopped the truck and looked at him. Jeremy looked tired. The hot sun had gotten to him, as sweat poured down his face. His clothes were a bit ripped, as he was working hard. Serena then pulled into the parking lot and got out of the truck. Jeremy came over and leaned his hand on the back, touching the tailgate.

"I thought that you would never come." Jeremy said.

"That's one way to say hello." Serena said.

"Well, hello."

"Hi."

"What do you think of this place? Everyone wants to turn it into a park or something. Others want to call it New Casper. What do you think?" Jeremy asked.

"I think that we know why I am here." Serena said.

Jeremy nodded and let out a sigh.

"Did you read the note?" Jeremy asked.

"Every word." Serena said.

"Then you are probably wondering what Clyde promised me. You know that he owes me a favor." Jeremy said.

"Clyde can explain it to me himself." Serena said.

Jeremy's eyes went wide.

"What?" Jeremy asked.

Serena went into the truck, pulled out Clyde's ashes, and The Hooks.

"We are going to bring Clyde back. We also made a deal before you came along." Serena said.

"Don't tell me that you are mad at me. How was I supposed to know that you two had those strange powers?" Jeremy asked.

"We wouldn't have bothered you, however, you compromised the entire situation and Clyde thought that you were going to tell everyone." Serena said.

"I never wanted any of this to happen." Jeremy said.

"Neither did I."

"How can you say something like that? You were never real, you were my friends imagination and now here you are, saying that you can bring him back to life and reverse everything. I don't believe you." Jeremy said.

Serena stepped forwards.

"I don't want you to believe me, however, you are the only one that I know right now. I need you to help me bury Clyde's ashes so we can bring him back to life. Will you help me? If you do, then you don't have to see me again." Serena said.

Jeremy looked at Serena and smiled. He stepped forward.

"I guess I could help you bury Clyde, but there is one thing I would like from you." Jeremy said.

"What?" Serena asked.

Jeremy ran a hand down Serena's face. Serena shuddered.

"One night with you. That is my deal." Jeremy said.

"No. I'm for Clyde." Serena said.

Jeremy shrugged.

"Ok, then I won't help you. There are tools down at the bottom of the crater. I guess you are going to have to get them yourself. I have my set in my trailer that I was going to give to you, but you want to do stuff the hard way."

"Fuck you." Serena said.

She put The Hooks and the ashes back into the GMC. Jeremy just stood there, watching Serena. Serena got into the truck and threw it in reverse. Jeremy had to dodge out of the way as Serena spun the truck around, then sped down the road. She slowed down and turned to the right, leaving Jeremy in the dust. Serena went back to where she was before, parked the truck, and went down the ramp. I need to get a shovel, Serena thought. A group of workers were going down the ramp, so Serena blended in with them. It was a miracle that she was not caught. Most of the workers wore uniforms, however, there were others that didn't. Military soldiers stood in various places, armed with weapons. I guess they don't want to take any chances, Serena thought. I'm such a fool for not asking where the tools were. Jeremy only mentioned his. He only said that because he wanted to get in your pants. He doesn't care about you, Serena thought. The tools were in a series of tool boxes, open for anyone to use. Serena went up to one of them and pulled out a shovel. Ok, now time to get out of here before anyone notices, Serena thought. Another group of workers were going up the ramp, so Serena blended in with them. When she reached the top of the ramp, Serena went over to the GMC. The doors were unlocked, and Serena put the tool down in the back seats of the truck. Clyde won't get mad at me if the truck is a bit dirty. Besides, he isn't alive yet, Serena thought. It's strange to me that I'm going to bring him back to life. He'll be grateful to me now, Serena thought. She jumped into the truck. I'll need a place to stay until nighttime. Again, the only person that I know is Jeremy and he just wants to sleep with me. No way, Serena thought. She threw the GMC intro drive and headed towards where Jeremy was. The parking lot was big enough for Serena to park the truck and just wait it out until nightfall. As she drove into the parking lot, Jeremy waited outside of his trailer. I bet its nice and cool in there, Serena thought. She parked the truck next to a group of others. Little by the little, the lot began to fill up with cars and trucks. Workers got out and headed towards the crater. They are working on this day and night, Serena thought. She kept the truck on, the air blowing into her face and all around. All the while, Jeremy just watched from the front step of his trailer.

"I can't just let the truck go on forever." Serena said.

Jeremy knows this. I know this. He's playing the waiting game. If I turn off the A/C, then I'll die in here. He knows that his trailer has A/C. Hell, all of them probably do. Fuck me, Serena thought. I'm stuck in a hard place. Do I go in and sleep with him or do I keep myself for Clyde. Clyde isn't here, Serena thought. I'm not sure if Clyde will even come back if I do this. I've slept with numerous guys who had The Hooks in their possession. I manifested for them so that they could fulfill their desires. The power of sex was a power that I wielded without remorse. I forced Clyde to fuck me when he couldn't. I broke a man using his own desire for it.

But what makes Clyde Holding so special?

He's just a man. He's like all the other men, who want sex, and move on. Clyde was surprisingly not like this, but Jeremy, that is a whole different story. Serena just stared at Jeremy. He hasn't moved, Serena thought. His stare.

God his stare is so annoying, Serena thought.

He knows that I'm going to break either way and he knows that he is right. I don't know how long I can hold out in the truck. If I give what he wants....

Don't think like that Serena. Don't play into his hand.

But what if I did.

What if I did play Jeremy. Used his desires against him. I did it to Clyde, but Clyde loves me for who I am, and he will love me even more when we are together. If I can break Jeremy, then I would have it made. Would that make me just as terrible as Mark? Just as terrible as the other owners of The Hooks? Would that make me a bad girl for going against Clyde's wishes? Why is this so fucking complicated!!! Serena thought. She pressed her hands to her head, as if she was trying to pop all the thoughts from her head and force them to explode. I could knock Jeremy out....

Serena then smiled.

It was devious. Knock Jeremy out, but let him touch me for a few minutes, just so that he thinks he is getting what he wants. Then knock him out, lock him in the bathroom of his trailer, then go bring him with me to bring Clyde back to life. It was a genius plan. A great plan. Jeremy was still out on the front step. Good, Serena thought. Let's go inside. It's hot out here. Serena switched off the GMC. Jeremy stood up on the porch. Serena watched him. Good. I want him to notice me, Serena thought. She went around and to the passengers seat of the truck, taking The Hooks with her. The Energy filled her body when she touched them. I'm still strong, Serena thought. Stronger than him, however, I must play to his desire, which won't be easy. Serena walked towards Jeremy and his trailer. The GMC was off now, and Serena put the key fob into her pocket. Jeremy cracked a smile.

"Too hot in the truck?" Jeremy asked.

"I can't let it run forever. I'll need the truck and its gas for later tonight." Serena said.

Now here is the moment of truth. Will he let me in or will I go back to the truck. Jeremy eyed Serena up and down.

"Would you like to come inside? I promise I wont touch you in anyway." Jeremy said.

"That would be fine. Thanks." Serena said.

Good, he took the bait. Now let's see how aggressive his bite is, Serena thought. Jeremy led her into the trailer. It was a simple one floor trailer, with a bed off to the right. There was a couch that was also a fold out bed. A TV was mounted to one of the walls. Two windows were behind the couch. A small sink and kitchen area were in front of the couch. At the back of the trailer was the bathroom and a set of small bunks.

"The US Government didn't spare any expense. They built most of this in a week, which was impressive for government workers." Jeremy said.

"It's nice."

Jeremy sat down on the couch. Serena stood by the door.

"Now they got so many workers here, there aren't enough jobs to go around. They have been promoting people to make more job openings. I don't know how that makes any sense, but it's working. More people arrive here by the day, hoping to work for a few hours or stay until the place is completely done. Do you want a drink or something?" Jeremy asked.

"That would be nice, please." Serena said.

Jeremy went to the fridge and grabbed two water bottles. Serena sat on the other end of the couch, staying far away from Jeremy as possible. I must ease myself into this, Serena thought. The A/C in the trailer was nice and Serena felt herself cooling off nicely. The TV was on, however, none of them were paying attention. Jeremy sipped on his water, then spoke.

"When do you plan on going out?" Jeremy asked.

"Tonight. When most of the workers are not working." Serena said.

"That's going to be hard." Jeremy said.

"Why?"

"They have a night shift cleaning out the garbage and emptying the dumpsters. Work does not stop here at night, it just continues."

"I see. So that would make the situation critical." Serena said.

She inched on the couch, closing the gap between Jeremy. Jeremy didn't say anything and just continued sipping his water. He suspects nothing. What an idiot, Serena thought.

"Serena?" Jeremy asked.

"Yes?" Serena asked.

"Is there another reason why you came into the trailer? It can't be because of the A/C or is it something more?" Jeremy asked.

Here is my chance, Serena thought.

Serena moved closer to Jeremy, sitting beside him. Serena finished off her water.

"You know what I realized in the truck. Want to know what it is?" Serena said.

Jeremy nodded.

"Sure."

Serena grabbed Jeremy's hand and placed it on her left thigh. Jeremy tensed, but didn't move.

"I realized that Clyde was not here, so I could do what I please with my body." Serena said.

Jeremy was in shock, his eyes wide. Serena smiled.

"You..you want....to?" Jeremy asked.

Serena moved Jeremy's hand to her shirt, his fingers just touching the top of her shirt, feeling her skin.

"I think we can kill a few minutes, don't you think?" Serena asked.

I got him! Serena thought. Now time for the kill.

"I think so." Jeremy said.

In a quick movement, Jeremy grabbed Serena and pulled her on top of him. Perfect! Serena thought. She felt his hands go under her shirt and she wrapped her arms around his neck. The two kissed, then pulled away, then kissed again, passionately. Jeremy managed to slip off Serena's shirt and bra with one movement. Completely bare chested, Serena then went for the kill. Smiling, she raised both hands over her head as Jeremy touched her chest. Then in a quick movement, Serena brought both hands down on Jeremy's head, knocking him out. Serena moved out of the way as Jeremy's body slumped to the floor. Serena reached for sports bra and shirt, putting them on quickly.

"Never in a million years, you creep." Serena said.

Serena got down and grabbed Jeremy's body. She created rope from the air and tied his wrists and ankles. To add a touch, Serena took a sock, stuffed it into Jeremy's mouth, then gagged him with a piece of duct tape. Serena looked at her handiwork, then picked up Jeremy and placed him on the bed. She found the shades and closed them all, then blocked the room with a moveable wall that separated the bedroom from the rest of the trailer. Thank goodness for those, Serena thought. She then turned the TV on and raided his fridge. There was nothing but snacks, so Serena took everything out and ate it while some war movie played on one of the channels. Serena grabbed a water bottle and swirled the water in her mouth, then spit it out in the sink, trying to get the taste of Jeremy out of her mouth.

"Now we wait for nightfall." Serena said.

She smiled. I fucking did it! I resisted a man!

Now let's hope that Jeremy doesn't spill the beans about this. Serena knew that her plan was good, however, she forgot about that crucial part. I don't want Jeremy to tell anyone what I did, not even Clyde. It could hurt our relationship.

Clyde doesn't have to know. Clyde isn't here, Serena thought.

Night came and Serena went to check in on Jeremy. He was awake, dazed and confused about the entire thing. Serena went onto the bed with him and lay next to him, teasing him with a touch.

"Are you going to be a good boy?" Serena asked.

Jeremy nodded furiously.

"Ok." Serena said.

She removed the gag, in which Jeremy almost threw up on the bed.

"What the hell was that for! First it was ok, then you fucking hit me in the head. What the hell Serena!" Jeremy shouted.

"Now, Jeremy, don't get upset with me. You knew that you couldn't have me, so I gave you the second-best thing. I let you touch me for a bit and then I knocked you out so that I could just chill in your trailer, eat your food, and now, I'm going to let you help me with Clyde." Serena said.

"That wasn't fair at all, Serena. Not fair." Jeremy said, struggling.

"Whatever." Serena said, getting off the bed.

"Are you going to untie me?" Jeremy asked.

Serena looked at him, then sighed.

"I might as well." Serena said.

I don't want to, but you must help me, Serena thought. She grabbed Jeremy by the front of his shirt, turned him around, and undid his wrists. Serena then undid his ankles. Surprisingly, Jeremy didn't try anything. Serena then got off the bed and let Jeremy rub the life back into his wrists. Jeremy got off the bed and noticed the pile of trash that accumulated next to the door.

"You ate my food?" Jeremy asked.

Serena shrugged.

"I was hungry." Serena said.

"I'm going to have to get more at the local store they set up." Jeremy said.

"Good for you. Let's go." Serena said.

"Are we doing this now?" Jeremy asked.

"Yup. We have no choice. It's now or some other time. Don't you want your friend back?" Serena asked.

Jeremy had nothing to say to this and followed Serena outside of the trailer. The air was cool, and it hit both like a truck. Serena did not bother to look back to see if Jeremy was following her. I don't care, Serena thought. She reached the truck first and unlocked it. Serena took The Hooks and the jars of ashes and put them in the front seat with her. Serena hopped into the drivers seat and started the truck. Jeremy just made it to the passenger side door and hopped in as Serena drove. The Hooks were across her lap and the jars were in the cupholders in the middle console. Jeremy strapped himself in and Serena drove out of the trailer park. There were not many vehicles out currently at night, which was a good thing for Serena.

"We need to find a quiet place to bury the ashes and hope that I can use the Energy to bring Clyde back to life." Serena said.

Jeremy only nodded.

"Whatever." Jeremy said.

"What you upset that you couldn't get into my pants?" Serena asked.

"Fuck you."

"I would never think of it." Serena said.

The two were quiet as Serena drove the truck away from the crater. There was another road that led away from the crater and Serena realized that it was a road that led to a makeshift cemetery. Everything is makeshift around here now, Serena thought. The cemetery was out of the way, with only one main entrance to it. The fencing around it was flimsy and Serena noticed that people were already breaking in, hoping to find something among the bodies. People make me sick, Serena thought. She pulled the truck through the road and stopped. Lines of grave stones were scattered on both sides. Serena pulled the truck halfway up the road and put the vehicle in park.

"Come on." Serena said.

She got out of the truck and grabbed the shovel. Jeremy was

reluctant to get out, however, one look from Serena convinced him otherwise. You would think that he would be concerned about his friend? Serena thought. No, he just wants his part of the bargain. I wonder what Clyde promised him? I'm going to find out very soon. Serena grabbed Clyde's ash jar and brought it out with her. The cemetery was created out a large patch of dried out dirt. Very little grass grew out here, as if the area was always a desert. Clyde created this mess. I hope he can fix it, Serena thought. She handed the shovel to Jeremy.

"Dig."

"Where?" Jeremy asked.

"Where I'm standing." Serena said.

She moved to allow him to dig. Jeremy scowled, then began to dig in the spot that Serena pointed at. Jeremy flung the piles of dirt off the side and made a hole deep enough for Serena to cover the jar. Serena placed the jar in the hole, then Jeremy covered it with the dirt. Serena took The Hooks and held them in her hand. She thought of Clyde, his look, his clothes, his personality. Everything about Clyde that Serena could think about, she did. The ground shook. Jeremy dropped the shovel, startled. A hand reached out of the dirt. The dirt rippled and moved, revealing Clyde Holding. Serena was in shock. The Hooks shook in her hand, the Energy flowing through her. Clyde stood there. His skin was all burnt. His clothes were tattered. Serena struggled to hold a gaze to him. He's truly back from the dead, Serena thought.

"Serena?" Clyde asked.

Serena tried to hold back tears, but she couldn't. She charged for Clyde and wrapped her arms around her. Clyde tensed, however, he awkwardly hugged her back.

"I missed you." Serena said, crying.

The tears from Serena hissed off Clyde's warm skin. He's warm, Serena thought. Clyde just gulped.

I can't believe I'm alive. I'm back, Clyde thought. Serena pulled away from Clyde.

"Clyde. It worked. Everything worked." Serena said.

"So you are Real now?" Clyde asked.

Serena nodded.

"Yeah. I am."

Clyde looked at Jeremy. Jeremy?

"Jeremy?" Clyde asked.

Jeremy was in shock this entire time and had no idea what to say.

"It's good to have you back man, but now that you are here, I want the thing that you promised me." Jeremy said.

Promised? Clyde thought.

"I don't understand, Jeremy. I may be back, but everything is a bit fuzzy to me." Clyde said.

Oh no, Serena thought. This isn't good. Does that mean he lost some of his memory? Jeremy sighed.

"You promised me that you would help me bring Alexandria back to life! That was the deal if I led you to Serena." Jeremy said, voice raised.

"I think I remember something like that." Clyde said.

"Well, you better remember."

"Are you going to kill me again?" Clyde asked.

Clyde does have a good point, Serena thought. Jeremy can't kill Clyde, as I would just bring him back again. Jeremy stood there, completely baffled and confused. Clyde looked at him.

"So what?" Clyde asked.

Jeremy shrugged.

"I'm not going to do anything. I'm going back to the Reservoir and bury Alexandria. I'll probably work here until the crater is filled and then find another job somewhere else. Good bye Clyde, Serena." Jeremy said.

He then left, walking away on the road by himself. At least he was nice enough to leave the shovel, Serena thought. Clyde looked at Serena. He looked at his skin, charred and burnt. When he rubbed an itch, bits of ash drifted to the ground. Clyde then sighed.

"Look at me. I'm a mess." Clyde said.

"Clyde. I don't care how you look. I'll still love you." Serena said.

Clyde was about to respond when The Hooks began to glow. Serena dropped them on the ground as a light came from them.

Serena and Clyde covered their eyes as the flash enveloped them. A blue-white figure appeared. He was an old man, with a long white beard and a lone blue robe that covered him. A hood was over his face, covering it.

"Greetings." The man said.

"Who are you?" Clyde asked.

The man looked at them and threw back his hood.

"My name is Bowryn. I was the first owner of The Hooks, long before any of you." Bowryn said.

"What do you want?" Clyde asked.

Bowryn laughed.

"What do I want? I want to congratulate you both."

"What?" Clyde and Serena said.

Bowryn continued to laugh, then stopped.

"Yes, I've come to congratulate you. For centuries, I have been possessed by many others, hoping to use the Energy for their desires, however, none of the owners were as ruthless as Mark." Bowryn said.

"What was his curse exactly? He never explained it right." Clyde said.

"Explained it? He interpreted it wrong. He wanted Energy to use for himself, in which I refused. So when he got upset, I cursed him to live forever and only forced him to cause bad things until he repented. This did the opposite effect and he turned to evil. Only by killing two lovers that were apart, could Mark reverse his curse and he didn't."

"Why did you choose that specifically? The lovers being apart?" Serena asked.

"Mark only had the capacity to kill after going through so many lifetimes. The power of love was one of his weaknesses. It was really your bond that killed Mark, not the Energy." Bowryn said.

"So all we had to do was say that we loved each other, and Mark would have died?" Clyde asked.

Bowryn nodded. "Yup."

"I'd wished I'd known sooner. It would have saved a lot of trouble." Clyde said, irritated.

Bowryn let out a nervous laugh.

"I know, I should have explained earlier, however, it was not my time to come out and reveal myself as long as Mark was here, but I come to you now to reveal something else."

"Go on." Serena said.

"You two have proven the ability to master the Energy, while also keeping a pretty stable relationship. I must destroy The Hooks, however, you two will keep your powers, if you promise to stay only with each other and love each other as much as you do now, for all of eternity. You two will never die and will always be young and have vibrant Energy. If you two choose to have children, your Energy will go away and it will pass to your children, so you must choose wisely. Now, I must do something to Clyde. You can't be looking like that." Bowryn said.

He stretched out his hand. Clyde was shocked as he was lifted into the air and when Clyde came back down, he was completely healed. His skin was vibrant, and he wore a new set of clothes. Clyde looked at himself. He looked nice. Serena too, was lifted into the air and was brought back down into new clothes. Clyde realized that he was wearing a white tux that was tailored to his body. Clyde, eyes wide, looked at Serena. She wore a beautiful white dress, with a few floral designs on it. The dress was tailored to her body, and it fit nicely. With every step she took, Clyde could have sworn that Serena was gliding.

"Now that is in order. I must get rid of The Hooks, therefore getting rid of myself." Bowryn said.

"Are you sure you want to do that?" Clyde asked.

Bowryn laughed.

"Clyde, I've seen enough of this world to know when it is time to go. Another thing before I go. Both of you can't use the Energy around others. It must be kept a secret amongst you two and your children must keep the secret as well. If it gets out, then something like this can happen again. The United States Government knows about me and why I keep strict rules, so I expect them to be followed." Bowryn said.

"How will we know that you are watching us if you go?" Serena asked.

"I have my sources." Bowryn said.

Clyde and Serena watched as Bowryn grabbed The Hooks and sighed.

"Well, it was a pleasure meeting you two. You both make a fine couple and I wish you all the best." Bowryn said.

"Wait..."

Bowryn smiled and The Hooks burst into flames. The blue spirit disappeared, leaving nothing behind. Clyde sighed.

"He's gone." Clyde said.

"I know."

Clyde turned to face Serena and the two kissed passionately. The two pulled away from each other and as the sun rose, they got into Clyde's GMC and drove away.

Clyde and Serena arrived in the town of Bourne, Massachusetts. The two agreed to start a new life there and it had to be far away from Casper as possible. The two found an old house that was cheap, and they moved in almost immediately. After moving in, they signed papers saying that they were married and proved the residency. Serena found a job as a pre-school teacher in town, while Clyde decided to work for the Town of Bourne, doing lots of the landscaping work. Clyde and Serena chose these jobs so that they could blend in as best as they could. None of their bosses could understand how they could work seven days a week or afford the new house. They were newly-weds for Chrissake! Clyde never heard from Jeremy again. He'll never know what became of his best friend and Alexandria. Clyde looked at the newspaper clip that hung from the wall of their room. THE BUTCHER OF CASPER, A MEMORIAM. The article went into details of the whole thing, the mess that Clyde caused, which was last month. That is what his new name was. The Butcher of Casper, he thought. It didn't matter. Everything was in the past. Serena matters now, Clyde thought. As Clyde and Serena climbed into bed for the night, a Great Horned Owl perched from a tree branch looking in with its yellow eyes. Clyde smiled. Bowryn kept his word after all.

About the Author

    Benjamin Mailloux was born in Methuen, Massachusetts. From a young age, he fell in love with fiction and fantasy books and, as a result, wrote many stories as a child, however, never finished any of them. He graduated from Northern Essex Community College, in Haverhill, with an Associates in English. He then attended the University of Massachusetts, Lowell, and received a Bachelor's Degree in English, with a Literature Concentration. He hopes to teach English at the High School level someday. He currently lives in Kingston, NH, with his soon to be fiancée and is expecting a newborn daughter.